Isa 58:1 Cry aloud, spare not, lift up thy voice like a trumpet, and shew my people their transgression, and the house of Jacob their sins.

THREE QUESTIONS

A STUDY OF THE LAST DAYS BASED ON MATTHEW 24

By Lance Rowe

THREE QUESTIONS

A STUDY OF THE LAST DAYS BASED ON MATTHEW 24

Lance Rowe

Cross Country Publishing

Dutton, Al 35744

This is a research work.
Information is drawn from many sources. I have been careful to make every effort to attribute credit where credit is due.
Unless otherwise noted all Scripture is taken from the King James Version of the Holy Bible.

Definitions for the Greek and Hebrew words contained herein are from Strong's Exhaustive Concordance of the Bible, Thayer's Greek Definitions, and Brown - Driver - Briggs' Hebrew definitions.

Commentaries used and quoted from in this work are:
Adam Clarke's Commentary
Jameson, Faucett and Brown
Keil and Delitz
F B Meyer
Ralph Woodrow, Ralph Woodrow Evangelistic Association

Library of Congress Control Number: 2015953366

I dedicate this book first and foremost to my Lord Jesus Christ, Whose Wisdom and Grace and Mercy are so beyond comprehension. Without Him, we wouldn't be. I pray that everything I do and everything I say will bring Honor to Him, and that He will be Glorified in this book.

Then I dedicate this book to my family. To my wife Michelle, who has stood by me for thirty two years. I could never have found a more perfect mate to spend my life with. Such patience with her husband, the preacher, the researcher and writer! I thank God for you, and I have never regretted that night that I had that one on One talk with my Father as I stood by the Great Salt Lake, and told Him I would like to spend my life with you. And when He spoke so loudly in my spirit, and gave me the O.K. to go get you, I didn't waste time in driving back to Minnesota. What were the odds of you being the very first person I saw as I pulled into Big Falls unannounced? 100% with God. What an adventure we have had so far. I love you, honey, and thanks for the memories!

To my children Talitha, Feather, Elijah, Grace, Noah, Abigail, and Hoshea; I love each one of you, and am honored that you are my sons and daughters. What an adventure it's been with you, as well. You gotta admit, your childhood years were definitely unique! Someday I will go the way of all flesh, and this book is a tangible thing that can carry on with you while I am rejoicing in the Presence of my Lord and Savior Jesus Christ. I truly pray that each one of you will join me there beside me. May you never forget this eternal Question: What does it profit a man if he gains the whole world and loses his soul?

To my grand children Jolie and Roma, and the one that is soon to be born. What a delight grand children are!

I also dedicate this book to everyone who I have had the privilege of working with in the ministry over the years. You know who you are. Pastors, musicians, evangelists, co-laborers and true yoke fellows. If I began to name each one of you, the chances are that I will forget to mention someone, and I want you all to know that I value your friendship and your influence in my life tremendously.

And likewise, to my friends and those of you who have supported us and our ministry in one way or another, this book is dedicated to you.

I also dedicate this book in memory of my mom, Faith. What a woman! She unselfishly raised two children and took care of her mother and handicapped brother in the toughest of situations, and she did a good job at that! She was one of the best hunters and fishers that have ever lived!

And finally, but certainly not in the least, I dedicate this book to you, the reader. Go ahead and say your name here. I want to sincerely thank you for taking the time to read this, because I know time is valuable, and it is my prayer that you will be edified, and encouraged to press on with Jesus even more than in the past. May the Lord richly bless you as you explore these pages.

Contents

Three Important Questions That Need To Be Answered

What is the significance of the letters to the Churches in Revelation 2 and 3?

When will the end of the world happen?

Who is the Anti Christ?

Those are three questions that are commonly asked by people, both Christian and non-Christian alike who have an interest in New Testament prophecy. There are a whole lot of other questions that are being asked beside these, and while I hope to answer these and other pertinent questions concerning the end times in this book, the three questions that this book is primarily meant to address are the ones the disciples asked Jesus:

Mat 24:3 And as he sat upon the mount of Olives, the disciples came unto him privately, saying, Tell us, when shall these things be? and what *shall be* the sign of thy coming, and of the end of the world?

To preface this study, I think it is necessary to explain that I personally believe that the accounts of the end time events, whether they be in Revelation, Thessalonians, Timothy, Peter, Jude, Isaiah, Jeremiah, Ezekiel, Daniel, Zechariah, Joel, Acts, or anywhere else in the Bible *should be interpreted according to the Words of Jesus*, the One Who is the Author and Finisher of our Faith, the One Who is our Savior, our Lord, and the King of Kings, the One For Whom and By Whom all things were created, the One Who is the Alpha and Omega, the Prophet above all Prophets, the Word manifested in the flesh.

Paul, John, Daniel, Peter, and all the others I mentioned above were not wiser or more knowledgeable than Jesus, the Author and Finisher of our Faith. And certainly, any current or past expositors of the end times are not wiser than Jesus, whether they be proponents of the Pre-trib, Mid-trib, or Post-trib rapture or those who are from the Preterist persuasion.

I don't presume to be smarter than any of the above, and I don't presume to have the whole picture, but what follows is my understanding of the prophetic word concerning the "end times" based on what Jesus taught His disciples, and what that prophetic word has to do with you, the reader.

The book you are holding is a book that will challenge you. There are some phrases I use that may seem to be offensive, and I have no doubt that some will take offense as they read this book. I write about "Pulpit Puppets", "Profits", and "Professional Pulpiteers". If you are one of these, then I can understand why you would be offended, and I make no apology to you, but if you are not, well, praise the Lord, there is no reason for you to take offense.

A lot of what you read will challenge doctrine that you have accepted as Truth for years. Chances are that if you have been thoroughly indoctrinated into a particular end times mindset, you will want to stop reading this book. I would encourage you not to do that.

Sometimes the foundation which we start with concerning a particular doctrine was a wrong foundation, but if we have just blindly accepted it as a fact, we will build our ideas and our doctrinal stance on that flawed foundation, not even realizing that is what we are doing.

The Christian who goes to the altar at a particular church will more than likely adopt it's eschatological doctrine without question. If he is a Baptist or a Church of God convert, he will be a dispensationalist pretribber. If he is a Lutheran, he will tend more to an amillennialist or a post millennialist position. On the other hand, a Presbyterian may tend more to a preterist position. And a host of non-denominational fellowships differ from one another in their position concerning end-times doctrine. Preachers generally preach the "denominational line", and read the Bible with their denomination-tinted glasses.

 Christ and His teachings should be the foundation upon which we build, since He is the Author and Finisher of our Faith. The sad truth is that we have a tendency to build on "church doctrine" or on "men's doctrines", instead of Christ's.

 Hence, the reason for his book. Get out your Bible, wipe the dust off it, and check out what I have written with what the Bible says. If your Bible is a Scofield or a Dake's, I would challenge you to just read the Biblical text, and not the commentary they offer.

I have been a Christian since September 6, 1983. It was on that date in 1983 that I bowed my knees to Jesus Christ in a motel room with a Gideon's Bible laying open on the bed, and asked Jesus Christ to be the Lord of my life. I crossed over the briar and thorn infested border of Self and Unbelief into a new land and became a citizen of the Kingdom of God that night. I didn't really know what all of that meant, as I had not been brought up in a church environment, so my walk with Jesus was a fresh walk, free of any doctrinal or denominational influence.

All I knew was that my experience with Jesus that night was undeniable, and my surrender to Him was complete, whatever that meant. A long haired, bearded, pot smoking, drug using, ex con had walked into that motel room that night and in the morning the guy who walked out of that motel room looked the same as the one who had entered, but a transformation had taken place in his mind that was undeniable.

Since that night I have had a hunger to learn the Word of God, not the word of God that has been filtered through the thought processes of a preacher or a philosopher, but the Word of God as it is written in the pages of the Bible. As I said earlier, I had not grown up in church. The man who entered that motel room was a full blooded heathen who grew up in taverns, and who began doing drugs and lost his virginity at the age of 11, and whose only happiness came from the gratification of his flesh in whatever form that took. If it felt good, he did it.

Two nights later I was in a park somewhere near Boulder Colorado, and it was raining. It was night time, and I had the dome light on in my rusted out 72 Chevy Vega, reading the Bible I had stolen from the motel room. I had ten hits of blotter acid in a cellophane cigarette wrapper in my shirt pocket. One of my friends that I had stopped to visit the day before in Blue Springs, Nebraska had given them to me. As I read that Bible, with the rain beating on the roof of the car, I suddenly had a thought come to me: "You have to get rid of that acid." THAT was weird. Why would I think that? Naturally, I ignored that thought, and continued reading the Bible. Pretty soon, that thought came to me again.

Prior to my experience in the motel room, I would have never had a thought like that, so you can imagine how strange that was to me. Why would I want to do something like that? Peyote, mushrooms, mescaline, LSD, PCP, THC and other forms of hallucinogenic drugs were all avenues of excitement to me, and I enjoyed the experience they brought. So now I have this crazy thought invading my space as I am reading the Word of God in the driver's seat of my Vega. I dismissed the thought once more, but a few minutes later there came this incredible sense of my stomach being twisted up in a knot, so much that I bent over and leaned my head against the steering wheel as the thought came once more, "*YOU'VE GOTTA GET RID OF THAT ACID!*"

Outside the rain was pouring down hard. I knew the minute I threw that cellophane out the window, there would be no changing my mind. The acid would dissolve into nothing, and I would have wasted ten good experiences (or so I thought at the moment). But I had never experienced what I was experiencing at the moment with my belly all in an uproar like that. I was sure it must have been God that was doing this to me. So I straightened up in my seat, reached in my pocket and grabbed hold of that wrapper. I remember saying as I rolled down the window, "God, I really hope this is You," and I tossed that wrapper outside and rolled the window back up.

God visited me in that moment like He had in that motel room. His Holy Spirit swept over me, and gave me the most awesome "Atta boy" I could have ever received. Hallelujah! What a wonderful adventure this has been! From that day on I knew that I was never to do any hallucinogenic ever again. And I didn't.

I will never forget what I read that next morning before I left the park. Elihu had been listening in silence to Job and his friends' dialogue as they discussed why all these things were happening to Job. Finally he couldn't contain himself anymore. What he described was exactly what I had experienced the night before.

Job 32:18 For I am full of matter, the spirit within me constraineth me.
19 Behold, my belly *is* as wine *which* hath no vent; it is ready to burst like new bottles.
20 I will speak, that I may be refreshed: I will open my lips and answer.

It wasn't until Elihu spoke that he found relief, and it wasn't until I threw that acid away that I found relief.

The rest of that passage has stuck with me ever since:

Job 32:21 Let me not, I pray you, accept any man's person, neither let me give flattering titles unto man.
22 For I know not to give flattering titles; *in so doing* my maker would soon take me away.

Jesus didn't esteem the titles of honor that men took upon themselves:

Mat 23:5 But all their works they do for to be seen of men: they make broad their phylacteries, and enlarge the borders of their garments,
6 And love the uppermost rooms at feasts, and the chief seats in the synagogues,
7 And greetings in the markets, and to be called of men, Rabbi, Rabbi.
8 But be not ye called Rabbi: for one is your Master, *even* Christ; and all ye are brethren.
9 And call no *man* your father upon the earth: for one is your Father, which is in heaven.
10 Neither be ye called masters: for one is your Master, *even* Christ.

While we should give honor where honor is due, there are some men and women who love their titles of honor and prestige, and work very hard at maintaining it, and many in the Body of Christ become the equivalent of Christian "groupies" when it comes to certain self proclaimed prophets or apostles, or evangelists or pastors and teachers.

They love the way they preach, they love the way they shroud themselves with a cloak of spiritual mysticism. Christians love to hear "something new", and will pay good money to be in on it. The sad truth is that the Western Church at large prefers to be hearers rather than doers of the word, and so they hear all of this information that floods the markets, and go from conference to conference, becoming parrots of the men they esteem so highly. Pastors and preachers jump on the band wagon of popularity and parrot the things that "big guys" are saying. If a person expresses the idea that the big guys "ain't all that", chances are he or she will be given the cold shoulder or rebuked.

But God is looking for the Elihus who will speak up despite the popular opinion, and will speak the truth. Since that morning in the park in Colorado, my desire has been to be an Elihu in my walk with Jesus.

Food For Your Consideration

Did you realize that nowhere in the Bible does it say "God helps those who help themselves", yet many Christians believe that it's somewhere in there. The Bible also doesn't say "Cleanliness is next to godliness". Nor does it say that money is the root of all evil. Many more believe that the Bible says "God works in mysterious ways;" a great number of Christians quote the phrase "I am just a sinner saved by Grace" as if it is in the Bible; and Adam and Eve didn't eat an apple, and Saint Peter isn't going to be standing by the Pearly Gates to ask you why he should let you in. I realize that those who do read the Bible will silently scoff and say, " I know that", but a lot of professing Christians don't because they don't really read the Bible for themselves. I have heard a number of preachers mention the Peter and the Pearly Gates scenario, as well as the other things mentioned above.

By the same token, a lot of pastors and other ministers of the Gospel don't really study the issue of the "last days" for themselves, but glean the bulk of their knowledge from denominational doctrine (the party line), or "end time" experts. A lot of what is preached from the pulpit is denominational doctrine (read traditions of men) rather than Foundational Biblical Truth. As I write this, I am sure a few names would pop up in one's mind concerning someone who is reputed to be an expert in last days prophecy. You probably hold him in high esteem and have quoted a lot of what he said.

The truth is, a lot of preachers (not all) are just parrots of one another as they teach end times doctrine. A lot of pastors rely on other men's sermons to feed the sheep, like buzzards who regurgitate their rotten road kill for their little chicks to eat, rather than seeking God for fresh Manna for their message to the Body of Christ. Instead of equipping the Body of Christ to do the work of the ministry, they entertain them with flowery speeches and "fiery" preaching. I call them "pulpit puppets" or "professional pulpiteers". Let me illustrate one relatively simple example here. It's a simple example, but improper interpretation of a Biblical passage can lead to many doctrinal errors.

Did you know that Revelation 2 and 3 are not letters to the churches?

Yet most teachers refer to them as such. Chances are that you the reader have referred to these chapters as "the letters to the seven churches". But each of the messages actually begin like this: "To the *angel* of the church of Ephesus", "To the *angel* of the church of Smyrna", "To the *angel* of the church of Pergamos", "To the *angel* of the church of Thyratira", "To the *angel* of the church of Sardis", "To the *angel* of the church of Philadelphia", and "To the *angel* of the church of Laodocea". Now, that might seem to be "nit-picking" but the distinction is very significant, especially when it comes to your end times theology.

The Greek word translated as "angel" actually doesn't refer exclusively to heavenly beings. The word can also refer to human messengers. Jesus used that word when He referred to John, and the translators of the King James translated the Greek word "angellos" (angel) as "messenger":

Mat 11:10 For this is *he,* of whom it is written, Behold, I send my messenger *(angellos)* **before thy face, which shall prepare thy way before thee.**

See also Luke 7:24, 9:52, Gal 4:14, and Jas 2:25, for other examples where men were referred to as "angels".

The Book of Revelation as a whole is written to the seven churches which were then extant in John's time. It was written to address things that were already happening, and those things which were shortly to come to pass:

Rev 1:1 The Revelation of Jesus Christ, which God gave unto him, to shew unto his servants things which must shortly come to pass; and he sent and signified *it* by his angel unto his servant John:

Rev 1:4 John to the seven churches which are in Asia: Grace *be* unto you, and peace, from him which is, and which was, and which is to come; and from the seven Spirits which are before his throne;

Revelation 2 and 3 are *parenthetical*, and were written to the *leadership* of those churches, and five of the seven were warned to repent of the things they were allowing or neglecting in their fellowships. Polycarp may have been the bishop of Smyrna at the time, and no doubt he would have read that letter as a personal word to him.

I point this out because a great degree of *dispensational* doctrine rests on the idea that these letters are written to the "churches", and according to those who hold a dispensationalist view point, each church mentioned in these chapters is representative as a "church age".

According to dispensationalists, we are now in the age of the *Laodocean* or the lukewarm church. But while it sounds good, and has made for some "good" preaching content, the whole premise is wrong and based on a wrong interpretation of the chapters. The letters are to the *leadership* of the churches. Those letters also pertain to those who are in leadership today. And in each one of the areas in which these messengers were told to repent, we can see the doctrinal error that is being taught today by some messengers.

Lukewarm pastors beget lukewarm pew warming Christians, but all pastors are not lukewarm. I personally know several who equip their members to make a difference in their communities for the sake of the Kingdom of God.

When one reads the letters in the way they are supposed to be read, the dispensationalist will have to go elsewhere to prove his position of "Seven Church Ages", but that will be tough, because it is in these letters that the concept of seven church ages is found.

We are commanded to rightly divide the Word of truth, not to tear it up and make it something it is not.

The things that are coming upon the world is because the current messengers to the churches won't repent of their hidden agendas, their wrong doctrine, their conformity to this world, and their failure to equip their congregation to do the work of furthering the Kingdom of God in their cities or neighborhoods.

If pastors and ministers of the gospel would carefully examine themselves in the light of these letters, they would probably find a cause for repentance. But as long as they are conditioned to believe that these letters are to the churches and not to *them*, then this world will continue on its slippery descent into moral degradation because the congregations these pastors lead are themselves on the same slope.

At this moment a couple of questions may arise, one of which is "But each of the letters end with the admonishment *'He that hath an ear, let him hear what the Spirit saith unto the churches'*; doesn't that show that these letters were written to the churches?"

No, to the contrary, it is saying that those who are in leadership should be attuned to what the Holy Spirit would have them to teach their congregations. God doesn't want those who have been given the responsibility of feeding His sheep to feed them wrong doctrine, and He is calling those who have been given the responsibly of leading His people to repent of their negligence, and if they have an ear to hear the Holy Spirit, they should be teaching the Church right doctrine, and prevent wrong doctrine from creeping in. My website deals with these letters to the messengers. You can go to *crosscountry4jesus.com/index57.html* to read about them.

There is a great responsibility for those who are messengers to the Church. Many see it as a "vocation", a career opportunity. Jesus calls those type of messengers "hirelings".

A lot of preachers believe and teach their congregation that there is no hope for our nation or the world. They are convinced that the end times are upon us, and that there is no remedy. Yet throughout the Bible, God says that if His people repent of their wickedness, He Himself will intervene and heal their land. Dispensationalists teach there is no remedy, while at the same time saying that God is the same today as He was yesterday and will be tomorrow. The Word of God says that God Himself is not willing that *any* should perish, but that *all* should come to repentance. The majority of the preachers today are preaching "Come Lord Jesus, take us out of here and let the rest of the world go to hell!" Like James and John, they don't know what spirit they are of.

**Luk 9:53 And they did not receive him, because his face was as though he would go to Jerusalem.
54 And when his disciples James and John saw *this,* they said, Lord, wilt thou that we command fire to come down from heaven, and consume them, even as Elias did?
55 But he turned, and rebuked them, and said, Ye know not what manner of spirit ye are of.
56 For the Son of man is not come to destroy men's lives, but to save *them.* And they went to another village.**

I am not proclaiming "Thus Saith the Lord", but instead I am endeavoring to present to the reader of this book a balanced look at "end times" doctrine from a different perspective, which obviously I believe is correct, since I am taking the time to write this book. I am not a Doctor of Theology, nor am I a seminarian, and this book is not a comprehensive study of the Last Days, but I have endeavored to answer many questions that may come to the reader's mind as he or she reads this.

There will probably be some discrepancies in this book, or even some error that I am personally not aware of. I am not infallible.

There will be many issues and theological sacred cows (read "traditions of men") that are addressed here, and the reader will be challenged to rethink his or her opinion concerning "the last days".

Col 2:8 Beware lest any man spoil you through philosophy and vain deceit, after the tradition of men, after the rudiments of the world, and not after Christ.

You may find yourself getting angry or perplexed because some of your sacred cows may be getting slaughtered, or at least, wounded. Six of these cows are commonly held views pertaining to Premilliennial Dispensationalism and the Seventieth Week of Daniel, The

Letters to The Churches, The Antichrist, the Mark of the Beast, and the Beast of Revelation 13.

Pray before you read this. I do believe it is possible that your perspective on the part you are to play in the Kingdom may be radically changed. You don't have to agree with everything I write here, and you probably won't, because chances are you have been conditioned for years to believe something different than what I am writing here. And to a degree, I can say "that's O.K.", but *I think it is very important that you don't miss the underlying message of this book, and that is that the majority of the Body of Christ has been sidetracked from its' purpose of obeying the Great Commission by focusing too much on what may or may not be coming than walking in obedience to the Command of our Lord Jesus Christ.*

Mat 28:18 And Jesus came and spake unto them, saying, All power is given unto me in heaven and in earth.
19 Go ye therefore, and teach all nations, baptizing them in the name of the Father, and of the Son, and of the Holy Ghost:
20 Teaching them to observe all things whatsoever I have commanded you: and, lo, I am with you alway, *even* unto the end of the world. Amen.

A little over 2,000 years ago, the disciples were gathered around Jesus on the mount of Olives, looking down at Jerusalem, and asked Him three questions concerning the end times.

Throughout His ministry, Jesus referred to the last days, or the Day of Judgment, but He didn't hold any end times conventions or pass the plate after he taught about the end times, and He certainly didn't make the "end times" the cornerstone of His teaching. I believe if He was walking on this planet in the flesh today, He still wouldn't, and He would solidly rebuke those who have fashioned their ministries as "end time ministries".

Christ's message concerning the end times was *ALWAYS* accompanied with a warning that when He does return, He will be coming back for those who are busy furthering the Kingdom of God on earth. That doesn't mean faithfully occupying a pew every Sunday or Saturday or whenever the "church" doors are open. What it does mean, is that He is looking for His people to *be the Church* to those who are yet living their lives outside of His Kingdom.

The truth is there are a lot of books and films that have raked in millions, probably billions of dollars with the "end times" as their selling point, and I believe that for the most part, the devil would love for that industry to grow even more as long as it keeps Christians arguing with each other, and being tossed to and fro by every wind of doctrine while they neglect the most important thing; *the commission to do their part in establishing the Kingdom of God.*

Some Transparency Here

As I write these words, I acknowledge that I am writing still another book to add to the others. And just to be up front about it, the proceeds to this book are not going to go to some charity, but they *will* help support my family and help finance the ministry the Lord has called us to. We have been in ministry since 1988 and have never solicited funds from anyone to support our ministry. I am not going to promise you a copy of my book if you send in a donation for the support of "my ministry". The Lord has blessed me with the ability to write, and the Word of God says that he who does not provide for his family is worse than an infidel. This may be one of those means whereby I may provide for my family. Ours truly has been a "Faith Based Ministry". God has always supplied our needs, and this book may or may not be another means that God uses to do so (I guess it depends on how well it sells), but having said that, I want to assure the reader that making money is NOT the purpose of this book.

My suggestion to the reader of this book would be to go out and tell somebody about the Kingdom of God, lay hands on the sick, minister healing and deliverance to some broken soul in the Name of Jesus, and save the reading of this book to your bathroom time or while you are eating your breakfast, or before you go to sleep at night (but please don't substitute the reading of your Bible with this book!).

THAT is the purpose of this book, to compel the reader to understand that there is a world waiting for the Church to manifest the Power of God in this current age and if you are in Christ, YOU the reader are a very important part in God's Plan to see humanity reconciled to God. God wants to use you for the furtherance of His Kingdom here on earth.

I would invite the reader to momentarily park your preconceived ideas concerning the "end times" as you read this book. Pray first, and ask the Holy Spirit to give you understanding. This book is NOT a detailed exposition on the end times, but since it is a probe into the answers of the three questions posed by the disciples, we will be taking some necessary detours down some rabbit trails, looking with some detail at the books of Daniel and Revelation.

By no means is this to be seen as an exhaustive study of these books, and there will undoubtedly be a lot of questions left unanswered, but hopefully the reader will be able to get enough of a glimpse "behind the veil" so to speak, that they will be able to see more clearly their part they are to play in responding to their calling and purpose as citizens of the Kingdom of God in these times we find ourselves living in.

THREE IMPORTANT QUESTIONS

In Matthew 24, Jesus deals with three questions that were asked of Him by His disciples, and He answers each one.

Mat 24:3 And as he sat upon the mount of Olives, the disciples came unto him privately, saying, Tell us, when shall these things be? and what *shall be* the sign of thy coming, and of the end of the world?

The questions that were asked by the disciples were:

1) When shall there not be left one stone upon another.

2) What is the sign of your coming?

3) What is the sign of the end of the AGE; not the physical sphere which we live upon and what we refer to as "the world". That sphere would be referred to in the Greek as "Kosmos", but the disciples use the word "Aion" here which gives a total different meaning.

DEFINING TWO IMPORTANT TERMS FOR CLEARER UNDERSTANDING

Age = Gr. Aion. In the Greek they are asking about the end of the age. What age? The age in which Satan has control of the world.

Kosmos = World, the circle of the earth, the earth, or the Universe.

2 Corinthians 4:4 references Satan as the "god of this age". He is NOT the god of this "world" as in the physical sphere upon which we live, but he would love you to believe that he is. Satan's time is short, and he is doing everything he can to keep your mind blinded to the truth of the Gospel of the Kingdom of God.

2Co 4:3 But if our gospel be hid, it is hid to them that are lost:
4 In whom the god of this world (read "age") **hath blinded the minds of them which believe not, lest the light of the glorious gospel of Christ, who is the image of God, should shine unto them.**

The disciples are asking about the end of that period of time when the god of this age no longer rules. Most commentators and preachers translate it as *"the end of this world"*...which would be "*Kosmos*", and not AION.

The first sacred cow to be killed:

IT IS VERY IMPORTANT TO UNDERSTAND THAT THE MATTHEW 24 DIALOGUE IS NOT ABOUT THE END OF THE WORLD, BUT THE END OF AN "AGE".

There is a difference.

The disciples knew what they were asking.

I personally prefer the King James version of the Bible. There are a lot of tools available that help me do more of an in depth study of the Word of God when I read the King James. But in studying the Word of God, often times you will find that a word translated one way is not the best word to use, as in this case. Many translations have it translated as follows, which I believe is the best translation:

Mat 24:3 While Jesus was sitting on the Mount of Olives, the disciples came to him privately and said, "Tell us, when will these things take place, and what will be the sign of your coming and of the end of the age?" (*International Standard Version*)

Hebrews 9:26 uses the word Kosmos and the word Aion in the same sentence.

Heb 9:26 For then must he often have suffered since the foundation of the world: but now once in the end of the world hath he appeared to put away sin by the sacrifice of himself.

When the author speaks of the "foundation of the world", he uses the Greek word "Kosmos", which is literally speaking of this physical world on which we live. But when he speaks of the "end of the world", he uses the same terminology that the disciples used when questioning Jesus: "The end of the age".

Goodspeed's translation of the New Testament reads like this:

Heb 9:26 for then he would have had to suffer death over and over, ever since the creation of the world. But, as it is, once for all at the close of the age he has appeared, to put an end to sin by his sacrifice.

With the understanding that the question asked by the disciples isn't addressing the end of the world, as the majority of modern day teachers hold, one's view of Biblical Christianity and the individual Christian's responsibility as a citizen of the Kingdom of God will be (should be) radically transformed.

The Sunday morning "orator/audience" scenario that we see in most churches today will no longer be seen as "normal" Christianity, because it is not.

Christianity as it is understood in America is very abnormal in the light of Biblical Christianity. Hopefully you will understand what I mean by that by the time you finish reading this book.

Once Pastors and believers understand that each one of them have an important role to play NOW in the furtherance of the Kingdom of God today, your fellowship will be (should be) radically transformed into a group of men and women of God who are used of God to turn this world we live in upside down.

Just A Word Of Caution.

During the course of the reading of this book, there will be mention of those who stand in the pulpit, and of a backslid church, but the reader is not to suppose that I am saying that everyone who preaches behind a pulpit are deceivers or that all "churches" are out of the Will of God. But there are certainly some (I would say many in the United States) who are, and if you happen to be a "Puppet in the Pulpit", serving your own personal agenda, while expounding on the "new revelation" that *profit* so and so brought forth in his last best seller or You Tube video, or if you are blindly giving credence to or parroting denominational doctrine that may be contrary to Biblical doctrine because that denomination is what "butters your bread", you need to repent. Like Elihu, I realize this is a time when men of God cannot afford to esteem an man's person above the Word of God. If I step on your toes during the course of this book, there are three options left to you.

1) Stop reading. If you read any farther, you *may* find yourself guilty of leading the people of God astray from their purpose, and it will be your responsibility to repent.

2) Get some steel toed shoes and keep on reading. Then dismiss this book as irrelevant to your denominational position.

3) Refuse to be offended and if anything I write pertains to you, repent, and get busy about the furthering of the Kingdom of God.

Job 32:21 Let me not, I pray you, accept any man's person, neither let me give flattering titles unto man.
22 For I know not to give flattering titles; *in so doing* **my maker would soon take me away.**

It is also important to understand that I am NOT "anti-church". I believe that there must be serious reformation of the Church to get back to where we are supposed to be as the Body of Christ, but I am a firm believer that the individual Christian needs to find a place of fellowship in the area they live in where they can grow in their calling and help others to grow as well.

I also find it necessary to point out to the reader that there is a futurist and a preterist view of the events Jesus mentions in Matthew 24. I suppose my position would be somewhat of a futurist/preterist. In the Appendix under the section titled *An Overview of Eschatological Positions Concerning The Millennium,* you can find my doctrinal position on the end times, as well as definitions of the various end times doctrines that people hold.

Although I have my own thoughts on the "end times", I myself personally am not overly concerned about the positions others hold.

I AM concerned enough to write this book, and I believe it is a prophetic call for the Church to wake up and to be about furthering the Kingdom of God before it is too late, but I am not so concerned that I refuse to fellowship with those who hold a different view point than I do - unless you are one of those parroting pulpit puppets that purposely clothe yourself in sheep's clothing to hide the fact that you are a wolf.

I may seem rough in my writing, and occasionally seem hard in some of my terminology, ("pulpit puppets", "professional pulpiteers", "hirelings") but the truth needs be told without apology. If you aren't one of those, then I am not talking about you. **And if you don't agree with the content of this book, that doesn't automatically classify you as one of those, either.** I have a lot of friends who are pastors and who do not see eye to eye with me in these matters, but we still love each other, and I don't stand in judgment of them if they preach a different end times message than I do. I will probably make sure they get my book, though!

If you believe that Jesus is coming in a month or two, or if you believe He has already come, or if you believe you will be raptured out before the tribulation, or if you believe there are some perilous times ahead; if you believe that there is no such thing as the rapture, or if you believe the mark of the Beast is a chip or a tattoo or an ideology; if you believe that the United States is Babylon, or the Catholic Church or the apostate church; if you are a historic premillennialist, a dispensational premillenialist, or a post millennialist or an amillinnealist, it really doesn't matter that much to me. Obviously I have my own thoughts on the subject or I wouldn't write this book. I could be wrong. But so could you. Obviously I don't think I am wrong. And obviously you don't think you are wrong. I hope we can walk in love toward one another and agree to disagree.

My concern is whether or not the doctrinal position that you hold is leading you to a state of apathy in your walk with Jesus, or if it is causing you to forsake fellowshipping with those who disagree with your eschatological (doctrine concerning the end times) viewpoint. Personally, I can (and do) fellowship with anyone who is in Christ regardless of their eschatological viewpoint. How about you?

As a dear evangelist friend of mine often says: "One more thing":

Since there is an index, it is pretty common for people to look at the index and say "Oh, that topic interests me. I think I will read that", and in the process bypass a lot of other pertinent information. Please don't do that. I believe that if you do that you will miss some very essential points, and will have a tendency to misunderstand what has been written.

To avoid a lot of rabbit trails (although there are some) I added notes in the appendix. I would suggest that you refer to those appendix notes once you have finished with the main body of the section that refers to that note. If you wait until the end of the book to read the appendix notes, you will probably find yourself having to reread that section that it deals with anyway. For the reader who insists on waiting until the end to read the appendix notes, I have included page numbers from the main body of the book that deals with those subjects. It will be easier and maybe even save some confusion to just read them as you go.

I am trying to be very diligent each time I edit this book to make sure the appendix numbers and the page numbers that I refer to throughout this book line up with the actual pages, but there is a possibility that I might miss some. If I do mess that up, I ask you to forgive me. Once I publish it, and it is printed, the formatting process MAY throw everything off kilter. I hope not. But don't let that distract you from the main content and message of the book. I want to thank you for your patience in advance.

I have an e-mail listed on my copyright page. You can feel free to contact me about any matters of concern you may have regarding this book. I pray the Peace of God which passes all understanding will be yours as you read this book.

Don't be deceived. Jesus *IS* coming back sometime to get His Bride. But He is coming back for a people who are surrendered to His Will in their lives. Are you surrendered? It is my prayer that this book will help you honestly assess that question.

SECTION 1

THINGS TO KNOW CONCERNING THE END OF THE AGE

ANSWERS: CONCERNING "WHEN SHALL BE THE END OF THE AGE", JESUS REPLIES:

Mat 24:4 And Jesus answered and said unto them, Take heed that no man deceive you. 5 For many shall come in my name, saying, I am Christ; and shall deceive many

Deceivers Abound

I don't believe that Jesus is saying here that there would be many who declare that they are Christ, as some have interpreted this. Some translations have quotation marks around the words "I am Christ", which would lead the reader to believe that Jesus is teaching that these people would be saying *they* are Christ, but there were no quotation marks in the original Greek, so the individual translators placed them there at their own discretion and as a result of their personal interpretation as to what Jesus was referring to.

I believe He is saying that there would be many who come in the Name of Jesus, who declare Him to indeed be the Christ, and who would deceive many. He addresses false Christ's later (verse 24), but right now He is speaking of those who confess Him to be the Christ, and who stand in the pulpits or on television or on social media and on-line videos with titles before their names (Pastor, Evangelist, Prophet, Apostle, Doctor, Reverend, Bishop, Elder) and who lead many astray.

There are a lot of preachers in the pulpits who deceive, sometimes intentionally, ***but more often than not***, unintentionally, who come in the Name of Christ and who preach another gospel than the gospel that Jesus preached (Read 1 Tim 4:1, Matt 7:22, Matt 24:11, 2 Tim 3:5-7), because of traditional or denominational doctrinal stances that aren't necessarily Biblical.

Because they stand behind the pulpit, or hold some degree or title, or are great sermonizers (preachers) doesn't qualify them as being infallible. Jesus said be careful that you don't be deceived.

There is a professionalism which has replaced the servant hood of ministry today, and that professionalism serves to elevate men to a place of veneration and glory that was never intended to be theirs. The majority of Christians listen to the "man of God's" speeches without searching the Scriptures themselves to determine if what he is saying is true or not.

Statistically, the odds are that the person who is reading this book spends more time reading other books or listening to the preachers (whether live or on cd or dvd or social media) than the time he or she spends reading the Bible.

Although the Bible repeatedly warns against being in ministry for the sake of personal financial gain, there are plenty of ministers who are about financial gain. These are referred to in the Word of God as "hirelings". A nine to five job is not a ministry. It is a job. Service (which is what "ministry" means) to God is a lifestyle, not a vocation.

**Joh 10:11 I am the good shepherd: the good shepherd giveth his life for the sheep.
12 But he that is an hireling, and not the shepherd, whose own the sheep are not, seeth the wolf coming, and leaveth the sheep, and fleeth: and the wolf catcheth them, and scattereth the sheep.
13 The hireling fleeth, because he is an hireling, and careth not for the sheep.**

The qualification of those who are in ministry is that they are not to be about gain for themselves.

**1Ti 3:2 A bishop then must be blameless, the husband of one wife, vigilant, sober, of good behaviour, given to hospitality, apt to teach;
3 Not given to wine, no striker, not greedy of filthy lucre; but patient, not a brawler, not covetous;**

**Tit 1:7 For a bishop must be blameless, as the steward of God; not selfwilled, not soon angry, not given to wine, no striker, not given to filthy lucre;
8 Likewise *must* the deacons *be* grave, not doubletongued, not given to much wine, not greedy of filthy lucre;
9 Holding the mystery of the faith in a pure conscience.**

It is the lust for money (translated as "filthy lucre" in the verses above; the Greek translation actually being "greedy for money") that spurs men to look for new and exciting ways to market themselves in order to get more opportunities to have preaching engagements where they can get more money.

**Tit 1:10 For there are many unruly and vain talkers and deceivers, specially they of the circumcision:
11 Whose mouths must be stopped, who subvert whole houses, teaching things which they ought not, for filthy lucre's sake.**

Jesus Himself told His disciples these words when He sent them out to minister:

**Mat 10:7 And as ye go, preach, saying, The kingdom of heaven is at hand.
8 Heal the sick, cleanse the lepers, raise the dead, cast out devils: freely ye have received, freely give.**

It is the love of money that clouds the truth and brings in error.

1Ti 6:6 But godliness with contentment is great gain.
7 For we brought nothing into *this* world, *and it is* certain we can carry nothing out.
8 And having food and raiment let us be therewith content.
9 But they that will be rich fall into temptation and a snare, and *into* many foolish and hurtful lusts, which drown men in destruction and perdition.
10 For the love of money is the root of all evil: which while some coveted after, they have erred from the faith, and pierced themselves through with many sorrows.
11 But thou, O man of God, flee these things; and follow after righteousness, godliness, faith, love, patience, meekness.

It is very significant that the first thing Jesus warns His disciples about concerning their questions was that they were to **"Take heed that no man deceive you. For many shall come in my name, saying I am Christ; and shall deceive many."**

Many professional pulpiteers are being used by Satan to render the Body of Christ ineffective for the work of the Kingdom of God. "How", you may ask? A few pages from now you will encounter a section that discusses about the *Cloward-Piven Strategy of Manufactured Crises*. Carefully read this section when you get there, and keep this in mind as you read this book. ***The truth is a lot of what Christians are taught from the pulpit is designed to keep them from realizing their potential and their Purpose in Christ, and Satan loves to keep it that way.***

2Ti 3:13 But evil men and seducers shall wax worse and worse, deceiving, and being deceived.

Mat 24:6 And ye shall hear of wars and rumours of wars: see that ye be not troubled: for all *these things* must come to pass, but the end is not yet. (Answer to Question 3 = "the end of the age is not yet").
7 For nation shall rise against nation, and kingdom against kingdom: and there shall be famines, and pestilences, and earthquakes, in divers places.
8 All these *are* the beginning of sorrows.

Notice He says it is the *beginning* of sorrows (birth pains), not the end. We will address these birth pains a little later, but at this point, it is important to see what 2 Thessalonians says concerning the Coming of the Lord:

2Th 2:1 Now we beseech you, brethren, by the coming of our Lord Jesus Christ (Remember that one of the questions asked by the disciples was "What is the sign of your coming?"), **and *by* our gathering together unto him**
2 That ye be not soon shaken in mind, or be troubled, neither by spirit, nor by word, nor by letter as from us, as that the day of Christ is at hand (Note what Jesus Himself said

in Matthew 24:6: "See that ye be not troubled: for all *these things* must come to pass, but the end is not yet")

3 Let no man deceive you by any means: (Jesus Himself said "take heed that no man deceive you" Matt 24:4) **for *that day shall not come,*** (What day? The Day of the Coming of our Lord; vs 1) **except there come a falling away first, and that man of sin be revealed, the son of perdition** (most commentators say it is the "Antichrist" who is being referred to here, but dispensational premillennialist preachers believe that the appearance of the antichrist comes at Revelation 13, by which time (according to them) the "Church" has been raptured, which is typically understood by dispensationalist preachers to take place at Revelation 4:1, when *JOHN* is called to "come up hither'. But here it says that the "Anti Christ" [if that is really who the man of sin is] will be revealed first, ***before*** Christ's coming.) **4 Who opposeth and exalteth himself above all that is called God, or that is worshipped; so that he as God sitteth in the temple of God, shewing himself that he is God.**

In the appendix I deal with this passage more extensively,[1] and I address the various details concerning the Coming of the Lord as mentioned here and in the light of what Jesus taught, but for now, the point I want the reader to see is that Paul confirms what Jesus said; that no matter what it looks like, and no matter what deceivers may say concerning Christ's Coming, don't be troubled. There are a lot of things that need to happen first, and the primary thing will be a "falling away" from the truth. Some preachers are saying that is happening already. And to a degree it is, but that *falling away* (apostasy) will be because of this "*man of sin*" that is mentioned. As I said, we will discuss this in more detail later in the appendix section of this book[1].

For now let's hop off this rabbit trail and continue down the original path we began on. We continue with Jesus' teaching in Matthew 24:

Matthew 24:9 Then shall they deliver you up to be afflicted, and shall kill you: and ye shall be hated of all nations for my name's sake.
10 And then shall many be offended, and shall betray one another, and shall hate one another.
11 And many false prophets shall rise, and shall deceive many.
12 And because iniquity shall abound, the love of many shall wax cold.
13 But he that shall endure unto the end, the same shall be saved.

To the end of what? To the end of the age. To the end of one's ministry. To the end of one's life.

It is interesting that Jesus uses the same phrase in verse 13 as he does when He commissions the disciples to preach the Gospel in Matthew 10:

Mat 10:22 And ye shall be hated of all *men* for my name's sake*: but he that endureth to the end shall be saved.*

"Endure" means to persevere, to undergo, to hold fast to one's faith in Christ, remain, (and interestingly) *to tarry behind*. There is no easy way out of the persecution and the challenges that will accompany the ministry that is centered on the message of the Gospel. It is the message of the Gospel that results in persecution.

But What Is The Gospel?

It was the *Gospel of the Kingdom of God* that the disciples were told to preach:

Matt 10:7 And as ye go, preach, saying, The kingdom of heaven is at hand.

Some might argue that the passage in Matthew says "The Kingdom of Heaven", and not the Kingdom of God. That the phrases are interchangeable can be seen in Luke 9 and elsewhere:

Luk 9:2 And he sent them to preach the kingdom of God, and to heal the sick.

Jesus warns us that true discipleship in the Ways of the Kingdom of God will result in persecution.

Joh 15:19 If ye were of the world, the world would love his own: but because ye are not of the world, but I have chosen you out of the world, therefore the world hateth you.
20 Remember the word that I said unto you, The servant is not greater than his lord. If they have persecuted me, they will also persecute you; if they have kept my saying, they will keep yours also.
21 But all these things will they do unto you for my name's sake, because they know not him that sent me.

The Gospel of the Kingdom of God threatens the way things are done in the political, economic, and social realms of the kingdoms of this world. The Gospel of the Kingdom of God threatens cultures, traditions and lifestyles.

Matt 24:14 AND THIS GOSPEL OF THE KINGDOM SHALL BE PREACHED IN ALL THE WORLD FOR A WITNESS UNTO ALL NATIONS; AND THEN SHALL THE END COME

It is only when the Gospel of the Kingdom of God is preached in all the world that the end of the age will come.

It is important to note here that it is the same Gospel of the Kingdom that Jesus and His disciples preached that will usher in the end of the age. He said *THIS* GOSPEL OF THE KINGDOM shall be preached in all the world (kosmos).

A study of Matthew 10 will reveal how Jesus intended for the ministry to be conducted.

In Matthew 10, the disciples are told to preach the Gospel of the Kingdom of God in Israel:

Mat 10:5 These twelve Jesus sent forth, and commanded them, saying, Go not into the way of the Gentiles, and into *any* city of the Samaritans enter ye not:
6 But go rather to the lost sheep of the house of Israel.
7 And as ye go, preach, saying, The kingdom of heaven is at hand.

In Matthew 24, Jesus is telling the disciples that the Commission in the end of the age will be the same as it was for them, except that instead of being LOCAL and confined to ISRAEL, the scope of the ministry of the Gospel of the Kingdom of God will be global, and there will be an increase in persecutions, and false prophets, and many declarations of the Coming of Christ as well.

Matthew 24:14 tells what the sign of the end of the age is, and *that is that the Gospel of the Kingdom of God will be preached in all the world*! It is important that the reader grasp the significance of that truth.

THERE IS A MARKED DIFFERENCE BETWEEN THE GOSPEL THAT IS GENERALLY PREACHED FROM THE PULPIT TODAY AND THE GOSPEL THAT JESUS AND THE DISCIPLES PREACHED.

The Gospel that Jesus and the Disciples preached included going out into the cities and the towns, healing the sick, cleansing the lepers, raising the dead, and casting out devils, with the proclamation that the Kingdom of God or the Kingdom of Heaven was at hand.

It is important to understand this fact: *The Gospel that Jesus preached was the Gospel of the Kingdom of God,* and it wasn't about some future Kingdom that would come after we all died or got raptured out of here; it was a Gospel that proclaimed that the Kingdom of God is at hand, present tense, *NOW.*

This is how Jesus commissioned His Disciples:

Mat 10:5 These twelve Jesus sent forth, and commanded them, saying, Go not into the way of the Gentiles, and into *any* city of the Samaritans enter ye not:
6 But go rather to the lost sheep of the house of Israel.
7 And as ye go, preach, saying, The kingdom of heaven is at hand.
8 Heal the sick, cleanse the lepers, raise the dead, cast out devils: freely ye have received, freely give.
9 Provide neither gold, nor silver, nor brass in your purses,
10 Nor scrip for *your* journey, neither two coats, neither shoes, nor yet staves: for the workman is worthy of his meat.

11 And into whatsoever city or town ye shall enter, enquire who in it is worthy; and there abide till ye go thence.
12 And when ye come into an house, salute it.

Most Churches today are preaching different gospels than the Gospel of the Kingdom of God. What do I mean by that?

There are whole denominations that preach a *Cessationist doctrine* and present it as the Gospel.

They say that the miraculous gifts aren't needed any longer because we have the Bible written down for us to instruct us in the Way of perfection.

Some go so far as to say that technological advances negate the need for the Gifts of the Spirit today. But that is *not* the Gospel of the Kingdom.

The Kingdom of God comes with demonstration of the Power of God, not mere philosophy and doctrinal thesis'.

The Cessationist gospel is actually paving the way for the anti-Christ spirit of unbelief that will (and already has) eventually infect many "mainstream denominations", where people will have a form of godliness but deny the Power thereof. These same people will say that they believe the Bible is inerrant and infallible, while allowing their doctrine to teach them that much of the Bible is irrelevant for the Christian today.

Paul writes "Covet earnestly the best gifts" (1 Cor 12:31), but what would be the point of that if the Gifts have been done away with? If he was only writing to the Corinthian church at that particular point in time, and it has nothing to do with us today, then I would suggest high-lighting the entire 1st and 2nd Corinthians with black magic marker, so you won't get any more confused than you already are.

One man I spoke to recently was adamant about the necessity to obey Mark 16:16, and to be baptized in order to be saved.

Mar 16:15 And he said unto them, Go ye into all the world, and preach the gospel to every creature.
16 He that believeth and is baptized shall be saved; but he that believeth not shall be damned.

But when we were talking about the Gifts of the Spirit, he told me that they went away with the apostles. I said what about "Mark 16:17 and 18?" He explained to me that wasn't for us today.

Mar 16:17 And these signs shall follow them that believe; In my name shall they cast out devils; they shall speak with new tongues;
18 They shall take up serpents; and if they drink any deadly thing, it shall not hurt them; they shall lay hands on the sick, and they shall recover.

I told him it was Jesus speaking these things in the same dialogue that He spoke of being baptized. If you are going to pick and choose what you want to believe and what you don't want to believe, you are treading on dangerous ground. Either all of what Jesus said here applies, or none of it does.

Cessationism is *another* gospel.

For centuries the bulk of what was preached was the gospel of Catholicism and the *Nicolaitan* heresy of a clergy/laity division that teaches that only certain men are granted a special "anointing" to do the work of the ministry.[2]

Then came the gospel of Anabaptists, then the gospel of the Lutherans, or the Protestant gospel, then the Baptist, the Calvinist Gospel, the Armenian gospel, the Quaker gospel, the Methodist gospel, the denominational gospel, the non denominational gospel, the Pentecostal gospel, the Charismatic gospel, the Holiness gospel, the snake handling and poison drinking gospel, the tongue speaking gospel, the social gospel, the prosperity gospel, the seeker friendly gospel, the legalistic gospel, the Universalist gospel, the Unitarian gospel, the end times gospel, the preterist gospel, the futurist gospel, the pre-trib, mid-trib and post-trib gospel, the gospel of church membership, the anti-homosexual gospel, the all-inclusive gospel, and a thousand other gospels have been and are being preached. Paul's concern that he expressed to the Church has come to pass:

2Co 11:3 But I fear, lest by any means, as the serpent beguiled Eve through his subtilty, so your minds should be corrupted from the simplicity that is in Christ.
4 For if he that cometh preacheth another Jesus, whom we have not preached, or *if* ye receive another spirit, which ye have not received, or another gospel, which ye have not accepted, ye might well bear with *him*.

While all of these other "gospels" are being preached in the pulpits to a passive tithe paying membership, the Gospel of the Kingdom of God was and is being to a large degree neglected.

Rather than making and commissioning disciples to "go into all the world" with the same power and authority as the original disciples had, to proclaim that the Kingdom of God *is at hand* as laid out in Matthew 10, Christianity has become a religion with statutes and ordinances (read dress codes, church attendance, membership requirements, and a whole spectrum of do's and don'ts) instead of a world-changing force or lifestyle (read "culture") to all who embrace it.

The gospel that is preached today requires the passing of a collection plate or a guaranteed "honorarium" for those who preach it. Jesus taught that if we make the Kingdom of God our priority, God will take care of our expenses (See Matthew10:9 and Matt 6:33).

But in the Last Days the Gospel of the Kingdom of God will once again be preached.
That is the sign of the end of this present age and the end of the rule that the god of this age has over this world.

Matt 24:14 AND THIS GOSPEL OF THE KINGDOM SHALL BE PREACHED IN ALL THE WORLD FOR A WITNESS UNTO ALL NATIONS; AND THEN SHALL THE END COME

The correlation to this occurrence is found in Revelation 14:6,7:

**Rev 14:6 And I saw another angel fly in the midst of heaven, having the everlasting gospel to preach unto them that dwell on the earth, and to every nation, and kindred, and tongue, and people,
7 Saying with a loud voice, Fear God, and give glory to him; for the hour of his judgment is come: and worship him that made heaven, and earth, and the sea, and the fountains of waters.**

When the Gospel of the Kingdom of God is preached and received by enough individuals in a region, it changes the culture of that region. It changes the landscape. It changes how society looks, and the world view of those who embrace it. It changes the economy.

When the Gospel of the Kingdom of God was preached in the Book of Acts, those who believed had all things in common. No one lacked anything. But it was not a gospel of "having all things in common". It was the Gospel of the Kingdom of God that caused those who embraced it to be cheerful givers out of the genuine love and concern that they had for one another.

The Gospel of the Kingdom of God does NOT preach the necessity of paying a tithe of one's income. When one has become impacted by the profound Truths of the Kingdom of God, his or her lifestyle will be a lifestyle of cheerfully giving of their substance for the furtherance of the Kingdom. Those who are part of a ministry that is equipping them to fulfill their purpose in Christ, will gladly invest their resources into that ministry. The Kingdom minded person is a cheerful giver. A mere ten percent of their income isn't enough to invest in the Kingdom and in those around them. The early Church (read citizens of the Kingdom of God) gave all:

**Act 2:44 And all that believed were together, and had all things common;
45 And sold their possessions and goods, and parted them to all *men,* as every man had need.**

Those who preach the Gospel of the Kingdom of God are actively involved in a warfare against the kingdoms of this world. Where the Kingdom of God takes root, worldviews change.

The other gospels that are so prevalent today are of little concern to the devil, the "god of this age". As long as the Christians stay contained in their buildings, he is not really overly concerned. But the Gospel of the Kingdom goes out into the market place, into the highways and the byways, the hedges, and the street corners. The Gospel of the Kingdom invades the devil's turf, and that is of great concern to him.

When the open air preacher preaches repentance in the market square, people who are under the influence of the god of this age begin to gnash their teeth, and to rail on the preacher. "Keep that in your church, not out here!" they will yell. Warfare is taking place. Seeds are being planted in hearts that may never hear the Gospel otherwise.

Satan wants the gospel to remain contained in the four walls of the "church", because it isn't a threat to his kingdom as long as it is kept in the building. And the majority of Christians comply with his demands.

Those who are truly Born of the Spirit of God are transformed from a carnal worldly mindset, and they begin to see things through the Eyes of God, as long as they don't allow their understanding to become blinded by the deception that the god of this age tries to get them entangled in, sometimes through well meaning but deceived preachers.

Satan wants to keep Christians in the carnal realm, being spoon-fed feel good messages about how God wants to bless them or how Jesus is coming soon to take you out of this mess. That is NOT the gospel of the early Church. Paul told Timothy to endure hardness as a good soldier of Jesus Christ (2 Tim 2:3). There is no feel good message there.

Paul and Silas preached the Gospel of the Kingdom of God in the market place as well as from house to house and the synagogues, and people began getting rid of things that were a part of their world-centered culture. That impacted the social-economic realm of their world. Businesses were shutting down because people weren't buying their idols any more. As a result, Paul and Silas and those who followed them were persecuted for their faith, and were accused of turning the world upside down.

Act 17:5 But the Jews which believed not, moved with envy, took unto them certain lewd fellows of the baser sort, and gathered a company, and set all the city on an uproar, and assaulted the house of Jason, and sought to bring them out to the people.
6 And when they found them not, they drew Jason and certain brethren unto the rulers of the city, crying, These that have turned the world upside down are come hither also;

The Gospel of the Kingdom of God will turn the world upside down. It will be preached by a vibrant world changing Body of Christ before the Coming of the Lord, and it will usher in the end of the age, a transition from the rule of the god of this age, to the establishment of the Millennial Kingdom of Jesus Christ. The Lord is just waiting for His people to start walking in obedience to His Commission to "Go and preach the Gospel".

Psa 146:9 The LORD preserveth the strangers; he relieveth the fatherless and widow: but the way of the wicked he turneth upside down.
10 The LORD shall reign forever, *even* thy God, O Zion, unto all generations. Praise ye the LORD.

There is currently a myriad of types of another gospel (read "agendas") being preached that have rendered the Church at large ineffective and irrelevant in the Western world. Hence there is currently very little persecution happening in the West, because Western Christianity is not presently a danger to the kingdoms of this world/age, but that could change if the Church awakens to and begins to fulfill its Purpose.

The goal of the god of this world is to eradicate Christianity from the face of the earth, either through great persecution (read tribulation) or through rendering the Church completely ineffective and irrelevant.

He uses his puppets that he has planted in the pulpits (read "tares") to do that. Satan's puppets stress church membership, church activities, and faithfulness to tithe. Servants of God equip those who are in their care to do the work of the ministry, not to be admission paying spectators. There are considerably more puppets in the pulpits of America who are more eager to build their own kingdoms than they are the Kingdom of God. And so the Western Church is of little significance in America, as long as the preachers are fat and comfortable with their fat and comfortable congregations.

But Christians are being slaughtered elsewhere for the Name of Christ, not because they are helpless, but because the truth of Christianity is a threat to the cultures that worship other gods.

Anti Christ Influences Abound

Islam is a culture in nations whose socio-economic-political worldview is influenced by its religion. True Christian faith threatens that culture, so one of the pivotal doctrines that adherents of Islam are taught is that their god *ALLAH* has no son, whereas Christianity's God has a Son, and so Christianity is viewed by adherents of Islam as an attempt to turn their culture upside down.

They say the God of the Bible is the same god as theirs, yet they join forces with other Anti Semite and Anti Christian ideologies in an attempt to eradicate Jews and Christians (the People of the Book) from the face of the earth, or at the least, to make them pay a tax (Jizya, a tax exacted from non-Muslims) for the privilege to exist.

Islam by its nature is a religion of the Anti Christ spirit. Christians throughout the world are being slaughtered and persecuted by adherents of Islam because of the Anti Christ spirit behind their religion.

1Jn 2:22 Who is a liar but he that denieth that Jesus is the Christ? He is antichrist, that denieth the Father and the Son.
23 Whosoever denieth the Son, the same hath not the Father: *(but) he that acknowledgeth the Son hath the Father also.*

The Hindu faith is a culture in nations whose socio-economic-political worldview is influenced by its religion. Whereas Hinduism has many gods, Christianity teaches that there is only one God, and Jesus Christ is the only way to that one God. For this reason Christians are being slaughtered in Hindu nations. It is the same in other countries around the world whose culture is influenced by their religion.

Christianity in the West has to a large degree become conformed to the worldliness of those who pursue the American Dream (worshipping the created thing instead of the Creator), and instead of being a world-changing influence that would transform the Western culture from its idolatry of material pleasure to the worship of the God of all creation, the culture of the "American dream" has influenced Christianity to conform to it.

American Christians are all about owning their home and their two car garage and the debt that goes with it. The Bible teaches about debt that lasts no more than seven years (read Deuteronomy 15). But Christians in the Western world are caught up in 30 year loans in order to possess things that moth and rust will one day corrupt, or thieves will steal, even though the One they profess to serve taught against that very thing.

Today in Western nations, Christianity is simply one of many religions, as opposed to a cultural lifestyle (with the possible exception of those who adhere to the Amish and Mennonite faith), and it only holds relevance to those who embrace that religion. But elsewhere, Christianity is a culture changing lifestyle, a driving force that influences the socio-economic-political worldview of the region in which it exists.

Whether modern historians wish to acknowledge it or not, the truth is that our nation was founded on Judeo-Christian values, and not so long ago it was acknowledged by other nations as being a Christian nation, and the laws and society in general were pretty much centered around Judeo-Christian values. There are still those in the United States who wish to maintain those Christian values, but because of compromise from the pulpit in the interest of '"seeker-sensitivity" and "church growth", that reality is eroding fast.

The Gospel that Paul Preached. 1 Cor 15

Some people will say that the "Gospel" is defined in 1 Corinthians 15:1-8. They say this because Paul prefaces that chapter with these words:

1 Co 15:1 Moreover, brethren, I declare unto you the gospel which I preached unto you, which also ye have received, and wherein ye stand;
2 By which also ye are saved, if ye keep in memory what I preached unto you, unless ye have believed in vain.

This follows what Paul wrote concerning the Gifts and the order of the service in a typical fellowship gathering (1 Cor 12-14). It is important to understand that the Gifts and the order of service are integral parts of the function of the Kingdom of God in this world.

He then says,

1Co 15:3 For I delivered unto you first of all that which I also received, how that Christ died for our sins according to the scriptures;
4 And that he was buried, and that he rose again the third day according to the scriptures:
5 And that he was seen of Cephas, then of the twelve:
6 After that, he was seen of above five hundred brethren at once; of whom the greater part remain unto this present, but some are fallen asleep.
7 After that, he was seen of James; then of all the apostles.
8 And last of all he was seen of me also, as of one born out of due time.

Some people are content with keeping the Gospel at that; that Christ died for our sins, that He was buried and that He rose again, that many eyewitness saw Him after His resurrection, and that sometime in the future He will return for His Church (15:32). And Paul deals extensively in chapter 15 with the Truth of the resurrection and Christ's return.

But Paul says that this was the "first thing that he shared with them" (verse 3). A lot of preachers park their theology in this lot, and they think that is the whole gospel. But Paul didn't say this is the whole of the gospel.

The truth is that Christ reigns.

To reign means to be sovereign. Supreme over all.

Jesus is sitting at the Right Hand of the Father in the Heavenly Places. God wants His Church to understand what that means and what that entails.

In his letter to the Ephesians, Paul's prayer was that the eyes of their understanding would be enlightened:

Eph 1:18 ...that ye may know what is the hope of his calling, and what the riches of the glory of his inheritance in the saints,
19 And what is the exceeding greatness of his power to us-ward who believe, according to the working of his mighty power *(Kratos = Governing Authority. This speaks of the Kingdom of God).*
20 Which he wrought in Christ, when he raised him from the dead, and set him at his own right hand in the heavenly places,

In verse 19, Christ's Sovereignty is mentioned in the light of God's Governing Authority. What is the Hope of your calling? Those who have been called can have confidence (really what the word "hope" means) that their calling is accompanied with everything they need to fulfill that calling.

On a personal note, I offer this testimony to verify that statement: Anyone who knows me and is familiar with the ministry God has called me to knows I don't make appeals for money, asking people to help me do what the Lord has Called me to do. That is not because I am rich and self sufficient. I just have confidence in His Faithfulness. A few days ago at the time of this writing, we were down to 38 cents to our name after groceries. BUT no one knew that, except God. And I have confidence that He has called me to do the Work He has called me to, and as such, I have access to His riches which enable me to do that work. *Confidence* allows me to rest, and enables me to concentrate on HIS Kingdom work. Anyway, God spoke to a brother and a sister who live a long way from us, and they heard Him, and although they didn't realize it, they took our 38 cents to 200+ dollars. Michelle and I chuckled at how the Lord always comes through at the perfect time. This is not an isolated incident in our lives. This is a common testimony for us as we put the furtherance of the Kingdom of God top priority in our lives. *Yahweh Yireh* (some say Jehovah Jireh). That is one of His Names. He is Provider for all of the children of His Kingdom. He is El Shaddai. The God who is all sufficient. He is more than enough for any of our needs. And since He is no respecter of persons, He is more than enough for any of *your* needs as well, if you are a child of God who has resolved to seek *FIRST* His Kingdom and His Righteousness (Matt 6:33).

He wants us to understand what is the exceeding greatness of His Power to us-ward who believe.

The Father has exalted His Son

Eph 1:21 Far above all principality, and power, and might, and dominion, and every name that is named, not only in this world, but also in that which is to come:
22 And hath put all things under his feet, and gave him to be the head over all things to the church,
23 Which is his body, the fulness of him that filleth all in all.

ALL things are under His feet. His Name is greater than every principality, every authority (translated as "power" in verse 21), every power, and every government (dominion) that rules over this age; and that exact list is mentioned in 1 Cor 15:24 in that exact order (principality, power and might) where it mentions that there will be a day when He will have put down all principalities (same word as "rule" in 1 Cor 15:24), authority, and power.

1Co 15:24 Then cometh the end, when he shall have delivered up the kingdom to God, even the Father; when he shall have put down all rule (principality) **and all authority** (power) **and power** (might)**.**

Remember this is the gospel Paul is reminding us that he preached.

How does He put down all rule and all authority and all power in this world?

Through those men and women of God who respond to His Commission to "Go and preach the Gospel in all the world to every creature" (Mark 16:15, Matthew 28:19). If you are a Christian and you are reading this book, you are one of those men and women of God who are intended to respond to His Commission.

His Work of establishing the Kingdom on this earth has not come to an end. It is still ongoing, and the Gospel we are to preach is still the Gospel of the Kingdom of God. The American Church has just been side tracked for a while. This book is written in the hopes that it will open our eyes to the necessity to get back on track.

In this life, in this time, on this earth, His Kingdom will be established once His Body (the Church) begins to be what the Church needs to be. And I am not talking about those little Sunday morning domiciles when I use the word "Church". I am talking about YOU. You are the Church. It is time to get serious.

1 Cor 15:25 For he must reign, till he hath put all enemies under his feet.

The Truth is Christ is reigning NOW (look at Ephesians 1:19-22 again). We are seated with Christ in the heavenlies, right where He is with the Father. I understand that is hard for a carnal mind to grasp, but what it means is this: His Authority, Dominion and Power is here at this moment for our employment for the furtherance of His Kingdom.

Eph 2:5 Even when we were dead in sins, hath quickened us together with Christ, (by grace ye are saved;)
6 And hath raised us up together, and made us sit together in heavenly places in Christ Jesus:
7 That in the ages to come he might shew the exceeding riches of his grace in his kindness toward us through Christ Jesus.

The Gospel is not just about Christ's death, burial, and resurrection.

It is about His Kingdom. His Power. His Authority. NOW.

All enemies are to be put under His feet. Everything that opposes Him. Christ is the Victor, not Satan.

The Gospel is about the privilege *you* have of working with Him to further His Kingdom here on this earth. There are other ages to come (vs 7 above) after the end of this age in which Satan rules. There is an age of a thousand year reign of Christ, and there is an age in which God will dwell with His people forever just as He intended in the Beginning. But rather than looking forward to that, we need to be busy in the fields of harvest for His Glory, and to see His Kingdom come, His Will be done, on earth, as it is in heaven.

There is a real battle taking place in the heavenlies.

Satan's puppets are active in the earth (whether they are atheists, Satanists, pagans, religious adherents, or Christian pretenders), furthering his agenda of ungodliness, while the servants of God are being lulled to sleep and complacency by Satan's pulpit puppets who are busy holding seminars on the end times and on feeling good about yourself and about becoming prosperous and successful Christians.

Silence in the face of evil is itself evil: God will not hold us guiltless. Not to speak is to speak. Not to act is to act.—Dietrich Bonhoeffer

The Church in America has been largely silent concerning the slaughter of innocent babies. One will rarely find many who will stand in front of a clinic to be a witness against the horrors of our nation's legalized infanticide industry. Yet behind the pulpits, preachers who never raised their voice in a public forum against the atrocity will speak to a congregation that has been publicly silent over the years, about how our nation is going to experience God's Judgment for the murder of millions of innocent lives. In your silence you have been a part of the industry. God's Judgment begins at the House of God.

The Church in America has sat inside the four walls howling in protest with loud Amen's as they listen to a preacher condemning homosexual marriage as the straw that broke the camel's back, and judgment is coming to America as a result of this great abomination, yet the preachers and the congregation have never ventured into a Gay Pride festival or a Gay district, or have avoided one on one conversations with those who are in that lifestyle in an attempt to warn them from their sin. It's been easier to talk about it among each other than having compassion on the soul that needs to be saved. Oh, did I mention that a third of the congregation has been divorced and remarried? Jesus called that adultery. God's Judgment begins at the House of God.

In its' silence, the Church in America has allowed evil to thrive in America, and yet it is quick to agree with the fiery speaking preacher who talks about the judgment that is soon to come on this evil nation, and Hallelujah! Jesus is coming to take us out of this sin-sick world to reward us for our faithfulness to attend church every week and to tithe our ten percent while we look with disdain at those who are wallowing in their sin, instead of trying to minister to them the Love of Christ in order to rescue them from their bondage.

Do you really think Jesus is coming for a wicked and slothful servant who chooses to hide his or her gifts in the four walls of the church rather than contending for the furtherance of the Kingdom of God? God's Judgment begins at the House of God.

Make no mistake. The Judgment that comes on America will come because we who profess to be Christians have been too busy playing church a couple of times a week instead of being the Church 24/7. Chances are good that your preacher has been lulling you to a place of comfort in your pews telling you that you'll fly out of here before it gets *too* bad.

It's interesting that recently I have been hearing those who once guaranteed a quick trip out before it got bad are now changing their tune and saying "We are going to go through some stuff..." but still salve our ears with the "I'll fly away" before its *really* bad. Remember you were supposed to be outta here *before* the mark of the beast came on the scene? Now we hear it's here and by 2017 according to some profits the mark will be mandatory. So if you are still here after 2017, and the chip system is in place, you better reconsider your position.

Of course, that would have to mean the Blood moons just came and went. And society continued as usual after the shimetah. And we will continue in our cubicles sitting on our pews with our loud "Amens" when we are cued to shout "Amen" by the preacher who preaches a "powerful word" to the choir. We hear dates, and are taught about the "fulfillment of prophecy" through world events, but as the Church we remain silent.

Yes, Judgment is coming. And it begins at the House of God. Every Christian should have a healthy fear of being found a wicked and slothful servant when He comes.

It's not too late to repent. Resolve today to be the Church every day to someone you encounter while about your daily business. Exercise the power and authority you have been given by Christ and lay hands on the sick, and pray for their healing. Cast out some devils. Feed some hungry people in the Name of Jesus. Devote your life to further the Kingdom of God while you are living this life.

Section 2

WHEN SHALL THERE NOT BE LEFT ONE STONE UPON ANOTHER?

The Anti Christ, the Abomination of Desolation And the Great Tribulation

ANSWERS: WHEN SHALL THERE NOT BE LEFT ONE STONE UPON ANOTHER?

It's time to put on your thinking hat. This next section is going to be dealing a lot with various end-times passages, and will require patience and prayer on the part of the reader in order to follow along, as it will be necessary to cover a significant portion of the Book of Daniel and the Book of Revelation in the following discussion concerning the Abomination of Desolation and other things that Jesus mentions.

A lot of what you have been taught concerning the "end times" will be challenged. Follow along in your Bible. Don't let "tradition" get in your way. Pray right now for the Lord to give you wisdom and insight as you read this.

Jesus continues His discourse on the Mount of Olives, teaching now about the first question the disciples had asked. "When shall these things be (that there will be no stone on top of another)?" The phrase "the abomination of desolation" and the reference to Daniel is what tells us that the next verses are in regard to the first question they had asked.

Mat 24:15 When ye therefore shall see the abomination of desolation, spoken of by Daniel the prophet, stand in the holy place, (whoso readeth, let him understand:)

That parenthetical statement in verse 15 **(whoso readeth, let him understand)** sets the stage for understanding what Jesus is referring to here. It is in Daniel that we first read about the abomination of desolation:

Dan 12:9 And he said, Go thy way, Daniel: for the words *are* closed up and sealed till the time of the end
10 Many shall be purified, and made white, and tried; but the wicked shall do wickedly: and none of the wicked shall understand; but the wise shall understand.
11 And from the time *that* the daily *sacrifice* shall be taken away, and the abomination that maketh desolate set up, *there shall be* a thousand two hundred and ninety days.

This abomination that makes desolate is also referred to in Daniel 8:13, and 9:27.

Dan 8:13 Then I heard one saint speaking, and another saint said unto that certain *saint* which spake, How long *shall be* the vision *concerning* the daily *sacrifice,* and the transgression of desolation, to give both the sanctuary and the host to be trodden under foot?
14 And he said unto me, Unto two thousand and three hundred days; then shall the sanctuary be cleansed.

History tells us that what Daniel had foretold in Daniel chapter 8 had actually happened during the time of the Maccabees 150 years before Christ.

The translators of the Bishop's Bible and the Geneva Bible (both of which predated the King James translation) included the *Apocrypha* in their Bible, among which were the Books of the Maccabees. These books give a historical account of the period that took place between the Old Testament and the New Testament.

 In 1 Maccabees, we read about a man named Antiochus Epiphanes who desecrated the temple and put a statue of Jupiter Olympus in the temple and offered swine's blood on the altar, desecrating the sanctuary and the vessels with the blood and entrails of the pig. From the Geneva Bible we read:

1 Maccabees 1:57 The fifteenth day of Casleu, in the hundreth and fiue and fourtieth yeere, they set vp the abomination of desolation vpon the altar, and they buylded altars throughout the cities of Iuda on euery side.

In the Greek Septuagint (the Greek Old Testament), we find that reference in verse 54:

1 Maccabees 1:54 Now the fifteenth day of the month Casleu, in the hundred forty and fifth year, they set up the abomination of desolation upon the altar, and builded idol altars throughout the cities of Juda on every side

A more detailed account of what happened at that time follows (from the Septuagint):

**1 Maccabees 1:41 Moreover king Antiochus wrote to his whole kingdom, that all should be one people,
42 And every one should leave his laws: so all the heathen agreed according to the commandment of the king.
43 Yea, many also of the Israelites consented to his religion, and sacrificed unto idols, and profaned the sabbath.
44 For the king had sent letters by messengers unto Jerusalem and the cities of Juda that they should follow the strange laws of the land,
45 And forbid burnt offerings, and sacrifice, and drink offerings, in the temple; and that they should profane the sabbaths and festival days:
46 And pollute the sanctuary and holy people:
47 Set up altars, and groves, and chapels of idols, and sacrifice swine's flesh, and unclean beasts:
48 That they should also leave their children uncircumcised, and make their souls abominable with all manner of uncleanness and profanation:
49 To the end they might forget the law, and change all the ordinances.
50 And whosoever would not do according to the commandment of the king, he said, he should die.
51 In the selfsame manner wrote he to his whole kingdom, and appointed overseers over all the people, commanding the cities of Juda to sacrifice, city by city.
52 Then many of the people were gathered unto them, to wit every one that forsook the law; and so they committed evils in the land;**

53 And drove the Israelites into secret places, even wheresoever they could flee for succour.

54 Now the fifteenth day of the month Casleu, in the hundred forty and fifth year, they set up the *abomination of desolation* upon the altar, and builded idol altars throughout the cities of Juda on every side;

55 And burnt incense at the doors of their houses, and in the streets.

56 And when they had rent in pieces the books of the law which they found, they burnt them with fire.

57 And whosoever was found with any the book of the testament, or if any committed to the law, the king's commandment was, that they should put him to death.

58 Thus did they by their authority unto the Israelites every month, to as many as were found in the cities.

59 Now the five and twentieth day of the month they did sacrifice upon the idol altar, which was upon the altar of God.

60 At which time according to the commandment they put to death certain women, that had caused their children to be circumcised.

61 And they hanged the infants about their necks, and rifled their houses, and slew them that had circumcised them.

62 Howbeit many in Israel were fully resolved and confirmed in themselves not to eat any unclean thing.

63 Wherefore the rather to die, that they might not be defiled with meats, and that they might not profane the holy covenant: so then they died.

64 And there was very great wrath upon Israel.

Daniel's prophetic word concerning the Abomination of Desolation was fulfilled in this event which took place in Jerusalem about 150 years Before Christ.

Keil and Delitzsch's commentary which was published somewhere around 1860 presents much evidence of the prophecy being fulfilled by Antiochus Epiphanes, and also deals with the various interpretations then extant concerning the time frames mentioned in Daniel (1290 days, 1300 days, 1335 days, and three and a half weeks).

In Daniel 8 we see Antiochus Epiphanes prophetically referred to in verse 9 as the notable little horn (not to be confused with the little horn mentioned in Daniel 7) which exalted itself up to heaven.

Dan 8:5 And as I was considering, behold, an he goat came from the west on the face of the whole earth, and touched not the ground: and the goat *had* a notable horn between his eyes.

6 And he came to the ram that had *two* horns, which I had seen standing before the river, and ran unto him in the fury of his power.

7 And I saw him come close unto the ram, and he was moved with choler against him, and smote the ram, and brake his two horns: and there was no power in the ram to stand before him, but he cast him down to the ground, and stamped upon him: and there was none that could deliver the ram out of his hand.

8 Therefore the he goat waxed very great: and when he was strong, the great horn was broken; and for it came up four notable ones toward the four winds of heaven.

9 And out of one of them came forth a little horn, which waxed exceeding great, toward the south, and toward the east, and toward the pleasant *land.*

10 And it waxed great, *even* to the host of heaven; and it cast down *some* of the host and of the stars to the ground, and stamped upon them.

11 Yea, he magnified *himself* even to the prince of the host, and by him the daily *sacrifice* was taken away, and the place of his sanctuary was cast down.

F.B. Meyer (1847-1929) in his commentary wrote:

The Books of the Maccabees, included in the Apocrypha, should be studied to understand more clearly what is intended in Dan 8:11-12. The explanation of these obscure verses is also given in Dan 8:24-25. Antiochus was obsessed with hatred against the spiritual worship of the Jews, and their refusal to admit his image into the Temple. He stayed their sacrifices, though they were restored for a season, to be finally suspended during the present age.

I mention Keil and Delitzsch and FB Meyer here because their views concerning the prophecies of Daniel are typically in agreement with most commentators of their time, and of those who wrote commentaries in the centuries leading up to the 19th century.

In the 1800s, many "end time" teachers arose who declared that the end of the world was at hand. Jehovah's Witnesses, Mormonism, Christian Science, Seventh Day Adventism, and other cults arose with a message that the end was near, and that it was time to prepare for the Coming of the Lord. But there were other groups and teachers who were more mainstream in doctrine than the cults just mentioned who also jumped on the end times band wagon as well.

DARBY'S "END TIMES" DOCTRINE

It was also in the early 1800's that John Nelson Darby formulated the theory of a secret rapture that would happen before the visible return of Christ. This new doctrine, which had never been mentioned in the 1800 years prior to Darby's revelation (1830) eventually became known as the Pre-tribulation rapture. Prior to Darby's introduction of this secret return of Christ, most commentators agreed that the prophecies spoken of in Daniel had already been fulfilled, either by Antiochus Epiphanies or with the Roman destruction of Jerusalem in 70 AD.

The *Scofield Reference Bible* is perhaps the single greatest contributor to the popularization of Darby's doctrine.

In doing ministry on the streets of Chattanooga in the early 1990's I would regularly encounter theological students who would engage me in conversation about various subjects, more often than not, concerning the end times. I would often have to remind them that they were quoting from Scofield rather than the Biblical text. People have a tendency to do that with their "reference Bibles" - they glean most of their information from the commentary around the text than they do from the Word of God itself. I often hear people echoing Dake's sentiments rather than the Word of God.

I acknowledge that I myself refer to the commentaries of Adam Clarke, Jamieson-Faucet and Brown, and F.B. Meyers throughout this book, but I include them only because I have studied the Word of God first, and found that I am in general agreement with the bulk of their observations.

One of the common verses that are quoted when someone goes against the current flow of accepted interpretation of prophecy is 2 Peter 2:10, which says "that no prophecy of the scripture is of any private interpretation. "

A lot of teachers today use this verse to insulate themselves from accusations that they may be wrong in their deductions. The one who believes in a pretrib rapture will use this verse against someone who doesn't believe that position, saying in essence, "Our whole denomination believes in a pre-trib rapture, and now you are coming in here with some foreign idea that goes against what we believe. But the Bible says that no prophecy of the scripture is of any private interpretation. " The fact that I often quote these various scholars should be proof to the skeptic that the majority of what I write is not from my own "private revelation".

It is only after I come up with a conclusion about a specific passage of the Word of God, that I read a commentary to see if I am not "way out there" in my conclusions. Having said that, I do understand that there are some who will read this book, and think that I *am* way out there in my conclusions, but if they read this with an honest mind, I do think they will have to admit that I don't dance around and pluck scripture out of context to prove my point. I don't read a commentary as "Thus saith the Lord", and neither should you.

Since I am hunting sacred cows, I have to say this: I personally think it is pretty irresponsible for anyone to buy into the commentator's view that the Church is raptured at Revelation 4:1, when the verse is plainly saying it was *John* who was caught up in the spirit to behold the vision that he was shown. The truth is, if it wasn't for those who embraced Darby and Scofield's line of thought in their commentaries, no reader would ever come up with the conclusion that this was talking about anyone else *but* John.

Rev 4:1 After this I looked, and, behold, a door *was* opened in heaven: and the first voice which I heard *was* as it were of a trumpet talking with me; which said, Come up hither, and I will shew thee things which must be hereafter.
2 And immediately I was in the spirit: and, behold, a throne was set in heaven, and *one* sat on the throne.

If anyone violated the principle of 2 Peter 2:10, it was certainly John Darby.

Prior to Darby's introduction of his doctrine of the secret rapture of the Church, there was no idea of a separation between the sixty ninth and seventieth weeks of Daniel that modern day dispensationalist premillenials teach. To read more about the 70th week, please refer to my appendix concerning the Seventieth week.

R. Sandeen: *"Darby introduced into discussion at Powerscourt (1833) the ideas of a secret rapture of the church and of a parenthesis in prophetic fulfillment between the sixty-ninth and seventieth weeks of Daniel. These two concepts constituted the basic tenets of the system of theology since referred to as dispensationalism" (E.R. Sandeen, The Roots of Fundamentalism 1800-1930, University of Chicago Press, 1970).*

The reader can reference the Appendix at the back of this book for more observations from contemporaries of Darby regarding Darby's doctrine[3.]

The truth is, there are a variety of interpretations (as many as there are of commentators) as to the meaning and the timing of Daniel's prophecies.

Whatever the true interpretation of Daniel's Prophecies may be, whether they are speaking of Antiochus Epiphanes, or some more distant future event (or both), Jesus said that there would be another occurrence of this (**whoso readeth, let him understand** Matthew 24:15).

The Septuagint and the Book of Maccabees were extant at that time, and no doubt Jesus and the rabbis knew the history of the Maccabees and what was said about the "Abomination of Desolation". That prophetic Word spoken by Jesus here in Matthew 24:15 was largely fulfilled in 70 A.D. when Jerusalem was destroyed by the Romans and the Temple was once again defiled and then leveled to the ground.

Jesus tells his disciples some wise advice concerning that time that was soon to come, when all of Israel would be scattered because of the Roman destruction, and of the future persecution that would arise:

Mat 24:16 Then let them which be in Judaea flee into the mountains:
17 Let him which is on the housetop not come down to take anything out of his house:
18 Neither let him which is in the field return back to take his clothes.
19 And woe unto them that are with child, and to them that give suck in those days!
20 But pray ye that your flight be not in the winter, neither on the sabbath day:
21 For then shall be great tribulation, such as was not since the beginning of the world to this time, no, nor ever shall be.

There Are Still Some Stones Remaining

While the prophetic word of Jesus concerning when the temple would be destroyed saw it's fulfillment in 70 AD in the Roman destruction of Jerusalem, it was NOT completely fulfilled, as is evidenced by the fact that the Wailing Wall or the Western Wall (which was part of the temple) is still standing in Jerusalem to this current day. Remember Jesus said there would not be one stone left upon another.

Preterists say that Jesus' Prophetic Word was fulfilled in 70 AD, because the temple was completely destroyed, but I personally believe the wall that remains is testimony to the fact that Jesus' Prophecy has not been completely fulfilled, and is another indication of a sign as to when the end of the age would take place.

I believe the wall will collapse either naturally or through violent means (most likely the latter) sometime in the relatively near future, and when it does, then we can expect the end of this age to be drawing quickly to a close.

Jesus' words concerning the Temple and it's buildings are what spurred the disciples to ask the three questions in the first place:

Mat 24:1 And Jesus went out, and departed from the temple: and his disciples came to _him_ for to shew him the buildings of the temple.
2 And Jesus said unto them, See ye not all these things? verily I say unto you, There shall not be left here one stone upon another, that shall not be thrown down.

MORE ON THE ANTI CHRIST AND THE ABOMINATION OF DESOLATION

In Daniel, the prophetic word was that the daily sacrifice would cease (Dan 8:12), then a period of time would pass, and the Abomination of Desolation would be set up (See verse 44 and 45 of 1 Maccabees chapter one above [at the beginning of this section], and then verse 54).

The Abomination of Desolation that Jesus spoke of _was not_ that which Daniel prophesied, because that was already fulfilled in Antiochus Epiphanes.

The New Testament speaks of how things that happened under the Old Covenant were _types and shadows_ of the New (see 1 Cor 10:11, Col 2:17, Heb 8:5, 9:5, 10:1), and I see the prophetic word in Daniel which was fulfilled in the person of Antiochus Epiphanes before the time of Christ as being a type and shadow of that which Jesus prophesied in Matthew 24.

Just as the daily sacrifice ceased in the days of the Maccabees, it also ceased when Jerusalem was razed by the Roman armies in 70 AD, and most commentators agree that the Abomination of Desolation was the Roman standard consisting of a graven image of an Eagle (an unclean bird) mounted on top of a pole on which flew a flag containing the image of Caesar who was worshipped as a god.

It is _my opinion_ that the ensign of the Roman Legions was only another shadow of what would come, and what would be set in place six hundred and ten years later when the Dome of the Rock was erected on the temple mount (689-691 AD).

Why Didn't Jesus Give Dates?

Unlike Daniel's prophecy about Antiochus Epiphanes, Jesus didn't give specific time periods in which these things were to take place. That is an important factor to understand. Jesus gave signs whereby we could tell the end of the age was near, but he didn't give specific time periods. Why?

I believe the reason Jesus didn't give dates is because *those who would follow Jesus have been granted an authority and power that Israel was not given.*

That Authority and Power was given to those who professed faith in Christ in order to equip them to further the Kingdom of God on earth. Lay hands on the sick, cast out devils, raise the dead, and thus demonstrate the existence of God to a world lost in vain religion and philosophical ideologies. The Commission given in Mark 16:15-18, Matthew 28:18-20 and Acts 1:8 has not changed. Paul walked in the Power and Authority that accompanies the Great Commission:

1Co 2:1 And I, brethren, when I came to you, came not with excellency of speech or of wisdom, declaring unto you the testimony of God.
2 For I determined not to know any thing among you, save Jesus Christ, and him crucified.
3 And I was with you in weakness, and in fear, and in much trembling.
4 And my speech and my preaching *was* not with enticing words of man's wisdom, but in demonstration of the Spirit and of power:

It would be at some time in the future, when the love of Christians would wax cold, and when they would be more concerned with their personal agendas rather than the furtherance of the Kingdom of God that the stage would be set for the end of the age.

Mat 24:12 And because iniquity shall abound, the love of many shall wax cold.

Iniquity would increase because the Church ceased to be the light and hedge between good and evil. Compromise and conformity with the world would grey the lines between sin and holiness. Morality would decay, and Christians would blend in with a godless society.

Throughout history, men and women of God who would not be conformed to this world have stood as the hedge between the Judgment of God and the future of humanity.

It was their love for God that compelled people like Polycarp, Ignatius, Aristides, Tertullian, the Waldensians, Jan Hus, John Wycliffe, John Knox, Martin Luther, John Wesley, Charles Finney, Jonathan Edwards, Evan Roberts, and thousands of other names, some famous, others not so famous to stand up in times of great persecution or apostasy and to be the hedge between God's Judgment and humanity.

I believe that Christ gave no dates, because it is left to the Church to determine the state of the world in their generation. When an apostate Church would forsake the commission to further the Kingdom of God, wickedness would increase. When God's people would humble themselves and repent of their wickedness, and return to the Business of the Kingdom, then God would stay His Hand of Judgment.

If you read the accounts of men like Jonathan Edwards, Charles Finney, George Whitfield, John Wesley, and others who were instrumental in ushering in the First and Second Great Awakening, the Welsh revival, the Hebrides Revival, the Azuza Street Revival, and to a degree the tent Revivals of the 1940s and 1950's, you will discover that in their day, the Church was in a very dire state of moral decay and complacency. In each of these times, a few men gave all to effect a change in the Church, and I believe may have stayed the Hand of God from Judgment on the world.

The leaders of these great revivals (with the exception of some of the tent revivalists of the 40's and 50's) were either post millennialists or historic premillennialists. They believed that it was their responsibility to further the Kingdom of God during their existence on this earth, and it was with that purpose and that commitment to fulfill their Lord's Will by the Power of the Holy Spirit that they accomplished those great moves of God in history.

Whereas Jesus didn't give dates, most of Daniel's dates and time periods have been fulfilled, even down to the "seventieth week" of Daniel 9:24-27 that many modern (dispensationalist) commentators say has not been fulfilled in an effort to prove their eschatological position (I refer the reader again to the entry regarding the *seventieth week* in the Appendix. This would be a good time to read that). But Jesus never gave any dates, because He put that in the care of the Church. The Church is meant to be the hedge that keeps wickedness at bay. If you are a Christian, then that means YOU. If you are not doing anything to impact your world for Christ, then you are responsible for the darkness that is creeping in. That is not written to condemn you, it is written so you will repent and do something about it!

It is interesting to note what Meyer has to say concerning the 2300 days mentioned in Daniel 8:14 (although I myself am inclined to side with Keil and Delitsch's observations concerning the 2300 days - that the tyrant Antiochus Epiphanes' reign lasted 6 years and a few months - [see my note in appendix 4], I include Meyer's here, because it also has some degree of credibility, since he maintains a consistency in the "day for a year" measurement of time):

"The day for a year system, Dan 8:14, may refer to the desolations of the Turkish or Ottoman empire, of which Antiochus was the representative." *(Through the Bible Day By Day by F.B. Mayer)*

The Ottoman empire was an Islamic empire that was started in 1293 AD and extended to 1918.

I have never been inside the Dome of the Rock, but many sources say that on the walls of the Dome of the Rock is an inscription from Sura 19:33-35 of the Qu'ran that shows the *Anti Christ* nature of the Islamic faith. (***https://en.wikipedia.org/wiki/Dome_of_the_Rock; http://www.islamic-architecture.info/WA-IS/WA-IS-001.htm***).

According to this passage, Jesus Himself as an infant in Mary's arms says these words to the people who behold Him:

19:33. "So peace is upon me the day I was born, and the day I die, and the day I shall be raised alive!" 34. Such is Jesus, son of Mary. It is a statement of truth, about which they doubt. 35. It is not befitting to (the majesty of) Allah that He should beget a son. Glory be to Him! when He determines a matter, He only says to it, "Be", and it is.

Later in the same Sura (chapter) of the Quran we read this:

19:83 Do you not see that We have sent the devils upon the disbelievers, inciting them to [evil] with [constant] incitement?
84 So be not impatient over them. We only count out to them a [limited] number.
85 On the Day We will gather the righteous to the Most Merciful as a delegation
86 And will drive the criminals to Hell in thirst
87 None will have [power of] intercession except he who had taken from the Most Merciful a covenant.
88 And they say, "The Most Merciful has taken [for Himself] a son."
89 You have done an atrocious thing.
90 The heavens almost rupture therefrom and the earth splits open and the mountains collapse in devastation
91 That they attribute to the Most Merciful a son.
92 And it is not appropriate for the Most Merciful that He should take a son.
93 There is no one in the heavens and earth but that he comes to the Most Merciful as a servant.
94 He has enumerated them and counted them a [full] counting.
95 And all of them are coming to Him on the Day of Resurrection alone.
(Sahib international)

To the Muslim, Christians are deceived by the devils, because they believe that God the Father sent His Only Begotten Son into the world to atone for the sins of humanity. Christians are criminals who are destined for Hell.

It is important to remember that the Qu'ran was written over 500 years after the Gospels were written. It is obvious that the prophet of Islam's intention was to rewrite history and to thwart the intent of the Almighty God concerning His Plan of redemption for humanity.

According to Mohammed's account there was no birth in a manger; it took place under a tree. There were no wise men. The nativity account of the Bible is non-existent in the Qu'ran.

As I said earlier, the very foundation of the religion of Islam is Anti Christ in nature. Muslims are conditioned to deny the Fatherhood of God and the Sonship of Jesus Christ. 1 John tells us that those who deny the Father and the Son are antichrist.

1Jn 2:18 Little children, it is the last time: and as ye have heard that antichrist shall come, even now are there many antichrists; whereby we know that it is the last time.
19 They went out from us, but they were not of us; for if they had been of us, they would _no doubt_ have continued with us: but _they went out,_ that they might be made manifest that they were not all of us.
20 But ye have an unction from the Holy One, and ye know all things.
21 I have not written unto you because ye know not the truth, but because ye know it, and that no lie is of the truth.
22 Who is a liar but he that denieth that Jesus is the Christ? He is antichrist, that denieth the Father and the Son.
23 Whosoever denieth the Son, the same hath not the Father: _(but) he that acknowledgeth the Son hath the Father also._
24 Let that therefore abide in you, which ye have heard from the beginning. If that which ye have heard from the beginning shall remain in you, ye also shall continue in the Son, and in the Father.

THE BIBLICAL IDENTIFICATION OF THE ANTI CHRIST

For the reader's information, it may come as a shock to realize that the "Anti Christ" who should come that modern day prophets speak of isn't even referenced in the book of Revelation or in the book of 2 Thessalonians, yet many preachers refer to the antichrist in reference to these two books. The Truth is that the only place "antichrist" is mentioned is in 1st John and 2nd John, and it is denoted as a spirit that influences those who oppose Christ (1 Jn 4:3); primarily those who deny the doctrine of the Father and Son relationship of the One True God.

1Jn 2:22 Who is a liar but he that denieth that Jesus is the Christ? He is antichrist, that denieth the Father and the Son.
23 Whosoever denieth the Son, the same hath not the Father: _(but) he that acknowledgeth the Son hath the Father also._
24 Let that therefore abide in you, which ye have heard from the beginning. If that which ye have heard from the beginning shall remain in you, ye also shall continue in the Son, and in the Father.

Those who deny the Fatherhood of God and the Sonship of Jesus Christ embrace an antichrist doctrine. If one denies the Sonship of Jesus Christ, they are denying the Father, hence they cannot be children of God.

There are Christian denominations whose doctrine teaches them to deny the Triune Nature of God. This is not to be taken to mean three gods, or a three headed god as some of the teachers who operate in a spirit of Antichrist allege.

It is the same position Islam takes, whose foundational belief declares that "Allah has no son", which contradicts the foundational belief of Christianity:

Joh 3:16 For God so loved the world, that he gave his only begotten Son, that whosoever believeth in him should not perish, but have everlasting life.
17 For God sent not his Son into the world to condemn the world; but that the world through him might be saved.
18 He that believeth on him is not condemned: but he that believeth not is condemned already, because he hath not believed in the name of the only begotten Son of God.

Those who deny the Fatherhood of God and the Sonship of the Lord Jesus Christ are walking in condemnation, because they have rejected the Truth of the Word of God and have embraced the Spirit of Anti Christ. There are even "Christian" Denominations that embrace the Anti Christ doctrine. For a more detailed look at the Triune Nature of God, I would refer the reader to the appendix[5].

God's purpose is to bring humanity into the place of an adoption status with Him as their Father, whereby we who were once alienated from God can be reconciled to Him as sons. Satan does not want that Truth to be known, so the spirit of antichrist prevails in the minds and hearts of many who are under his sway.

Rom 8:15 For ye have not received the spirit of bondage again to fear; but ye have received the Spirit of adoption, whereby we cry, Abba, Father.

The whole creation is awaiting the reconciliation of humanity to God the Father. Jesus Christ, God's only BEGOTTEN Son was the avenue through which that would happen.

Rom 8:19 For the earnest expectation of the creature waiteth for the manifestation of the sons of God.
20 For the creature was made subject to vanity, not willingly, but by reason of him who hath subjected *the same* in hope,
21 Because the creature itself also shall be delivered from the bondage of corruption into the glorious liberty of the children of God.
22 For we know that the whole creation groaneth and travaileth in pain together until now.
23 And not only *they*, but ourselves also, which have the firstfruits of the Spirit, even we ourselves groan within ourselves, waiting for the adoption, *to wit*, the redemption of our body.

Before Jesus, we were alienated and enemies of God. But Jesus came to reconcile us to God and to redeem us from the power of sin which separated us from God.

Eph 1:3 Blessed *be* **the God and Father of our Lord Jesus Christ, who hath blessed us with all spiritual blessings in heavenly** *places* **in Christ:**

4 According as he hath chosen us in him before the foundation of the world, that we should be holy and without blame before him in love:

5 Having predestinated us unto the adoption of children by Jesus Christ to himself, according to the good pleasure of his will,

6 To the praise of the glory of his grace, wherein he hath made us accepted in the beloved.

7 In whom we have redemption through his blood, the forgiveness of sins, according to the riches of his grace;

8 Wherein he hath abounded toward us in all wisdom and prudence;

9 Having made known unto us the mystery of his will, according to his good pleasure which he hath purposed in himself:

10 That in the dispensation of the fulness of times he might gather together in one all things in Christ, both which are in heaven, and which are on earth; *even* **in him:**

11 In whom also we have obtained an inheritance, being predestinated according to the purpose of him who worketh all things after the counsel of his own will:

12 That we should be to the praise of his glory, who first trusted in Christ.

It is no wonder that Satan, the enemy of God would put antichrist religions in place that deny the Sonship of Jesus Christ.

The Kingdom of God consists of sons and daughters of the Most High who walk in His Authority and who have power to subdue (not physically as other religions would understand the word, but spiritually through overcoming the power of the demons that control those who are blinded to the Truth that is in Christ) the enemies of Christ, once they understand their identity in Christ. It is Satan's goal to stop that from happening.

Eph 6:12 For we wrestle not against flesh and blood, but against principalities, against powers, against the rulers of the darkness of this world, against spiritual wickedness in high *places.*

Casting out devils, healing the sick, raising the dead, preaching the Gospel of the Kingdom of God, making disciples, feeding the hungry, clothing the naked, helping the poor, loving the unlovable, blessing those who curse you, praying for those who despitefully use you. Those are the weapons of our warfare. And the Kingdom of God advances with every soul that is impacted by that engagement.

Time to kill a sacred cow:

When someone speaks about "the Anti Christ" as being that man of sin that is prophesied in 2 Thessalonians 2:3, and connects him with the beast or the false prophet of Revelation 13, *they are adding things to the Word of God that don't exist.*

They are being distracted from the truth of what the essence of Anti Christ really is, and are being sucked into a *manufactured crises*, where every president or pope is said to be the Antichrist, so the rapture of the Church must be around the corner, and Christians get so caught up in the crises of the moment that they fail to obey the Great Commission.

Others begin to stockpile food and ammunition, while the furtherance of the Kingdom of God on earth (the Great Commission) is neglected.

Rev 22:18 For I testify unto every man that heareth the words of the prophecy of this book, If any man shall add unto these things, God shall add unto him the plagues that are written in this book:
19 And if any man shall take away from the words of the book of this prophecy, God shall take away his part out of the book of life, and out of the holy city, and *from* the things which are written in this book.

Ask yourself; where outside of the Book of 1 John or 2nd John do we find the term "Antichrist" mentioned?

Where in the Bible do we see a man labeled as the Beast who is the Anti Christ who is going to rule over the world?

How many books have you read or messages have you heard about this entity that isn't mentioned in the Bible?

Even more to the point, wouldn't it stand to reason if the Beast was the antichrist as so many allege, that John would have identified him as such since he also recorded the Book of Revelation?

I know right now that there are many who are taking exception to this statement, because it goes against everything you have been told. Remember: *Adam and Eve didn't eat an apple, either, and Saint Peter won't usher you into the Pearly Gates.*

Imagine for a moment that you are a new Christian and have had no access to anything but the Bible. You have never watched any of the popular pretrib rapture movies or heard any messages from preachers about the end-times.

You read the Bible for two years with no outside influence to sway you one way or another, and after the two years, I submit to you that you will conclude that there are some bad things that are going to take place in the end times, but you will never come up with a beast named Antichrist or a rapture of the Church that takes place in Rev 4:1.

Where did that idea come from? Let that soak in for a minute. Once you do, you might be ready to read on.

Cloward - Piven Strategy

Have you ever heard of the Cloward - Piven Strategy of manufactured crisis? Cloward and Piven didn't like the fact that there were people who were being overlooked by the welfare system. So they formulated a strategy that would result in a guaranteed annual income for all Americans; whether they worked or not. Wikipedia explains it like this:

The Cloward–Piven strategy is a political strategy outlined in 1966 by American sociologists and political activists Richard Cloward and Frances Fox Piven that called for overloading the U.S. public welfare system in order to precipitate a crisis that would lead to a replacement of the welfare system with a national system of "a guaranteed annual income and thus an end to poverty".

More from Wikipedia:

Michael Reisch and Janice Andrews wrote that Cloward and Piven "proposed to create a crisis in the current welfare system – by exploiting the gap between welfare law and practice – that would ultimately bring about its collapse and replace it with a system of guaranteed annual income. They hoped to accomplish this end by informing the poor of their rights to welfare assistance, encouraging them to apply for benefits and, in effect, overloading an already overburdened bureaucracy."

The idea was to overthrow capitalism.

This "manufactured crisis" didn't happen, but it seems like a lot of people have grabbed hold of that "manufactured crisis" idea to achieve a desired end. Satan is the biggest pro at this.

There is a manufactured crisis regarding racism, and as I write this, the confederate flag is one of the casualties. The truth is that there is really a small minority in comparison with the total population that has a hang up with racial issues. But when a black person gets injured or killed by a white person in authority, it's big news. When the situation is reversed, it's not so big news. A minority of the populace, consisting of the national media and other politically motivated individuals who have an ulterior hidden agenda are manufacturing a crisis in an effort to start a race war, and to rewrite or obliterate history.

There is more at issue with the Confederate flag than slavery. The South didn't want the Federal Government meddling in their business. There was something called States' Rights that was a real issue in the war between the states. There are some who are in authority who feel that the people of the United States don't need a flag to remind them of States' Rights, so get rid of the thing by associating it with racism. No doubt there are injustices done that are racially motivated, but that actually happens on both sides of the spectrum.

1Pe 2:9 But ye *are* a chosen generation, a royal priesthood, an holy nation, a peculiar people; that ye should shew forth the praises of him who hath called you out of darkness into his marvellous light:

I have news for you. In Christ there is no race...we are all ONE Holy ethnic group. The word "nation" is the Greek word "ethnos", from whence we get our word "ethnic". If that reality would sink into the Body of Christ, what an impact that would be in the world. But Christians allow themselves to become impacted by Satan's manufactured crisis and to a great degree remain divided over the "race" issue. In the Kingdom of God there is no such thing as different races.

It was a manufactured crisis that legalized abortion. Some women were dying because they tried to murder their children in their womb with coat hangers. Such a cruel way to die! Not for the baby, but the mom. The crises painted a grim picture that made it look like these deaths were everywhere, an epidemic that could only be solved through making abortion legal - and safe. The Bible teaches us that we are to take responsibility for our actions.

There is a manufactured crisis regarding flu's and other sicknesses every year. Who benefits? Medical professionals and Pharmaceutical giants who sell vaccines and other medicinal "cures". Then when the people get their vaccinations, often times they get the flu! Last year (2014-2015) that happened to many. Not only that, but there appears to be a definite link between childhood vaccines and Autism and other terrible side effects.

A lot of prescription drugs have terrible side effects. An Anti-depressant may lead a person to commit suicide. Blood pressure medication may result in heart conditions. I would venture to say that most people don't read up on the side effects that their medication could bring to them. Doctors get a kickback for the product they prescribe. Christians have become just as dependant on medication as the people who are in the world system are. The Greek word translated as "sorcery" in the Bible is the word "pharmakeia". The Bible declares that the love of money is the Root of all evil. The Pharmaceutical industry is booming, even in economically challenging times, because people have become dependent on their meds.

Unfortunately Christians have learned to put more trust in their doctors in medications than they do the Promises of God. **I am not inferring that doctors are unnecessary.** My point is simply that a lot of the medical problems people have are manufactured crises that could be remedied by a change of diet or a lifestyle or an environmental change. It's just ironic that a lot of the preachers who preach about having faith for God to heal His people have themselves a lot of prescription medications in their medicine cabinets. I have known preachers who stand behind the pulpit and preach about the peace of God while they themselves are on anti-depressants. One of the benefits that we have as citizens of the Kingdom of God is that God heals all our diseases:

Psa 103:1 *A Psalm* of David. Bless the LORD, O my soul: and all that is within me, *bless* his holy name.
2 Bless the LORD, O my soul, and forget not all his benefits:
3 Who forgiveth all thine iniquities; who healeth all thy diseases;
4 Who redeemeth thy life from destruction; who crowneth thee with lovingkindness and tender mercies;

Yep. The world and all of its manufactured crises, designed by a few to influence the masses. It's a common ploy.

And Americans fall for it over and over again.

I can understand that. But what I have a hard time understanding is why Christians fall for the manufactured crises' that Satan's puppets who occupy many pulpits promote. What do I mean by that?

Before every election, the "powers that be" come up with some kind manufactured crisis whereby they can build a political platform. And Christians jump on the bandwagon of the one who quotes the Bible the most, instead of looking deeply into the issues.

If your pastor or preacher has you more concerned about what might happen to the economy than about the souls around you who may be going to hell, you are being played by Satan's manufactured crisis.

If your pastor or preacher has you more concerned about looking for the pre-trib escape instead of preparing others who don't know God to be ready for the day of Judgment, you are being played by Satan's manufactured crisis.

If your pastor or preacher has you so focused on blood moons and shemitahs or years of Jubilee that you are too preoccupied with storing up your food and ammo, while neglecting ministering to those you meet on the street, you are being deterred from God's Purpose by Satan's manufactured crisis.

If your pastor or preacher has you giving those sacrificial offerings to finance his new jet or his new Bently, because a representative of the gospel like him should only have the best, and he isn't equipping you to further the Kingdom of God yourself, then you are being deterred from God's Purpose by Satan's manufactured crisis.

Or if the TV preacher says send in your best seed offering right now to get a financial blessing from God that you will not be able to contain...

If it doesn't have to do with the KINGDOM OF GOD, chances are you are being distracted from your purpose by Satan's manufactured crisis.

A lot of the last days scenarios that are being proclaimed from puppets in the pulpits are merely manufactured crisis' that serve to render the Church powerless while the god of this world continues his destructive work in an effort to thwart God's Plan for the furtherance of His Kingdom here on earth.

If you are not following and obeying Christ's Great Commission, you are walking in league with the enemy of God and are part of the problem, rather than the solution.

Chicken Little was a victim of a manufactured crisis, which resulted in those who bought into his story being devoured by the fox.

I received Jesus Christ as my Lord and Savior in 1983. Since 1983 I have heard dozens of end-times scenarios being played out from the preachers in the pulpits. We chuckle at them now, but the "88 reasons Christ is returning in 1988" was a very real concern for many who professed Jesus Christ. The impending Y2K disaster was being echoed from the pulpits. In 2001, many prophetic voices said the World Trade Center attacks were the beginning of the end. In 2005, with the devastation of Katrina, prophetic voices again sounded off, saying the end of the world was near.

At the time of this writing we are in the process of going through a tetrad or a series of four blood moons coupled with the 7 year of release, the shemitah, and more prophetic voices have been raised about the Lord's imminent Coming to rapture His Church out of this mess. There are others who are projecting into 2016 (Jubilee), 2017 and 2018 as being the time of the Lord's Return. I see these all as manufactured crises' (time will tell) that serve as a distraction from the Purpose of the Church to further the Kingdom of God. The Bride hasn't even begun to make herself ready.

The United States may well fall sooner or later, or be radically changed, but even if the United States of America is totally taken out of the world picture, it doesn't mean that Jesus is coming back tomorrow.

What it does mean is that we as the Church need to be getting busy about furthering the Kingdom of God and being the hedge against evil that God has called us to be.

Eze 22:25 *There is* **a conspiracy of her prophets in the midst thereof, like a roaring lion ravening the prey; they have devoured souls; they have taken the treasure and precious things; they have made her many widows in the midst thereof.**
26 Her priests have violated my law, and have profaned mine holy things: they have put no difference between the holy and profane, neither have they shewed *difference* **between the unclean and the clean, and have hid their eyes from my sabbaths, and I am profaned among them.**
27 Her princes in the midst thereof *are* **like wolves ravening the prey, to shed blood,** *and* **to destroy souls, to get dishonest gain.**
28 And her prophets have daubed them with untempered *morter,* **seeing vanity, and divining lies unto them, saying, Thus saith the Lord GOD, when the LORD hath not spoken.**
29 The people of the land have used oppression, and exercised robbery, and have vexed the poor and needy: yea, they have oppressed the stranger wrongfully.
30 And I sought for a man among them, that should make up the hedge, and stand in the gap before me for the land, that I should not destroy it: but I found none.
31 Therefore have I poured out mine indignation upon them; I have consumed them with the fire of my wrath: their own way have I recompensed upon their heads, saith the Lord GOD.

A STUDY OF THE TIME OF THE GREAT TRIBULATION

Matt 24:21 For then shall be great tribulation, such as was not since the beginning of the world to this time, no, nor ever shall be.

We have been conditioned by modern day prophets to look for a future seven year period of time which will be known as the Great Tribulation (based on their interpretation of Daniel's seventieth week - if you haven't yet read it, see the study in the Appendix), in which those who call on Christ after "the rapture" will have to suffer great persecution as a punishment for not receiving Christ sooner.

Remember, Jesus warned in verse 11:

Matt 24:11 And many false prophets shall rise, and shall deceive many.

From the time of 70 AD to the present time, the age that the disciples had asked about continues.

Since 70 A.D. the Jewish people and true Christians have suffered great tribulation every century at the hands of evil men.

All of the original disciples were killed as a result of persecution, with the exception of John, who tradition says was boiled in oil under Domitian's reign, and didn't die, so he was exiled to the island of Patmos, where he recorded the Book of Revelation.

Nero and Domitian had Christians burned by the hundreds because they would not recognize the Caesars as gods to be worshipped. Persecution by Domitian began in 81 AD. In 98 AD, Emperor Trajan persecuted the Christians. Under his reign in 161, Marcus Aurelius stepped up the persecution of Christians, and had them actively hunted. During the reign of Septimius Severus (193-211), Christians were told to either curse Jesus, and make an offering to Roman gods or be executed. Conversion to Christianity or Judaism was outlawed during his reign.

Persecution was widespread in Africa during this time as well. Decius reigned in 249, and began an empire wide persecution of Christians and Jews, followed in 257 by Valerian who continued Decius' work. In 303, the Emperors Diocletian, Maximian, Galerius, and Constantius issued a series of edicts rescinding the legal rights of Christians and demanding that they comply with traditional Roman religious practices. The resulting persecution ended in 313 with Licinius ousting Maximian, and putting an end to it. By 325, Constantine had made Christianity the State Religion, and thus was born the Roman Catholic Church.

From 325 on, the Roman Catholic gospel prevailed for centuries over humanity, another antichrist spirit (1 John 2:18 says there are many antichrists) united with the world system (Babylon) that tortured and killed all who would not comply with the Roman Church, and a large number of those who were tortured and killed were Jews. That antichrist spirit coupled with a counterfeit of Christianity is a part of what we see described as the Whore of Babylon in Revelation 18[6].

It is important that the reader distinguishes Roman Catholicism from Christianity. Much that has been done historically in the Name of Christ by the Roman Catholic Church is not representative of True Christianity.

The Catholic Inquisition, the Muslims who hunted down the "People of the Book" ever since Mohammad started the religion of Islam, Hindu extremists, Communism, Hitler, and countless other persecutions that have plagued the true Church of God and the Jewish people since 70 AD could rightly be called an age or a time of Great Tribulation.

American Christians can't grasp the idea of an age of Great Tribulation extending from 70 AD to the present time, because of our relative comfort and prosperity. But through the centuries even to this present time Christians and Jews have been slaughtered mercilessly at the hands of wicked men, in the name of some god or gods who call good evil and evil good. I recently heard a news report that said in these last two centuries, more Christians have been killed because of their faith than all the previous centuries combined.

America itself was founded by pilgrims who sought to escape the tyranny of the Church of England. Our constitution's First Amendment was written to ensure the freedom of religion in order to ensure that something like what had happened under the tyrannical reign of King George and the Church of England would not happen in this new country. An honest look at the history of the Church would reveal that Christians and Jews worldwide have endured great tribulation after the fall of Jerusalem in 70 AD to this present time.

As a matter of fact, the same word translated as "tribulation" in Matthew 24:21 is seen again in Acts 11:19, where persecution (same word translated elsewhere as "tribulation") against the church arose as a result of Stephen's bold words against the religious leaders of the Jewish faith. Read "tribulation" instead of persecution here:

Act 11:19 Now they which were scattered abroad upon the persecution that arose about Stephen travelled as far as Phenice, and Cyprus, and Antioch, preaching the word to none but unto the Jews only.

Before his name was changed to Paul, Saul was at the forefront of those who persecuted the Church. Later, Paul and Barnabas would tell the Church that it was through much tribulation that we enter the Kingdom of God.

Act 14:22 Confirming the souls of the disciples, *and* exhorting them to continue in the faith, and that we must through much tribulation enter into the kingdom of God.

John, the author of the Book of Revelation, identified himself as a companion in tribulation to the seven Churches who were enduring tribulation themselves at the time of his writing:

Rev 1:9 I John, who also am your brother, and companion in tribulation, and in the kingdom and patience of Jesus Christ, was in the isle that is called Patmos, for the word of God, and for the testimony of Jesus Christ.

Sometimes the Greek word that Jesus used in Matthew 24:21 which was translated as "tribulation" is translated elsewhere as "affliction". The writer of Hebrews acknowledges that those who he wrote to (the early Christians, in this instance, Messianic Jews) had endured reproaches and tribulations (Heb 10:33).

Heb 10:33 Partly, whilst ye were made a gazingstock both by reproaches and afflictions; and partly, whilst ye became companions of them that were so used.

James reminds his readers that pure religion is to visit the fatherless and the widows in their tribulation while keeping oneself unspotted from the world (James 1:27).

Jas 1:27 Pure religion and undefiled before God and the Father is this, To visit the fatherless and widows in their affliction, *and* to keep himself unspotted from the world.

In 2 Thessalonians 1:3-6, Paul encourages the Church that is suffering tribulation at the hands of ungodly men. He ensures the Church that God will repay those evil men.

2Th 1:3 We are bound to thank God always for you, brethren, as it is meet, because that your faith groweth exceedingly, and the charity of every one of you all toward each other aboundeth;
4 So that we ourselves glory in you in the churches of God for your patience and faith in all your persecutions and tribulations that ye endure:
5 *Which is* a manifest token of the righteous judgment of God, that ye may be counted worthy of the kingdom of God, for which ye also suffer:
6 Seeing *it is* a righteous thing with God to recompense tribulation to them that trouble you;

In 1 Thessalonians 1:6, Paul commends the Christians in that they had received the word in much tribulation (affliction), with joy of the Holy Spirit.

1Th 1:6 And ye became followers of us, and of the Lord, having received the word in much affliction, with joy of the Holy Ghost:

In 2 Co. 8:2, Paul mentions the great trial of tribulation that the churches of Macedonia were enduring.

2Co 8:2 How that in a great trial of affliction the abundance of their joy and their deep poverty abounded unto the riches of their liberality.

In 2 Co 1:4 he mentions the fact that God is his comfort in all his tribulation, and in verse 8, he speaks of the tribulation (translated as "trouble" in the KJV) that came to them in Asia, so much so that they despaired even of life (thought they were going to die). By any one's standards, that is Great Tribulation.

In Romans 12:12, Paul encourages Christians to be patient in tribulation. Paul understood that in the course of his ministry tribulation would follow (Act 20:23), and read in the light of the entire New Testament witness, any Christian should be able to see that the tribulation that the Bible speaks of isn't just a seven year period of time which we will escape by a "rapture" event.

I do believe that there will be an increased time of persecution on the Church in the last days before the end of the age, as the god of this age attempts to wipe out every vestige of Christianity that exists in this world. I believe Revelation 13 warns us of that.

Americans live in an isolated bubble and fail to understand that the last 15 years of this current century has seen wide spread Christian persecution (read 'slaughter') throughout the world at the hands of Muslim, Hindu and atheistic extremists.

It is important to understand that from the conception of the Church to the present time, there has been great tribulation against those who believe. For more references to the word "tribulation", check out the following verses: **Rom 5:3 Rom 8:35 2Co 2:4 2Co 4:17 2Co 6:4 2Co 7:4 2Co 8:13 Eph 3:13 Php 1:16   Php 4:14 Col 1:24 1Th 3:3 1Th 3:7 Rev 2:9 Rev 2:10 Rev 2:22 Rev 7:14**

Concerning the Great Tribulation that would follow the destruction of Jerusalem, Jesus says:

THE DAYS ARE SHORTENED

Matt 24:22 And except those days should be shortened, there should no flesh be saved: but for the elect's sake those days shall be shortened.

"Days" can mean individual units of time consisting of 24 hours, but it is usually used to describe a period of time encompassing the days that combine to make up a number of years. As an example, consider the Genesis chapter five accounts of the number of years men lived, defined as "all the days" that they lived, summed up as a specific number of years:

Gen 5:4 And the days of Adam after he had begotten Seth were eight hundred years: and he begat sons and daughters:
5 And all the days that Adam lived were nine hundred and thirty years: and he died...
....8 And all the days of Seth were nine hundred and twelve years: and he died.
....11 And all the days of Enos were nine hundred and five years: and he died.
....14 And all the days of Cainan were nine hundred and ten years: and he died.

....17 **And all the days of Mahalaleel were eight hundred ninety and five years: and he died.**
....20 **And all the days of Jared were nine hundred sixty and two years: and he died.**
.....23 **And all the days of Enoch were three hundred sixty and five years:**
.....27 **And all the days of Methuselah were nine hundred sixty and nine years: and he died.**

I have attempted to show the reader the possibility that the Great Tribulation mentioned in Matthew 24:21 could encompass a span of not simply seven years, but the period of time from 70 AD to the present day, but more specifically from the beginning of Christianity to the present day. So those "days" that are shortened (shortened means to cut off, or to abridge, or to curtail) for the "elect's" sake could mean a period of time such as a thousand years or two thousand years or more, possibly referring to the days of the current age in which we live.

 Remember that God's time table is not the same as ours:

2Pe 3:8 But, beloved, be not ignorant of this one thing, that one day *is* with the Lord as a thousand years, and a thousand years as one day.
9 The Lord is not slack concerning his promise, as some men count slackness; but is longsuffering to us-ward, not willing that any should perish, but that all should come to repentance.

In Revelation 12:12 we read that the devil has but a short time to accomplish what he needs to accomplish:

Rev 12:12 Therefore rejoice, *ye* heavens, and ye that dwell in them. Woe to the inhabiters of the earth and of the sea! for the devil is come down unto you, having great wrath, because he knoweth that he hath but a short time.

We will be taking more of an in depth look at Revelation 12 in a little bit. But first we need to define the Last Days from a Biblical perspective:

LAST DAYS

We know that the Word of God speaks of the "Last Days" as a time when there will be a great falling away from the Faith, because of the wicked one who is the god of this age wearing out the power of the saints (2 Thess 2:3,4, Dan 12:7, Dan 7:25).

Paul says that Jesus came in the fullness (or the completion) of the time (Time= *Chronos* a specific period set forth by God) in Galatians 4:4.

Gal 4:4 But when the fulness of the time was come, God sent forth his Son, made of a woman, made under the law,

The author of the letter to the Hebrews identifies the days in which he lived as the last days:

Heb 1:2 Hath in these last days spoken unto us by *his* Son, whom he hath appointed heir of all things, by whom also he made the worlds;

In his epistle Jude mentions how there are (present tense) those ungodly men who have crept in to the flock (verse 4). He then calls his readers to remember how the apostles had warned that these things would happen in the *last time*, obviously referring to the time in which he was writing.

Jud 1:17 But, beloved, remember ye the words which were spoken before of the apostles of our Lord Jesus Christ;
18 How that they told you there should be mockers in the last time, who should walk after their own ungodly lusts.

John identified his present day as being the "*last time*":

1Jn 2:18 Little children, it is the last time: and as ye have heard that antichrist shall come, even now are there many antichrists; whereby we know that it is the last time.

Peter identified his day as being the last times:

1Pe 1:19 But with the precious blood of Christ, as of a lamb without blemish and without spot:
20 Who verily was foreordained before the foundation of the world, but was manifest in these last times for you,

In the book of Acts, Peter identifies what was currently happening at Pentecost as being a fulfillment of an end times prophesy in Joel:

Act 2:16 But this is that which was spoken by the prophet Joel;
17 And it shall come to pass in the last days, saith God, I will pour out of my Spirit upon all flesh: and your sons and your daughters shall prophesy, and your young men shall see visions, and your old men shall dream dreams:

Again in Hebrews, the author uses another phrase which indicates that he understood the present time in which he lived as being the last days:

Heb 9:26 For then must he often have suffered since the foundation of the world: but now once in the end of the world hath he appeared to put away sin by the sacrifice of himself.

There is that phrase again that we saw at the beginning of this study: "*The end of the world*". Which should be translated as *"the end of the age"!*

Paul uses that phrase himself in his letter to the Corinthians (read "ends of the age").

1Co 10:11 Now all these things happened unto them for ensamples: and they are written for our admonition, upon whom the ends of the world are come.

The early Church fathers weren't confused or mistaken when they alluded to their days as being the *"last days"*. We know that God is longsuffering toward us, and that His Will is that none should perish (2 Pet 3:9).

He has commissioned the Body of Christ to join Him in that effort of seeing humanity reconciled to Him. As a matter of fact, we have already seen that in God's scheme of things, a day is as a thousand years and a thousand years is as a day (2 Pet 3:8).

Remember what we saw earlier about the phrase Jesus used regarding to "those days being shortened" - those days of the tribulation that would befall the children of the Most High God during this present age.

Let me just tell you right now that **Satan's time is short**. Whether it is a thousand years, two thousand or more, it is short. The end of the age is here, and the close of the end of the age is even closer now than it was in Jesus' time, and the devil knows that, and he is pulling out all the stops to try to prevent that from happening.

It is when the Gospel of the Kingdom of God is preached in all the world that the end of this present evil age will come to an end. The apathy and impotence of the spectator church mentality is a great contributor to the postponement of the end of the age.

Since we are discussing time here, I find it necessary to discuss a phrase found four times in the Word of God in order to put some thoughts into perspective concerning those days that would be shortened, and what that could look like.

That phrase is **"A Time, Times, and Half A Time"**.

TIME, TIMES, AND HALF A TIME: ANOTHER PERSPECTIVE. THEIR RELATIONSHIP WITH MATTHEW 24:22 (The Days That Are Shortened)

The first place this phrase is used in the Word of God is in Daniel 7:25.

Dan 7:24 And the ten horns out of this kingdom *are* ten kings *that* shall arise: and another shall rise after them; and he shall be diverse from the first, and he shall subdue three kings.

25 And he shall speak *great* words against the most High, and shall wear out the saints of the most High, and think to change times and laws: and they shall be given into his hand until a time and times and the dividing of time.

26 But the judgment shall sit, and they shall take away his dominion, to consume and to destroy *it* unto the end.

A majority of commentators believe that this expression, "a time and times and the dividing of time" represents three and a half years, which is largely derived from their dispensational premillenial viewpoint concerning the study of the end times, and determining that Nebuchadnezzar's "seven times" in the wilderness mentioned in Daniel 4 was defined as being seven years:

Dan 4:25 That they shall drive thee from men, and thy dwelling shall be with the beasts of the field, and they shall make thee to eat grass as oxen, and they shall wet thee with the dew of heaven, and seven times shall pass over thee, till thou know that the most High ruleth in the kingdom of men, and giveth it to whomsoever he will.

They deduce that since seven times were defined as seven years in Daniel 4, that a time, and times (1 + 2) and the dividing of times (+1/2) represents 3 1/2 years. The argument sounds viable, but in Daniel 2:8 and 9, the king uses the same word "time" in his discourse with the magicians and astrologers in the sense that they were using deception to "buy time", or stalling. Here we can see that he is not referring to a year.

Dan 2:8 The king answered and said, I know of certainty that ye would gain the time, because ye see the thing is gone from me.

9 But if ye will not make known unto me the dream, *there is but* one decree for you: for ye have prepared lying and corrupt words to speak before me, till the time be changed: therefore tell me the dream, and I shall know that ye can shew me the interpretation thereof.

Daniel mentions God, and says of Him that He changes the times and the seasons.

Dan 2:20 Daniel answered and said, Blessed be the name of God forever and ever: for wisdom and might are his:

21 And he changeth the times and the seasons: he removeth kings, and setteth up kings: he giveth wisdom unto the wise, and knowledge to them that know understanding:

Nebuchadnezzar passed an edict that declared that people would fall down and worship the golden image at a specific time. He wasn't saying they were to do this at one time every year, but it was at a specific time of the day in which they were supposed to do this.

Dan 3:4 Then an herald cried aloud, To you it is commanded, O people, nations, and languages,
5 *That* at what time ye hear the sound of the cornet, flute, harp, sackbut, psaltery, dulcimer, and all kinds of musick, ye fall down and worship the golden image that Nebuchadnezzar the king hath set up:

The word "time" here in the Hebrew corresponds with the Greek word Chronos, which means a *set period of time*. It could be a given time within a 24 hour day (like 3:00 - 4:00), it could be a month, a year, a century or a millennium.

I apologize if I seem so simplistic, but a "time" would be one time. "Times" would be a plurality of one time. From the advantage of looking back into time to Daniel's prophetic words, I believe that the time, times and half a time could possibly be a period of time extending two and a half thousand years, but whether it is or not, it is definitely a specific period of time designated according to God's time table, and I am inclined to believe it is more than three and a half years.

Dan 7:24 And the ten horns out of this kingdom *are* ten kings *that* shall arise: and another shall rise after them; and he shall be diverse from the first, and he shall subdue three kings.
25 And he shall speak *great* words against the most High, and shall wear out the saints of the most High, and think to change times and laws: and they shall be given into his hand until a time and times and the dividing of time.
26 But the judgment shall sit, and they shall take away his dominion, to consume and to destroy *it* unto the end.

There are some who believe that this one who shall speak great words against the Most High who is diverse from the rest represents the Roman Catholic Church, which was established in 325 AD under the rule of Constantine.

I am not convinced of that. I believe this one could better describe the Prophet Muhammad.

We will cover that a little more in detail in the section dealing with **The Ten Horns**.

Having said that, let me just add that Adam Clarke, who wrote his commentary in 1825 (he didn't subscribe to Darby's doctrine either) saw the time, times and half a time as spanning the period of one thousand two hundred and sixty years, or three and half "prophetic years" in which each day would be a year. The interesting thing about this is this observation he made:

If the papal power, as a horn or temporal power, be intended here, which is most likely, (and we know that that power was given in 755 to Pope Stephen II. by Pepin, king of

France), counting one thousand two hundred and sixty years from that, we are brought to a.d. 2015, about one hundred and ninety years from the present [a.d. 1825].

But before we begin to sound the alarm as though the "time" is upon us, let's read what else he says following this passage:

"But I neither lay stress upon nor draw conclusions from these dates. If the Church of Rome will reform itself, it will then be the true Christian Church, and will never be destroyed. Let it throw aside all that is ritually Jewish, all that is heathen; all that which pretends to be of God, and which is only of man, all doctrines that are not in the Bible; and all rites and ceremonies which are not of the appointment of Christ and his apostles; and then, all hail the once Roman, but now, after such a change, the Holy, Catholic Church! Every true Protestant would wish rather the reform than the extinction of this Church."

Adam Clarke understood that the ministry of the Church is about reconciliation, not division.

Outside of the Book of Daniel, the next place we see this phrase used is in Revelation 12:14:

Rev 12:14 And to the woman were given two wings of a great eagle, that she might fly into the wilderness, into her place, where she is nourished for a time, and times, and half a time, from the face of the serpent.

Revelation 12:1-14 corresponds with the first part of Daniel 12. In both of these passages we can see the phrase **"a time, times, and an half,"** and Michael the archangel mentioned. [7]

Dan 12:1 And at that time shall Michael stand up, the great prince which standeth for the children of thy people: and there shall be a time of trouble, such as never was since there was a nation *even* to that same time: and at that time thy people shall be delivered, every one that shall be found written in the book.
2 And many of them that sleep in the dust of the earth shall awake, some to everlasting life, and some to shame *and* everlasting contempt.
3 And they that be wise shall shine as the brightness of the firmament; and they that turn many to righteousness as the stars for ever and ever.
4 But thou, O Daniel, shut up the words, and seal the book, *even* to the time of the end: many shall run to and fro, and knowledge shall be increased.
5 Then I Daniel looked, and, behold, there stood other two, the one on this side of the bank of the river, and the other on that side of the bank of the river.
6 And *one* said to the man clothed in linen, which *was* upon the waters of the river, How long *shall it be to* the end of these wonders?
7 And I heard the man clothed in linen, which *was* upon the waters of the river, when he held up his right hand and his left hand unto heaven, and sware by him that liveth for ever that *it shall be* for a time, times, and an half; and when he shall have accomplished

to scatter the power of the holy people, all these *things* shall be finished.

In Revelation 12:7, we read that there is a battle taking place in heaven.

**Rev 12:7 And there was war in heaven: Michael and his angels fought against the dragon; and the dragon fought and his angels,
8 And prevailed not; neither was their place found any more in heaven.
9 And the great dragon was cast out, that old serpent, called the Devil, and Satan, which deceiveth the whole world: he was cast out into the earth, and his angels were cast out with him.**

Let's look at Daniel 12:

Dan 12:1 And at that time shall Michael stand up, the great prince which standeth for the children of thy people: and there shall be a time of trouble, such as never was since there was a nation *even* to that same time: and at that time thy people shall be delivered, every one that shall be found written in the book.

"...and there shall be a time of trouble, such as never was since there was a nation *even* to that same time"- It is an interesting choice of words, since Jesus referred to this time of trouble (He referred to it as Great Tribulation) in His discourse with the disciples on the mount of Olives:

Matt 24:21 For then shall be great tribulation, such as was not since the beginning of the world to this time, no, nor ever shall be.

No doubt Jesus was drawing once again from the prophetic word in Daniel chapter 12 in His dialogue with the disciples.

As I have mentioned earlier, while most commentators limit that time of the tribulation to 3 1/2 years at some point in the future, I am inclined to believe that the time of tribulation mentioned here in Matthew 24:21 has extended from the formation of the Church to the present time (read again Matt 24:15-21).

While Daniel 12:1 reads "at that time thy people shall be delivered", in the King James version of the Bible, the sense in the Greek Septuagint is that it is *in* that time or *during* that time of great trouble that the people would be delivered, all those who are found written in the Book (referring to the Book of Life, in which those names are written who have received Jesus Christ as their Lord and Savior Rev 13:8, Rev 20:12, 15). The Word "delivered" means to escape, or to be preserved. It doesn't necessarily mean that they will be protected from harm. But they will be delivered or protected from the Judgment of God.

The same definition can apply to the words to the messenger of the Church of Philadelphia:

Rev 3:10 Because thou hast kept the word of my patience, I also will keep thee from the hour of temptation, which shall come upon all the world, to try them that dwell upon the earth.

The dispensationalists say that this verse points to a pretrib rapture, but the definition of the word translated as "keep" really promises protection from the consequences of the "temptation", not the tribulation (different words).

Keep: **G5083**

τηρέω

tēreō

Thayer Definition:
1) to attend to carefully, take care of
1a) to guard
1b) metaphorically to keep, one in the state in which he is
1c) to observe
1d) to reserve: to undergo something
Part of Speech: verb

At that time, due to the Great Tribulation that would fall upon the people of God, many of those who had once rejected the Messiah will understand that He is the Messiah.

In Daniel 12:3 we read that God would use this time of trouble to bring His people to Him, because there would be those who were wise who would turn many to righteousness as the stars forever and ever (verse 3).

Daniel 12:3 And they that be wise shall shine as the brightness of the firmament; and they that turn many to righteousness as the stars for ever and ever.

I believe that is referring to the Christians who are wise in the ways of God, and who go into all the world to proclaim the gospel of the Kingdom of God even in the midst of persecution, and as a result are the light of the world, and are clothed in the Righteousness of Jesus Christ.

Pro 11:30 The fruit of the righteous *is* a tree of life; and he that winneth souls *is* wise.

Despite hardship, persecution and tribulation throughout history, Christians have hazarded their lives on the mission field for the furtherance of the Kingdom of God, and through their witness even in the face of death, the Church has grown. This is what Jesus meant when He declared that the gates of hell (Hades = the Grave) would not prevail against the Church.

Mat 16:18 And I say also unto thee, That thou art Peter, and upon this rock I will build my church; and the gates of hell shall not prevail against it.

In Revelation 12:11 we are told that the saints *overcome* the dragon (Satan) by the Blood of the Lamb and the word of their testimony. Notice it doesn't say they are defeated by Satan; rather, they *overcome* him. And it continues on to say that the true saints of God are not defeated even in death.

Rev 12:11 And they overcame him by the blood of the Lamb, and by the word of their testimony; and they loved not their lives unto the death.

As a result of their faithfulness to the Name of Jesus even in the face of death, despite the centuries of ongoing persecution, multitudes have come to a saving knowledge of Jesus Christ.

Daniel 12:3 And they that be wise shall shine as the brightness of the firmament; and they that turn many to righteousness as the stars forever and ever.

If you ever wondered what happens when the People of God die, I would invite the reader to go to the Appendix at the back of this book and read the article on that subject[8].

WHO IS THE WOMAN IN REVELATION 12?

I think this would be the appropriate spot to discuss the woman in Revelation 12:1 and the correlation between Daniel 12:3 with Revelation 12:1.

Rev 12:1 And there appeared a great wonder in heaven; a woman clothed with the sun, and the moon under her feet, and upon her head a crown of twelve stars:

The woman is said to be clothed with the sun and the moon under her feet and upon her head a crown of twelve stars.

There are, of course, differing opinions as to who this woman is, but I personally believe the woman is the Church, the Bride of Christ. She is the personification of Wisdom in the Book of Proverbs. The Wisdom of God is manifested in His Creation.

The crown of twelve stars is the twelve apostles (messengers) who are the builders of the foundation of the Church, Jesus Christ Himself being the Chief Cornerstone (Eph 2:20). The twelve apostles were foreshadowed by the twelve sons of Jacob, or Israel. The woman is clothed with the sun, a descriptive analogy of the righteousness of Jesus Christ, the Sun of Righteousness Who is depicted as the Light that the Church must reflect (Mal 4:2, see also Revelation 19:8 where the Bride of Christ is clothed in fine linen clean and white, which is the Righteousness of the Saints).

Adam Clarke writes this observation about the moon under her feet, and I am inclined to say that it is agreeable with my thoughts as well:

*"**The moon under her feet** - Bishop Newton understands this of the Jewish typical worship and indeed the Mosaic system of rites and ceremonies could not have been better represented, for it was the shadow of good things to come. The moon is the less light, ruling over the night, and deriving all its illumination from the sun; in like manner the Jewish dispensation was the bright moonlight night of the world, and possessed a portion of the glorious light of the Gospel. At the rising of the sun the night is ended, and the lunar light no longer necessary, as the sun which enlightens her shines full upon the earth; exactly in the same way has the whole Jewish system of types and shadows has been superseded by the birth, life, crucifixion, death, resurrection, ascension, and intercession of Jesus Christ."*

I would add this observation, that the Jewish days, festivals and years were reckoned by the lunar calendar. Gentiles incline toward the solar calendar of measuring time. *The picture here is both the Jew and the Gentile under covenant with God as the Church of the One True God.*

It is the Unity of the two covenant people under Christ the Messiah that will usher in the fullness of the Kingdom of God[9].

In Ephesians, Paul writes of the separation that existed between the Gentile and the Jew, but how Jesus Christ has broken down that wall of separation and made of twain (Jew and Gentile) one new man, in order to reconcile both Jew and Gentile to God. Now through the Holy Spirit, both Jew and Gentile have access to the Father.

Eph 2:12 That at that time ye were without Christ, being aliens from the commonwealth of Israel, and strangers from the covenants of promise, having no hope, and without God in the world:
13 But now in Christ Jesus ye who sometimes were far off are made nigh by the blood of Christ.
14 For he is our peace, who hath made both one, and hath broken down the middle wall of partition *between us;*
15 Having abolished in his flesh the enmity, *even* the law of commandments *contained* in ordinances; for to make in himself of twain one new man, *so* making peace;
16 And that he might reconcile both unto God in one body by the cross, having slain the enmity thereby:
17 And came and preached peace to you which were afar off, and to them that were nigh.
18 For through him we both have access by one Spirit unto the Father.
19 Now therefore ye are no more strangers and foreigners, but fellowcitizens with the saints, and of the household of God;

20 And are built upon the foundation of the apostles and prophets, Jesus Christ himself being the chief corner *stone*;
21 In whom all the building fitly framed together groweth unto an holy temple in the Lord:
22 In whom ye also are builded together for an habitation of God through the Spirit.

It is this picture of the Church that we see in Revelation 12:1.

At the present time, however, Israel is still resistant to Christianity, due largely in part to the abuses of Roman Catholicism that have gone under the guise of Christianity. To the people of Israel, Christianity is synonymous with Roman Catholicism, and throughout Israel one can find Roman Catholic shrines with statues of the "saints" and of Mary and of Jesus, which to the Jew is akin to idolatry.

This perception has been a tremendous stumbling block to the Jew, and Christians who go on tours to Israel do nothing to dispel that idea, rather, they encourage it by flocking to the shrines, and buying souvenirs from their gift shops. But there will come a time when Israel will come to grips with the Messiah, and the Church will be complete and the present Age will come to a close.

Paul alluded to this in Romans 11:25:

Rom 11:25 For I would not, brethren, that ye should be ignorant of this mystery, lest ye should be wise in your own conceits; that blindness in part is happened to Israel, until the fulness of the Gentiles be come in.
26 And so all Israel shall be saved: as it is written, There shall come out of Sion the Deliverer, and shall turn away ungodliness from Jacob:

We have already covered Matthew 24:5-8, but let me say at this point in our study that Jesus, in His discourse with His disciples on the Mount of Olives stated that the wars and rumors of wars, famines, pestilences and increased earthquake activity around the world are simply the beginning of "Birth Pains" (the word translated as "sorrows" in the King James is better translated from the Greek as "*Birth Pains*"):

Mat 24:8 All these *are* the beginning of sorrows.

Now we see that the woman described in Revelation is travailing in birth; same word, different tense. *In Matthew, these were the beginnings of the birth pains. Here in Revelation, the birth is imminent.*

Rev 12:2 And she being with child cried, travailing in birth, and pained to be delivered.

THE MANIFESTATION OF THE SONS OF GOD

The Church is travailing in birth. And what will she give birth to?

That which was intended from the foundation of the world:

She will give birth to the heirs of the Kingdom of God; the manifestation of the sons of God, when the Body of Christ, Jew and Gentile combined, will walk in the Power and the Glory of dominion over the world system just as God had intended from the beginning.

Rom 8:19 For the earnest expectation of the creature waiteth for the manifestation of the sons of God.
20 For the creature was made subject to vanity, not willingly, but by reason of him who hath subjected *the same* in hope,
21 Because the creature itself also shall be delivered from the bondage of corruption into the glorious liberty of the children of God.
22 For we know that the whole creation groaneth and travaileth in pain together until now.
23 And not only *they,* but ourselves also, which have the firstfruits of the Spirit, even we ourselves groan within ourselves, waiting for the adoption, *to wit,* the redemption of our body.

As I have pointed out earlier, *from the inception of the Church (which had been foretold in Genesis 3:15), there has been a great attempt by the god of this age (Satan) to stop the realization of that manifestation of the sons of God, and the restoration of mankind's God-given authority over the earth.*

Christ was the firstborn of that manifestation, and through the inward work of the Holy Spirit we who are yielded in obedience to Him are ourselves becoming conformed to the image of God's Son, that He might be the firstborn among many brethren, both Jew and Gentile alike. But Satan will do everything in his power to prevent that from taking place.

Romans 8:24 For we are saved by hope: but hope that is seen is not hope: for what a man seeth, why doth he yet hope for?
25 But if we hope for that we see not, *then* do we with patience wait for *it.*
26 Likewise the Spirit also helpeth our infirmities: for we know not what we should pray for as we ought: but the Spirit itself maketh intercession for us with groanings which cannot be uttered.
27 And he that searcheth the hearts knoweth what *is* the mind of the Spirit, because he maketh intercession for the saints according to *the will of* God.
28 And we know that all things work together for good to them that love God, to them who are the called according to *his* purpose.

29 For whom he did foreknow, he also did predestinate *to be* conformed to the image of his Son, that he might be the firstborn among many brethren.
30 Moreover whom he did predestinate, them he also called: and whom he called, them he also justified: and whom he justified, them he also glorified.

As His Ambassadors of the Kingdom of God here on this earth, we who are in Christ are granted that same dominion and authority that Christ has.

Most Christians will agree with that in theory, but in actuality they don't believe it. When the types and shadows that are depicted in the law of commandments and the ordinances are realized by the fulfillment of the Purpose of God, then both the Jew and the Gentile will be one Body, one man in Christ (See Eph 2:15 below).

And that man child (the Body of Christ) shall rule the nations with a rod of iron.

To maintain the premise of Scripture interpreting Scripture, it is important to note that Revelation 19 mentions one who is called the Word of God and Who rules the nations with a rod of Iron. It seems obvious that this one Who is described here is Jesus:

Rev 19:11 And I saw heaven opened, and behold a white horse; and he that sat upon him *was* called Faithful and True, and in righteousness he doth judge and make war.
12 His eyes *were* as a flame of fire, and on his head *were* many crowns; and he had a name written, that no man knew, but he himself.
13 And he *was* clothed with a vesture dipped in blood: and his name is called The Word of God.
14 And the armies *which were* in heaven followed him upon white horses, clothed in fine linen, white and clean.
15 And out of his mouth goeth a sharp sword, that with it he should smite the nations: and he shall rule them with a rod of iron: and he treadeth the winepress of the fierceness and wrath of Almighty God.
16 And he hath on *his* vesture and on his thigh a name written, KING OF KINGS, AND LORD OF LORDS.

No doubt this Person described above Who rules with a rod of iron is Jesus.

But don't let it escape you that those who comprise His Church are known as the Body of Christ, and we are told that we will live *and reign* with Christ.

Rev 20:4 And I saw thrones, and they sat upon them, and judgment was given unto them: and *I saw* the souls of them that were beheaded for the witness of Jesus, and for the word of God, and which had not worshipped the beast, neither his image, neither had received *his* mark upon their foreheads, or in their hands; and they lived and reigned with Christ a thousand years.

2Ti 2:12 If we suffer, we shall also reign with *him:* if we deny *him,* he also will deny us:

Rev 5:10 And hast made us unto our God kings and priests: and we shall reign on the earth.

How shall we reign with Christ? On earth, as sons of God, *with a rod of iron,* just like our older Brother:

Rev 2:24 But unto you I say, and unto the rest in Thyatira, as many as have not this doctrine, and which have not known the depths of Satan, as they speak; I will put upon you none other burden.
25 But that which ye have *already* hold fast till I come.
26 And he that overcometh, and keepeth my works unto the end, to him will I give power over the nations:
27 *And he shall rule them with a rod of iron;* as the vessels of a potter shall they be broken to shivers: even as I received of my Father.
28 And I will give him the morning star.
29 He that hath an ear, let him hear what the Spirit saith unto the churches.

God's Plan from the foundation of the world was that His creation would be under the dominion of His crowning creation, man. That as sons and daughters we would be fruitful, multiply and fill the earth with godly seed. God's Plan has taken the span of thousands of years to fulfill, but a thousand years to God is as a day (2 Pet 3:8).

Adam and Eve's fall did not take God by surprise. Even before they fell, God had a Plan laid in place for redemption and reconciliation. God has never had to go back to the chalkboard to come up with another plan. Satan is continually going back to the chalkboard to re-strategize. Just as Jesus knew from the beginning that Judas was a thief who would eventually be used by Satan to betray him, our Father knew that Satan would lead a revolt against His Kingdom, in an attempt to thwart God's Plan.

Let me say also that when the child of God backslides and falls into sin, that doesn't take God by surprise, either. Like the father in the parable Jesus told about the Prodigal Son, God waits with expectancy to see His sons and daughters come to their senses, to repent of their sin, forsake their wallowing in the mire, and come running back to Him. It is the Goodness of God that leads men to repentance.

From the beginning, God's Plan wasn't just to redeem a select few for His Kingdom, but all of humanity; Jew and Gentile alike. Of course, some will perish, but it won't be God's fault.

Eph 2:10 For we are his workmanship, created in Christ Jesus unto good works, which God hath before ordained that we should walk in them.

11 Wherefore remember, that ye *being* in time past Gentiles in the flesh, who are called Uncircumcision by that which is called the Circumcision in the flesh made by hands;

12 That at that time ye were without Christ, being aliens from the commonwealth of Israel, and strangers from the covenants of promise, having no hope, and without God in the world:

13 But now in Christ Jesus ye who sometimes were far off are made nigh by the blood of Christ.

14 For he is our peace, who hath made both one, and hath broken down the middle wall of partition *between us;*

15 Having abolished in his flesh the enmity, *even* the law of commandments *contained* in ordinances; for to make in himself of twain one new man, *so* making peace;

16 And that he might reconcile both unto God in one body by the cross, having slain the enmity thereby:

17 And came and preached peace to you which were afar off, and to them that were nigh.

18 For through him we both have access by one Spirit unto the Father.

19 Now therefore ye are no more strangers and foreigners, but fellow citizens with the saints, and of the household of God;

20 And are built upon the foundation of the apostles and prophets, Jesus Christ himself being the chief corner *stone;*

21 In whom all the building fitly framed together groweth unto an holy temple in the Lord:

22 In whom ye also are builded together for an habitation of God through the Spirit.

We who are heirs of the Promise (both Jew and Gentile) are a holy Temple in the Lord. But the enemy of our souls, the enemy of the Kingdom of God, that great dragon, the devil will do anything he can to keep the manifestation of the sons of God from happening.

But it will happen.

There will come a day when both Jew and Gentile will embrace Christ and those who walk in His Truth will walk in His Power and Authority and will be His Witnesses on earth[9] in the midst of great persecution, casting out devils, laying hands on the sick, raising the dead, and walking in authority over all the authority of the devil.

I realize that during the course of the reading of this book, I have really "pushed the envelope" as far as contemporary end times teachings are concerned. Most likely the reader has by this time had a lot of his or her "end times theology" challenged. Well, there is no time like the present to throw out another challenge and to shoot another sacred cow.

Most Bible expositors will agree that scripture should interpret scripture, and context is of utmost importance to rightly divide the Word of Truth, but when it comes to the study of the Book of Revelation, all of that seems to go out the window.

As I pointed out in the beginning of this book, most expositors of the book of Revelation refer to chapters 2 and 3 as the "Letters To The Churches", when in fact, they are the letters to the *messengers* of the churches.

While that may seem unimportant at first, the fact is that a great degree of dispensational doctrine regarding the teaching of the seven Church ages, the teaching of the pretrib rapture, and the idea that the Church is raptured out at Revelation 4:1 is based on the idea that these are letters to the Churches. When read as the letters to the *Messengers of the Churches*, as they truly are, perspective and understanding of the Book of Revelation is radically changed.

Using context and allowing scripture to interpret scripture, let me ask the reader this: did you know that the two witnesses are identified in Revelation as the two olive trees and the two candlesticks that stand before God?

Rev 11:4 These are the two olive trees, and the two candlesticks standing before the God of the earth.

Did you realize that the candlesticks are defined in Revelation 1?

Rev 1:20 The mystery of the seven stars which thou sawest in my right hand, and the seven golden candlesticks. The seven stars are the angels of the seven churches: and the seven candlesticks which thou sawest are the seven churches.

We see that the candlesticks are the seven churches.

In Revelation 2 and 3, there are only two messengers of the seven churches who were not told to repent of what they were allowing to go on in their churches; the messenger of the Church of Smyrna, and the messenger of the Church of Philadelphia. *It is the remnant who are equipped by their leaders to do the work of the ministry in the furtherance of the Kingdom of God with power and authority who are being referred to in Revelation 11.* Of course, the "Church Age" theory will not allow for that interpretation.

Satan continually strives to deceive the Church into passively waiting for a pretrib rapture, so the truth of the warfare that is taking place in the heavenlies will be hid to the Body of Christ. For this reason, Satan is wandering about, doing all in his power to deceive the nations, and to prevent that which is inevitable from happening.

But the Beast makes war with the saints in Revelation 13:7, and in 11:7 we see that the beast makes war with these two witnesses. I don't want to take the reader too far away from the subject at hand, so I will encourage the reader to read more concerning these two witnesses in the Appendix[9].

I personally believe that there will come a time when there will be a remnant in the Church at large, both Messianic Jew and Gentile who will begin walking in the Power and Authority that was once manifest in the Church. You could call it a Pentecostal reawakening, if you wish. These two *candlesticks* (churches) will be the ones who do exploits in the last days:

Rev 11:5 And if any man will hurt them, fire proceedeth out of their mouth, and devoureth their enemies: and if any man will hurt them, he must in this manner be killed.
6 These have power to shut heaven, that it rain not in the days of their prophecy: and have power over waters to turn them to blood, and to smite the earth with all plagues, as often as they will.

I realize that sounds "out there" to someone who has been conditioned to believe that the two witnesses will be two people, that the letters of Revelation two and three are letters to the churches, that the Beast is some president who is the Anti Christ, that the seventieth week of Daniel has yet to be fulfilled, and that the rapture of the Church takes place when John testifies that *he* was caught up in the spirit to see the things that were to come.

Rev 4:1 After this I looked, and, behold, a door *was* opened in heaven: and the first voice which I heard *was* as it were of a trumpet talking with me; which said, Come up hither, and I will shew thee things which must be hereafter.
2 And immediately I was in the spirit: and, behold, a throne was set in heaven, and *one* sat on the throne.

Moving On...

Rev 12:3 And there appeared another wonder in heaven; and behold a great red dragon, having seven heads and ten horns, and seven crowns upon his heads.
4 And his tail drew the third part of the stars of heaven, and did cast them to the earth: and the dragon stood before the woman which was ready to be delivered, for to devour her child as soon as it was born.

From this point on, I step into a greater field of controversy than I have so far.

Dates, timing of events, interpretation of types and shadows will vary depending on whose commentary you may read, and there may even be some discrepancies in calculations in the content that follows. I hope that isn't the case. There has already been numerous books written about these "end times" prophecies, and as I said before, this is another book added to the lot. I don't profess to have all the answers.

The Bible says we know in part, and we prophesy in part. It means that none of us have the whole picture, and if we try to convince people we do, we are deceiving ourselves. Whether I consistently hit the nail on the head here or not, shouldn't serve to distract from the primary message of this book, which is this:

Those who are Born Again saints of God are overcomers, and NOT victims.

We are engaged in warfare, and the warfare is NOT carnal, but spiritual.

We are called to further the Kingdom of God NOW, not to live a life of defeat waiting for some future day when we will finally enter the Kingdom of God.

The Kingdom of God is at hand, and God wants YOU to walk in His Authority more than you may understand.

If you are a Christian and you are not publically proclaiming the Gospel of the Kingdom of God, casting out devils, laying hands on the sick and seeing them recover, feeding and clothing the poor, sheltering the homeless, for the Glory of God, you are walking in disobedience to the commandments of Jesus. Jesus asked "Why do you call me Lord, Lord, and do not the things that I say?"

Luk 6:46 And why call ye me, Lord, Lord, and do not the things which I say?
47 Whosoever cometh to me, and heareth my sayings, and doeth them, I will shew you to whom he is like:
48 He is like a man which built an house, and digged deep, and laid the foundation on a rock: and when the flood arose, the stream beat vehemently upon that house, and could not shake it: for it was founded upon a rock.
49 But he that heareth, and doeth not, is like a man that without a foundation built an house upon the earth; against which the stream did beat vehemently, and immediately it fell; and the ruin of that house was great.

There is a flood of wickedness and immorality increasing in our nation and in our world, because the pulpiteers are teaching the people of God that it has to be that way, and sometime soon we will fly away. When the people of God repent and begin to do what the Lord has told them to do, that flood will not prevail against them.

If the people of God persist in their Sunday go to meeting mentality, while being assimilated into the world the rest of the week, the institutional church will soon crumble because we ignored Christ's commandment to "Go ye" and proclaim His Kingdom to a lost and dying world. If persecution comes to the Church in America, it may be because *YOU* allowed it by ignoring Christ's Commandment to be a doer of the Word, and not just a hearer (Lk 6:46).

Just know this: a lot of the end times scenarios that preachers are preaching today are manufactured crises' designed to distract us from fulfilling God's Purpose for our lives. We need to quit our Chicken Little ways, and move from being little chickens hiding in the chicken coop, and rise up as the eagles we are supposed to be.

2Ti 3:12 Yea, and all that will live godly in Christ Jesus shall suffer persecution.
13 But evil men and seducers shall wax worse and worse, deceiving, and being deceived.

THE TEN HORNS

Rev 12:9 And the great dragon was cast out, that old serpent, called the Devil, and Satan, which deceiveth the whole world: he was cast out into the earth, and his angels were cast out with him.

For more information on when this took place, I refer the reader to the Appendix[10] where I address this at length.

Rev 12:3 And there appeared another wonder in heaven; and behold a great red dragon, having seven heads and ten horns, and seven crowns upon his heads.

The dragon is defined as being the devil in Revelation 12:9. He has seven heads, because he is the god of this age, and his influence is over the seven continents of the world, and he influences the kingdoms of this world in this present age (seven crowns).

In Daniel 7:7 and in Rev 13:1 we read of a beast who has ten horns, but he is not to be confused with the dragon, because in Revelation 13:2 we are told that the dragon gives this beast his power.

Dan 7:7 After this I saw in the night visions, and behold a fourth beast, dreadful and terrible, and strong exceedingly; and it had great iron teeth: it devoured and brake in pieces, and stamped the residue with the feet of it: and it *was* diverse from all the beasts that *were* before it; and it had ten horns.

Rev 13:1 And I stood upon the sand of the sea, and saw a beast rise up out of the sea, having seven heads and ten horns, and upon his horns ten crowns, and upon his heads the name of blasphemy.
2 And the beast which I saw was like unto a leopard, and his feet were as *the feet* of a bear, and his mouth as the mouth of a lion: and the dragon gave him his power, and his seat, and great authority.

Most agree that this fourth beast of Daniel 7:7 (which is an extension of that beast mentioned in Revelation 13:2) was the Roman empire, which spread its influence throughout the world in ten primary spheres of influence (ten kingdoms).

Spain, Britain, France, Italy, Greece, Eastern Europe, Turkey, The Middle East, Egypt, and North Africa were all under Roman rule by 300 AD

Most commentators correlate the four beasts mentioned in Daniel 7 with the image that Nebuchadnezzar saw in his vision in Daniel chapter 2.

Dan 2:31 Thou, O king, sawest, and behold a great image. This great image, whose brightness *was* excellent, stood before thee; and the form thereof *was* terrible.
32 This image's head *was* of fine gold, his breast and his arms of silver, his belly and his thighs of brass,
33 His legs of iron, his feet part of iron and part of clay.
34 Thou sawest till that a stone was cut out without hands, which smote the image upon his feet *that were* of iron and clay, and brake them to pieces.
35 Then was the iron, the clay, the brass, the silver, and the gold, broken to pieces together, and became like the chaff of the summer threshingfloors; and the wind carried them away, that no place was found for them: and the stone that smote the image became a great mountain, and filled the whole earth.

The fourth kingdom of iron and clay correlates with the beast in Daniel 7:7 that has teeth of iron. Most commentators agree that this is the Roman kingdom. It was during the time of Roman rule that Christ came and preached the Kingdom of God.

Dan 2:44 And in the days of these kings shall the God of heaven set up a kingdom, which shall never be destroyed: and the kingdom shall not be left to other people, *but* it shall break in pieces and consume all these kingdoms, and it shall stand for ever.
45 Forasmuch as thou sawest that the stone was cut out of the mountain without hands, and that it brake in pieces the iron, the brass, the clay, the silver, and the gold; the great God hath made known to the king what shall come to pass hereafter: and the dream *is* certain, and the interpretation thereof sure.

We know that Christ is the Chief Cornerstone of our Faith. He is that Stone referred to here, and the Jewish people of Jesus' day understood this passage as a promise that God would one day establish His Kingdom over the earth and over all kingdoms. They believed that meant that Israel would be exalted above all other kingdoms, and that is the Promise they looked for in Christ. The disciples also expected Him to restore the Kingdom to Israel after His Resurrection.

Act 1:6 When they therefore were come together, they asked of him, saying, Lord, wilt thou at this time restore again the kingdom to Israel?

*What is important to keep in mind is that the common thread of all these visions in the Book of Daniel was that **the Kingdom of God would prevail over the kingdoms of men,** no matter how terrible and oppressive those kingdoms were.*

The Promise is that the kingdoms of this world will become the Kingdom of our God (Rev 11:15).

As I stated above, **Spain, Britain, France**, **Italy, Greece, Eastern Europe, Turkey, The Middle East, Egypt, and North Africa** were all under Roman rule by 300 AD, and eventually the Roman Catholic Church, which was founded by the emperor Constantine became an extension of the kingdoms of Rome through political and religious domination.

This enabled it's rule and influence to extend even to this present day throughout the world, as a result of the missionary efforts of the Catholic Church, which eventually encompassed all seven continents of the world (seven heads). Christianity (read Catholicism) became the official state religion. For all intents and purposes, the "Church" was Rome, but Rome wasn't the True Church.

Rome is the seat of the Vatican. France, England and Spain were under Papal influence in the Medieval times, and it was during this time that these three countries were very powerful and instrumental in exploring and conquering hitherto unchartered regions of the world in the name of the Catholic Church.

Dan 7:7 After this I saw in the night visions, and behold a fourth beast, dreadful and terrible, and strong exceedingly; and it had great iron teeth: it devoured and brake in pieces, and stamped the residue with the feet of it: and it *was* diverse from all the beasts that *were* before it; and it had ten horns.

Daniel says that this fourth beast was diverse or different from all the beasts that were before it. The former beasts were identified as types of animals (lion, bear and leopard). The lion, the bear and the leopard are all ferocious bests who take their prey through brute force, but this beast was different, in that it was not compared to an animal, and was without description, other than it had iron teeth and ten horns. Nebuchadnezzar's image that he dreamed of had feet of clay and iron. I believe both visions are referring to a kingdom which was established not by mere strength alone, but through the inventions of men, or technological advancements.

Another aspect that made this fourth beast different from the rest was because of the "Christian" influence it carried with it, but the influence was not Christian in actuality. It carried with it the name of Christian, but was in fact a State religion (Roman Catholicism) that was used by wicked men to conquer and to corrupt the Word of God in the Name of God.

Before the destruction of Jerusalem, we see the early Church's missionary efforts to evangelize the world in the midst of great persecution, primarily at the hands of the Jewish leaders (see Acts 7 and 17 for an example), but also the pagan Gentiles (Acts 19:24-41).

After the fall of Jerusalem and the ensuing persecution of the Church, Christianity spread even more throughout the world. In 325 AD, Constantine declared Christianity to be the state religion of Rome. By 600 AD, Christianity and Roman Catholicism were practically synonymous, and the religion of Rome had been preached throughout the known world, including those regions wherein dwelt the descendants of Ishmael.

ISLAM IN PROPHECY

I believe that the religion of Islam plays a part in this important prophetic word found in Daniel 7 and Revelation 13, and most commentators leave that alone, as if Islam is not of significance in the Biblical picture.

Dan 7:8 I considered the horns, and, behold, there came up among them another little horn, before whom there were three of the first horns plucked up by the roots: and, behold, in this horn *were* eyes like the eyes of man, and a mouth speaking great things.

At this point, it is important to remember the Crusades that were fought in the Medieval times. The Roman Catholic Church was at war with the kingdom of Islam, which I believe is the little horn that rose up in the passage above, whose eyes were like the eyes of a man and a mouth speaking great things.

Abraham had two sons. One son was the son of the Promise, Isaac, who was born of Abraham's wife Sarah, and the other was Ishmael, who was born of Hagar, an Egyptian hand maid to Sarah. Of Ishmael we read a prophetic word that was given to Hagar:

Gen 16:10 And the angel of the LORD said unto her, I will multiply thy seed exceedingly, that it shall not be numbered for multitude.
11 And the angel of the LORD said unto her, Behold, thou *art* with child, and shalt bear a son, and shalt call his name Ishmael; because the LORD hath heard thy affliction.
12 And he will be a wild man; his hand *will be* against every man, and every man's hand against him; and he shall dwell in the presence of all his brethren.

The descendants of Ishmael today are the Arabian people.

Their religion and culture is defined as Islam. Islam was founded in 610 AD by a man named Muhammad who said he had received visions from the angel Gabriel. These visions were recorded with the help of scribes, and eventually were compiled into what is now known as the Qu'ran, the holy book of Islam.

From 610 - 632, the prophet of Islam, Muhammad led a small group of followers in the religion of his god, Allah, whom he professed to be the God of Abraham, Isaac and Jacob, which he would not have known about had it not been for the widespread influence of

Christianity in the world through the dominance of Rome which conquered in the name of the Roman Catholic Church.

By the time of his death, most of Arabia had been converted from polytheism to the monotheistic religion of Islam. It was after his death (he was poisoned by a Jewish woman who sought revenge on him for the death of her family) that Islam spread under the rule of Abu Bakr and three succeeding caliphates, initially throughout the Middle East, Egypt and Turkey, three of the first horns that were originally part of the Roman empire.

In just a few centuries, the religion of Islam spread throughout much of the same region as the Roman Empire had held. But it's primary seat of influence was and still is that geographical area known as the Middle East (The Middle East today includes Turkey, Cyprus, Syria, Lebanon, Israel, Jordan, Egypt, Saudi Arabia, Yemen, Oman, United Arab Emirates, Qatar, Bahrain, Kuwait, Iraq, and Iran), North Africa, and Eastern Europe.

Adherants of Islam are anti Semitic in nature as well as anti-Christian.

Islam can be seen to be a religion of Anti-Christ, as is evidenced through the increasing persecution and slaughter of Christians in the world at the hands of Muslim fundamentalists. I would refer the reader once again to that portion which I wrote under the heading of **MORE ON THE ANTI CHRIST AND THE ABOMINATION OF DESOLATION**, in reference to the Anti Christ inscription that is in the Dome of the Rock.

Again, what is important to keep in mind is that *the common thread of all these visions that Daniel and John had was that the Kingdom of God would prevail over the kingdoms of men, no matter how terrible and oppressive those kingdoms were.*

The Promise is that the kingdoms of this world will become the Kingdom of our God, which is prophesied in Revelation 11 at the time of the seventh Angel's trumpet (the last trumpet).

Rev 11:15 And the seventh angel sounded; and there were great voices in heaven, saying, The kingdoms of this world are become *the kingdoms* of our Lord, and of his Christ; and he shall reign forever and ever.

How will the kingdoms of this world become the Kingdom of our God? Through the Body of Christ (of which YOU are a part, if you are a Christian) obeying and fulfilling the Great Commission that Jesus left with His disciples, even in the midst of great tribulation.

Dan 7:9 I beheld till the thrones were cast down, and the Ancient of days did sit, whose garment *was* white as snow, and the hair of his head like the pure wool: his throne *was like* the fiery flame, *and* his wheels *as* burning fire.
10 A fiery stream issued and came forth from before him: thousand thousands ministered unto him, and ten thousand times ten thousand stood before him: the judgment was set, and the books were opened.

11 I beheld then because of the voice of the great words which the horn spake: I beheld *even* till the beast was slain, and his body destroyed, and given to the burning flame.

Mat 24:14 And this gospel of the kingdom shall be preached in all the world for a witness unto all nations; and then shall the end come.

Not the gospel of denominationalism, men's traditions, religions, philosophical musings or speculation, but the gospel of the Kingdom of God!

What does that look like? Unfortunately it doesn't look like what much of the Western church would have you think it looks like. Jesus' Gospel of the Kingdom of God produces results suitable for the Kingdom of God.

Mat 11:5 The blind receive their sight, and the lame walk, the lepers are cleansed, and the deaf hear, the dead are raised up, and the poor have the gospel preached to them.
6 And blessed is *he,* whosoever shall not be offended in me.

Remember, Paul's Gospel was no different than Jesus'!

1Th 1:5 For our gospel came not unto you in word only, but also in power, and in the Holy Ghost, and in much assurance; as ye know what manner of men we were among you for your sake.

The warfare spoken about in Ephesians 6 and 2 Corinthians 10, as well as in Daniel and Revelation (the beast makes war with the saints Revelation 13:7, Daniel 7:21,25) is not just ideas to be preached about, but to be actively engaged in by the saints of God as they further the Kingdom of God in this world.

Every demon that is cast out, every physical body that is healed, every soul that is delivered from the power of sin is a victory for the Kingdom of God, and the Kingdom of God advances one soul at a time.

If you don't believe in demons, they won't be cast out, particularly that demon of unbelief that has possessed your mind.

If you don't believe in the Power of God to heal, you won't see any healings.

If you don't believe a person can be miraculously freed from the power of addiction or sin in their lives, you won't see them delivered.

The Christian that is not engaged in the battle for souls is akin to a deserter or a traitor to the Kingdom of God.

Mat 25:24 Then he which had received the one talent came and said, Lord, I knew thee that thou art an hard man, reaping where thou hast not sown, and gathering where thou hast not strawed:
25 And I was afraid, and went and hid thy talent in the earth: lo, *there* **thou hast** *that is* **thine.**
26 His lord answered and said unto him, *Thou* **wicked and slothful servant, thou knewest that I reap where I sowed not, and gather where I have not strawed:**
27 Thou oughtest therefore to have put my money to the exchangers, and *then* **at my coming I should have received mine own with usury.**
28 Take therefore the talent from him, and give *it* **unto him which hath ten talents.**
29 For unto every one that hath shall be given, and he shall have abundance: but from him that hath not shall be taken away even that which he hath.
30 And cast ye the unprofitable servant into outer darkness: there shall be weeping and gnashing of teeth.

The Pastor who fails to equip his flock to obey the Great Commission of Christ is guilty of being no more than a hireling whose interests are in his own gain and well being.

But the faithful Pastor will train the children of God to do exploits for the furtherance of the Kingdom of God, and to thrive in adversity.

The evangelist who travels exclusively from church engagement to church engagement more than he frequents the streets to minister one on or in a public forum isn't an evangelist. He is a professional orator for hire. His specialty audience just happens to be Christians.

But a true evangelist will encourage and train others to do the work of an evangelist in the market place, on the street corner, wherever opportunity presents itself.

The prophet who holds countless end times seminars and gives special words to individuals from church to church is not a prophet. He is a prognosticator, or a practitioner of divination whose Biblical expounding gives him credibility to the sheep.

A true prophet will call the Body of Christ to repentance, and speak words to build up and edify the Body of Christ to do the Work of the Kingdom of God, not words of flattery or words that will instill fear in the Body of Christ because of those things which may be coming. The Prophet will say "Rise up! Live for Jesus! Further the Kingdom!"

Concerning this end time *beast system* and the saints of God, we read this:

Dan 11:32 And such as do wickedly against the covenant shall he corrupt by flatteries: but the people that do know their God shall be strong, and do *exploits.*

There are a number of professing Christians who do not understand or who have no interest in the concept of Covenant. They walk in willful sin and negligence of Jesus' Commission, in which He commanded those who believe in Him to further the Kingdom of God, and are under the illusion that faithful attendance in their fellowship of choice is sufficient. They have a *form* of godliness, but deny the power of it through their apathy concerning the Kingdom of God.

There are plenty of pastors who will reinforce their indifference by assuring them if they said "the prayer" and are faithful tithe paying members of the church, they have a ticket to be raptured out of here when the going gets too rough.

Ask yourself, is the above description a picture of you? Are you actively doing all you can to further the Kingdom of God in this world, or have you contented yourself with the idea that church membership, attending your church functions, and tithing is sufficient? Where do you see that pattern in the New Testament?

Christianity isn't a religion of helpless souls waiting for the rapture to take them out of this evil world. It is a vibrant community of able bodied, power endued, life changing soldiers whose lives are devoted to being continually engaged in spiritual warfare with the aim of furthering the Kingdom of God throughout this world. "*The people that do know their God shall be strong and do exploits*".

Dan 7:12 As concerning the rest of the beasts, they had their dominion taken away: yet their lives were prolonged for a season and time.

I will probably repeat this point several times in this book: Most commentators agree that the former beasts were Babylon (the lion with the eagle's wings), Persia (the bear), and Greece (the leopard), respectively, bringing us to the place where Rome (the fourth beast) dominates.

In Revelation 13:2, we see the three kingdoms mentioned in Daniel 7 transformed into the fourth beast.

Rev 13:2 The beast that I saw had the body of a leopard, the feet of a bear, and the mouth of a lion. The dragon handed over its own power and throne and great authority to this beast.

Each beast lost its dominion, but whereas there were other kingdoms whose people were totally annihilated (genocide) or assimilated into the culture by the conquering force, the influence and identity of these kingdoms continued in the kingdom of the fourth Beast.

The influence and identity of the former kingdoms were anti Semitic in nature; kingdoms who were used of God to chastise His people, but who themselves were used of Satan in an attempt to utterly destroy them, and would have, had not God intervened, as in the case of Esther when the Jewish people were under Persian rule.

Persia is now the modern day Iran, and we know of the open hostility Iran has toward Israel. Geographically, Babylon is in modern day Iraq. At that time it's rule extended over modern day Syria, Iraq, Southern Turkey, Israel and bordered Iran in the East.

If you look at the maps of the three kingdoms mentioned earlier, you will be able to see the extent of their rule, and how the countries represented in those various areas still hold a hatred toward the modern day Israel. *Many study Bibles today have maps, and the reader should be able to reference them to see what I am talking about.*

If you look at the map of the Babylonian empire, you will see that it's influence did not encompass as large of an area as that of the Persian or the Grecian empires, but it certainly reflects the area which is of great concern and imminent threat regarding Israel in this current time.

Israel And Her Significance Today

There is debate among Christian circles as to whether Israel as we know it today is the Israel of the Bible. I don't want to take time to address those questions, because I am deviating from the intended scope of this book already.

What I do know is that there is a nation in the Middle East that is called Israel. That fact is undeniable. The people in that nation worship the God of Abraham, Isaac and Jacob. They observe the Jewish religion, and the Biblical feasts. There are a few who are still alive who were eyewitnesses to and who survived Hitler's Holocaust. These few were among many who came to this area known as Palestine and occupied it as the Nation of Israel.

This same land was originally established and occupied by the Nation of Israel before its people were dispersed in 70 AD.

On July 1950, the Israeli parliament (Knesset) enacted the "Law of Return", which declared the right of every Jew to come to Israel. In 1970, it was expanded to include non-Jews with a Jewish grandparent and their spouses, those with Jewish ancestry, and converts to Judaism. I am of the personal opinion that Israel today is Israel that was, and the residents of Israel today are descendants of those who were given that land by God Himself.

It is an undeniable fact that there is hostility toward that nation known as Israel from a particular people group who also profess to worship the God of Abraham, Ishmael and Jacob, but whose intent and purpose is to annihilate the nation called Israel. These people and their culture are identified by the tenants of Islam, the religion which they adhere to.

As I mentioned earlier, I believe the "little horn" of Daniel 7 is actually Islam. Islam is *not* the Beast, but is part of the anti-Christ system of the Beast described in Revelation 13.

It is important to keep in mind that the Beasts mentioned in Daniel 7 *are kingdoms*, and not individuals.

Dan 7:23 Thus he said, The fourth beast shall be the fourth kingdom upon earth, which shall be diverse from all kingdoms, and shall devour the whole earth, and shall tread it down, and break it in pieces.

Another Sacred Cow is about to be shot:

Who or What Is The Beast of Revelation 13:2?

There are a lot of teachers who say that the Beast of Revelation 13 is an individual, and as of this writing, I can say that during my 33 years of being a Christian, I have heard many Christian teachers proclaiming the "Beast" as being practically every United States President that has sat in office during those years, every pope, communist leaders, dictators, and even some religious leaders or celebrities. Preterists hold the position that the "Beast" was Nero or Domitian, who ruled at the time of John's writing.

A lot of people who call themselves prophets churn out books of secret Bible codes that "reveal" who this mystery man is. Did I call them prophets? They would be better termed as "profits", because that is what their endless litany of "fresh revelation" results in. The beast in Revelation 13:2 or in Revelation 13:11 is not a man, but a *kingdom* that will rule over the world, just as the beasts in Daniel seven were described as kingdoms.

Types, Allegories and Parables.

Some may object to a lot which is written here and mention that the "beast" of Revelation 13 is referred to as "he", instead of an "it", arguing that the beast could not be a kingdom, but is instead a person, because of the use of the personal pronoun, yet by the same token, some will say that the Bride of Christ is the New Jerusalem or the Church, and the harlot of Revelation 18 is the apostate Church, or Catholicism, or a one world governmental system. Each of these are identified with a personal pronoun.

Visions and dreams are highly symbolic, which is why there are countless commentaries (including the one you are now reading) that try to explain the symbolism of various prophetic passages in the Books of the Bible.

Rev 13:2 And the beast which I saw was like unto a leopard, and his feet were as *the feet* of a bear, and his mouth as the mouth of a lion: and the dragon gave him his power, and his seat, and great authority.

Dan 7:12 As concerning the rest of the beasts, they had their dominion taken away: yet their lives were prolonged for a season and time.

"**A season and time**" (Dan 7:12). A season is a period of change or transition. "A time" is a specific period of time, and corresponds to the Greek word "Chronos". A time could be a year or a thousand years, but it is a specified period of time, whether that is designated by a predetermined known number as in "one year" or if it is a predetermined time only known by the Father, as Jesus explained to His disciples:

Act 1:6 When they therefore were come together, they asked of him, saying, Lord, wilt thou at this time restore again the kingdom to Israel?
7 And he said unto them, It is not for you to know the times (Chronos) **or the seasons, which the Father hath put in his own power.**

Daniel's visions eventually take him to a time when none of the four kingdoms will have any influence over the world any longer. It will be a time when Jesus Christ rules over the world.

The age of this present kingdom will be replaced by the Age of the Kingdom of God.

Dan 7:13 I saw in the night visions, and, behold, *one* like the Son of man came with the clouds of heaven, and came to the Ancient of days, and they brought him near before him.
14 And there was given him dominion, and glory, and a kingdom, that all people, nations, and languages, should serve him: his dominion *is* an everlasting dominion, which shall not pass away, and his kingdom *that* which shall not be destroyed.

But before that time comes there will be an all out war between the Saints of God (the Kingdom of God) and the Beast (the kingdoms of this world).

The weapons of this one called the Beast are carnal; persecution, imprisonment, executions, suicide bombings, beheadings, and jihad. I believe the kingdom of the Beast includes for a time the religious culture known as Islam.

The weapons of the Saints are spiritual; the Blood of the Lamb and the Word of His testimony - their witness to those who are held captive to the dragon (Rev 12:11, 2Cor 10:4, Eph 6:11-18, 1 Thes 1:5, Mark 16:15-20).

For more on the Beast, and the harlot that rides the beast, I would again refer the reader to Chapter 6 in the appendix.

The Mark

It is interesting that the 36th Sura in the Qu'ran which was recited by Islam's prophet Mohammad, and recorded by the scribes that accompanied him during his recitations, declares Mohammad to be the prophet who was the messenger to declare the straight path to God. It also describes in length the final Judgment of God (the last days). And it reaffirms again in the 82nd verse that Allah is alone, and has no son.

3 Indeed you, [O Muhammad], are from among the messengers,
4 On a straight path.
5 [This is] a revelation of the Exalted in Might, the Merciful,
6 That you may warn a people whose forefathers were not warned, so they are unaware.

82 His command is only when He intends a thing that He says to it, "Be," and it is.

This same phrase in verse 82 was used earlier to disprove that Jesus was the Son of God:

It is not befitting to (the majesty of) Allah that He should beget a son. Glory be to Him! when He determines a matter, He only says to it, "Be", and it is. - 19:35

If one adds the number of Suras in succession up to this Sura, the final number will be 666[11] which is indeed the number of a man, and points to a prophet and a system that is intent on world conquest and submission.

The Beast kingdom of the last days is identified with a false prophet (Rev 16:13, 19:20, and 20:10). I have already pointed out that the Beast is not a man, but a kingdom. I believe the false prophet would be the one who serves to further that kingdom. If you are still not settled or convinced of this, I would once more invite the reader to read the article in the Appendix 6 concerning the Whore of Babylon.

The marvelous thing is to realize that this prophecy in Revelation was written almost 600 years before the founding of Islam, but any thinking person can easily see the correlation between Revelation 13 and a religious kingdom which would arise at some time in the future and which would be founded by a prophet, whose temple would sit in the Holy place of the original temple mount, and which would make war with the saints, those who are called sons and daughters of the Most High God.

Do I think that the Qu'ran *is* the mark of the Beast? No. But I believe it will be a precursor to the instituting of the Mark of the Beast.

Do I believe that Islam is the Beast? No. But I believe it is part of that system that ushers in the Anti-Christ Beast Kingdom.

For a more detailed explanation of all this, I would again refer the reader to the study on the harlot of Revelation 17[6] .

The beautiful thing is that even in the midst of the great tribulation that has taken place as a result of this kingdom's advancement, eyes have been opened to the Truth of Jesus Christ as the Saints of the Most High, empowered by the anointing of Holy Spirit turn many to righteousness.

Dan 12:3 And they that be wise shall shine as the brightness of the firmament; and they that turn many to righteousness as the stars for ever and ever.

Dan 7:13 I saw in the night visions, and, behold, *one* like the Son of man came with the clouds of heaven, and came to the Ancient of days, and they brought him near before him.
14 And there was given him dominion, and glory, and a kingdom, that all people, nations, and languages, should serve him: his dominion *is* an everlasting dominion, which shall not pass away, and his kingdom *that* which shall not be destroyed.

God's Grace For The Last Days

And, dear reader, here is God's Grace. As you read these words, and the scroll and the mystery of the Revelation is being unfolded before you, you can be assured that even if you have fallen into the error of the deception of the spirit of antichrist that prevails in the world today, and if you realize that you have rejected the Truth that is in Jesus Christ, it's still not too late for you. Regardless if you are a Muslim, an atheist, a Catholic, an adulterer, a fornicator, a homosexual, a satanist, a wiccan, a Hindu, a Buddhist, or an adherent of any other religion that opposes Biblical doctrine and Jesus Christ, it is still not too late for you to come to repentance and call on the One Who Alone is able to save your soul from eternal damnation.

If the words that have been written herein are an offense to you, be assured that God has promised that you would find the Truth if you seek Him with your whole heart. He will hear your prayers, if you ask Him to reveal His Truth to you.

God's Grace is Amazing. Whereas the Antichrist spirit resists the Truth of the Only Begotten Son of God, His Truth will and does prevail in the hearts of those who seek His Face.

In this moment, I know that there are many who will read these words, and who will be drawn to confess their sin of unbelief to the Almighty God, and who will surrender their hearts and lives to Jesus Christ as their Lord and Savior, and who will become a son or daughter of the Most High God.

Allah may have no sons. But the God of all creation and the God of Abraham, Isaac and Jacob has sent His ONLY begotten Son to reveal the Father to all mankind. He wants to call *you* son, or daughter.

If you feel that tug, it is the Holy Spirit Who is drawing you right now. Don't resist, friend. Call on the Name of Jesus Christ, and ask Him to forgive and to save you from your sins and your rebellion against the Will of God for your life and to be the Lord of your life. As you do that in sincere repentance, you will experience a Divine Touch from the Living God Who created you to be a part of His Kingdom and His Family.

Joh 3:16 For God so loved the world, that he gave his only begotten Son, that whosoever believeth in him should not perish, but have everlasting life.
17 For God sent not his Son into the world to condemn the world; but that the world through him might be saved.
18 He that believeth on him is not condemned: but he that believeth not is condemned already, because he hath not believed in the name of the only begotten Son of God.
19 And this is the condemnation, that light is come into the world, and men loved darkness rather than light, because their deeds were evil.
20 For every one that doeth evil hateth the light, neither cometh to the light, lest his deeds should be reproved.
21 But he that doeth truth cometh to the light, that his deeds may be made manifest, that they are wrought in God.

Heb 2:9 But we see Jesus, who was made a little lower than the angels for the suffering of death, crowned with glory and honour; that he by the grace of God should taste death for every man.
10 For it became him, for whom *are* all things, and by whom *are* all things, in bringing many sons unto glory, to make the captain of their salvation perfect through sufferings.

Heb 1:1 God, who at sundry times and in divers manners spake in time past unto the fathers by the prophets,
2 Hath in these last days spoken unto us by *his* Son, whom he hath appointed heir of all things, by whom also he made the worlds;
3 Who being the brightness of *his* glory, and the express image of his person, and upholding all things by the word of his power, when he had by himself purged our sins, sat down on the right hand of the Majesty on high;
4 Being made so much better than the angels, as he hath by inheritance obtained a more excellent name than they.
5 For unto which of the angels said he at any time, Thou art my Son, this day have I begotten thee? And again, I will be to him a Father, and he shall be to me a Son?

6 And again, when he bringeth in the firstbegotten into the world, he saith, And let all the angels of God worship him.

Joh 14:1 Let not your heart be troubled: ye believe in God, believe also in me.
2 In my Father's house are many mansions: if *it were* not *so,* I would have told you. I go to prepare a place for you.
3 And if I go and prepare a place for you, I will come again, and receive you unto myself; that where I am, *there* ye may be also.
4 And whither I go ye know, and the way ye know.
5 Thomas saith unto him, Lord, we know not whither thou goest; and how can we know the way?
6 Jesus saith unto him, I am the way, the truth, and the life: no man cometh unto the Father, but by me.

2Pe 3:8 But, beloved, be not ignorant of this one thing, that one day *is* with the Lord as a thousand years, and a thousand years as one day.
9 The Lord is not slack concerning his promise, as some men count slackness; but is longsuffering to us-ward, not willing that any should perish, but that all should come to repentance.
10 But the day of the Lord will come as a thief in the night; in the which the heavens shall pass away with a great noise, and the elements shall melt with fervent heat, the earth also and the works that are therein shall be burned up.
11 *Seeing* then *that* all these things shall be dissolved, what manner *of persons* ought ye to be in *all* holy conversation and godliness,
12 Looking for and hasting unto the coming of the day of God, wherein the heavens being on fire shall be dissolved, and the elements shall melt with fervent heat?
13 Nevertheless we, according to his promise, look for new heavens and a new earth, wherein dwelleth righteousness.
14 Wherefore, beloved, seeing that ye look for such things, be diligent that ye may be found of him in peace, without spot, and blameless.

Rom 10:6 But the righteousness which is of faith speaketh on this wise, Say not in thine heart, Who shall ascend into heaven? (that is, to bring Christ down *from above:)*
7 Or, Who shall descend into the deep? (that is, to bring up Christ again from the dead.)
8 But what saith it? The word is nigh thee, *even* in thy mouth, and in thy heart: that is, the word of faith, which we preach;
9 That if thou shalt confess with thy mouth the Lord Jesus, and shalt believe in thine heart that God hath raised him from the dead, thou shalt be saved.
10 For with the heart man believeth unto righteousness; and with the mouth confession is made unto salvation.
11 For the scripture saith, Whosoever believeth on him shall not be ashamed.
12 For there is no difference between the Jew and the Greek: for the same Lord over all

is rich unto all that call upon him.

13 For whosoever shall call upon the name of the Lord shall be saved.

14 How then shall they call on him in whom they have not believed? and how shall they believe in him of whom they have not heard? and how shall they hear without a preacher?

15 And how shall they preach, except they be sent? as it is written, How beautiful are the feet of them that preach the gospel of peace, and bring glad tidings of good things!

SECTION 3

THE SIGN OF HIS COMING

Mat 24:3 And as he sat upon the mount of Olives, the disciples came unto him privately, saying, Tell us, when shall these things be? and what *shall be* the sign of thy coming, and of the end of the world?

THE CLOUDS OF GLORY THE SIGN OF HIS COMING

Mat 24:29 Immediately after the tribulation of those days shall the sun be darkened, and the moon shall not give her light, and the stars shall fall from heaven, and the powers of the heavens shall be shaken:
30 And then shall appear the sign of the Son of man in heaven: and then shall all the tribes of the earth mourn, and they shall see the Son of man coming in the clouds of heaven with power and great glory.

When Jesus was questioned by the High Priest as to whether He was the Christ, Jesus' answer in Mark 14:62 was a direct reference to this passage in Daniel 7:13, and was seen as blasphemy by the priest.

This is what the passage Jesus quoted from says:

Dan 7:13 I saw in the night visions, and, behold, *one* like the Son of man came with the clouds of heaven, and came to the Ancient of days, and they brought him near before him.
14 And there was given him dominion, and glory, and a kingdom, that all people, nations, and languages, should serve him: his dominion *is* an everlasting dominion, which shall not pass away, and his kingdom *that* which shall not be destroyed.

This is what Jesus said that got the high priest upset:

Mar 14:61 But he held his peace, and answered nothing. Again the high priest asked him, and said unto him, Art thou the Christ, the Son of the Blessed?
62 And Jesus said, I am: and ye shall see the Son of man sitting on the right hand of power, and coming in the clouds of heaven.

Jesus spoke of His Coming in Matthew 24:30 as being on the clouds of heaven, which was understood by His disciples and the religious leaders of His day to be another reference to the prophecy in Daniel.

This is the High priest's reaction to what Jesus said:

Mar 14:63 Then the high priest rent his clothes, and saith, What need we any further witnesses?
64 Ye have heard the blasphemy: what think ye? And they all condemned him to be guilty of death.

Some commentators allegorize this passage of Jesus' coming on the clouds in various ways, but I believe the account in Acts 1:9-11 is a promise of the literal return of Christ on the clouds:

Act 1:9 And when he had spoken these things, while they beheld, he was taken up; and a cloud received him out of their sight.
10 And while they looked stedfastly toward heaven as he went up, behold, two men stood by them in white apparel;
11 Which also said, Ye men of Galilee, why stand ye gazing up into heaven? this same Jesus, which is taken up from you into heaven, shall so come in like manner as ye have seen him go into heaven.

Unless you want to allegorize these verses, and say that Jesus wasn't really taken up into a cloud, then the natural inference is that Jesus is coming back on the clouds of heaven just like He said he would. But if you insist on allegorizing it, then you will have to concede that you don't believe that Jesus was taken up into a cloud. That is treading on dangerous ground for a person who professes to be a Christian.

Remember, according to Jesus' Words, this would take place *after* the time of great tribulation (Matt 24:29). I believe the timing of this event is recorded in Revelation 14:

Rev 14:14 And I looked, and behold a white cloud, and upon the cloud *one* sat like unto the Son of man, having on his head a golden crown, and in his hand a sharp sickle.
15 And another angel came out of the temple, crying with a loud voice to him that sat on the cloud, Thrust in thy sickle, and reap: for the time is come for thee to reap; for the harvest of the earth is ripe.
16 And he that sat on the cloud thrust in his sickle on the earth; and the earth was reaped.

Note that this happens AFTER the account of the persecution of the saints in Revelation 13.

Some people maintain the view that these saints who are persecuted in Chapter 13 are those who come to the Lord during a seven year tribulation, but I see no firm Biblical premise for this, as there certainly is NO Biblical premise whatsoever that the "Church" is "raptured" out in Revelation 4:1, which the pre-tribulation rapture theorists allege.

Anyone who has not been deceived by the movie makers, the book sellers and the TV personalities can see that it is *John* who was caught up in his vision, and not the Church.

Rev 4:1 After this I looked, and, behold, a door *was* opened in heaven: and the first voice which I heard *was* as it were of a trumpet talking with me; which said, Come up hither, and I will shew thee things which must be hereafter.

Those who have been deceived by false profits of today say that the word "Church" is not mentioned any more after Revelation chapter 3, and they point to that as "proof" that the rapture has occurred. Most of those who hold this position are merely parroting what they have heard from other teachers. They say that Revelation 4:1 is really the Church being raptured up. But there really isn't anything at all to indicate that John was representative of the Church. And who does the Church consist of?

Saints.

In Revelation 13:7, we are told that the Beast makes war with the saints. We see the saints mentioned again in Revelation 13:10, 14:12, 16:6, 17:6, and 18:24. The pre-trib rapture theorists say that these "saints" are people who have called on the Lord during the 7 year end-times tribulation. That's the time that dispensationalists refer to as the 70th week.

There are all kinds of scenarios that are presented as to how this is going to happen, but they are just fictional events based on a fictional premise.

I would refer the reader to my study on the 70th week of Daniel in the Appendix at this point which addresses the dispensationalist's view of a "last days gap" between the sixty ninth week and the seventieth week of Daniel 9:24-27, and on which an end times seven year tribulation doctrine is formulated.

If you find yourself acknowledging that the seventieth year of Daniel 9 has already been fulfilled in Jesus, then you have to come to terms with the fact that the "seventieth week" of dispensationalist theory is based on flawed reasoning, and another Sacred cow may be dying in your field of dreams that some false teacher of Scripture has sold you.

Most of these theorists maintain the Holy Spirit is taken out of the earth at the rapture according to their interpretation of 2 Thessalonians 2:7 ("He who letteth" is supposed to be the Holy Spirit according to some dispensationalist pretrib profits).

2Th 2:7 For the mystery of iniquity doth already work: only he who now letteth *will let*, until he be taken out of the way.

So if this is the Holy Spirit being spoken of, how can anyone be saved, if He is taken out of the way? How can they be Born Again, or Born of the Spirit, if the Holy Spirit is removed? I would once again refer the reader to see the first entry in the Appendix concerning 2 Thessalonians.

Those who "let" or hinder the coming of the lawlessness which is to prevail over the world are those who are actively about furthering the Kingdom of God in this world. These will be taken out of the way by the slaughter or imprisonment of the Christians which are actively hindering Satan's kingdom from overtaking the world, which takes place in Revelation 11, and 13.

Jesus *is* coming in the clouds. But His coming will signal the end of the age, and NOT the end of the world.

Rev 1:7 Behold, he cometh with clouds; and every eye shall see him, and they *also* which pierced him: and all kindreds of the earth shall wail because of him. Even so, Amen.

1Th 4:17 Then we which are alive *and* remain shall be caught up together with them in the clouds, to meet the Lord in the air: and so shall we ever be with the Lord.

According to Matthew 24:29, this is going to take place *immediately after the tribulation*, or when the times of the Gentiles has been fulfilled.

Mat 24:29 Immediately after the tribulation of those days shall the sun be darkened, and the moon shall not give her light, and the stars shall fall from heaven, and the powers of the heavens shall be shaken:
30 And then shall appear the sign of the Son of man in heaven: and then shall all the tribes of the earth mourn, and they shall see the Son of man coming in the clouds of heaven with power and great glory.
31 And he shall send his angels with a great sound of a trumpet, and they shall gather together his elect from the four winds, from one end of heaven to the other.

God will take His people out before He pours His wrath out on the earth to purge the earth from its wickedness, just as He took Noah and his family out (by way of the ark) of the wrath of God while He purged the earth from its wickedness.

Remember the warning in Revelation 22:18:

Rev 22:18 For I testify unto every man that heareth the words of the prophecy of this book, If any man shall add unto these things, God shall add unto him the plagues that are written in this book:
19 And if any man shall take away from the words of the book of this prophecy, God shall take away his part out of the book of life, and out of the holy city, and *from* the things which are written in this book.

THE TRIBULATION AND THE WRATH OF GOD.

A common misconception held by a lot of people who study the "end times" is that the Great Tribulation and the Wrath of God are the same thing, but that isn't true. Pre-trib rapture proponents will say that Christians will be taken out before the tribulation because God hasn't appointed us to wrath.

1Th 5:9 For God hath not appointed us to wrath, but to obtain salvation by our Lord Jesus Christ,

Tribulation comes at the hands of man; and as I have pointed out earlier, the tribulation that Jesus spoke of has extended from the foundation of the Church and will continue to the end of the present age. The Wrath of God, on the other hand, comes from the Hand of God, and brings an end to the age that the dragon rules over, when the times of the Gentiles will be fulfilled. I believe that the account of Revelation 14:14-16 is the parallel to Matthew 24:30-31 and Daniel 7:13:

Rev 14:14 And I looked, and behold a white cloud, and upon the cloud *one* **sat like unto the Son of man, having on his head a golden crown, and in his hand a sharp sickle.**
15 And another angel came out of the temple, crying with a loud voice to him that sat on the cloud, Thrust in thy sickle, and reap: for the time is come for thee to reap; for the harvest of the earth is ripe.
16 And he that sat on the cloud thrust in his sickle on the earth; and the earth was reaped.

Mat 24:30 And then shall appear the sign of the Son of man in heaven: and then shall all the tribes of the earth mourn, and they shall see the Son of man coming in the clouds of heaven with power and great glory.
31 And he shall send his angels with a great sound of a trumpet, and they shall gather together his elect from the four winds, from one end of heaven to the other.

Dan 7:13 I saw in the night visions, and, behold, *one* **like the Son of man came with the clouds of heaven, and came to the Ancient of days, and they brought him near before him.**
14 And there was given him dominion, and glory, and a kingdom, that all people, nations, and languages, should serve him: his dominion *is* **an everlasting dominion, which shall not pass away, and his kingdom** *that* **which shall not be destroyed.**

Some people reject the idea of a Rapture or a "catching away" altogether, but I believe there are too many passages that allude to it to ignore.

Noah was found Righteous in the eyes of God, and he was taken out of the destruction that resulted as a consequence of God's Wrath, but he was eventually restored to the earth, a new earth that was cleansed from the wickedness that prevailed over it.

I believe that as soon as the Saints are caught up in the air to be with the Lord (immediately *after* the tribulation - [Matthew 24:29] the end of which will take place at an appointed time, that only the Father knows), there will be a time of Wrath that is poured out on the earth - a cleansing of the earth, just as it was in the days of Noah.

Revelation 14:14-16 tells of the gathering of the people of God to Jesus Christ.

Rev 14:14 And I looked, and behold a white cloud, and upon the cloud *one* sat like unto the Son of man, having on his head a golden crown, and in his hand a sharp sickle.
15 And another angel came out of the temple, crying with a loud voice to him that sat on the cloud, Thrust in thy sickle, and reap: for the time is come for thee to reap; for the harvest of the earth is ripe.
16 And he that sat on the cloud thrust in his sickle on the earth; and the earth was reaped.

Revelation 14:17-20 foretells of the Wrath of God which immediately follows.

Rev 14:17 And another angel came out of the temple which is in heaven, he also having a sharp sickle.
18 And another angel came out from the altar, which had power over fire; and cried with a loud cry to him that had the sharp sickle, saying, Thrust in thy sharp sickle, and gather the clusters of the vine of the earth; for her grapes are fully ripe.
19 And the angel thrust in his sickle into the earth, and gathered the vine of the earth, and cast *it* into the great winepress of the wrath of God.
20 And the winepress was trodden without the city, and blood came out of the winepress, even unto the horse bridles, by the space of a thousand *and* six hundred furlongs.

The "Cup" or the "wine" of the wrath of God is mentioned several times in the Bible. It will happen. There is a day when God will pour out His Wrath on the inhabitants of the world who have rejected him. And there is a day when He will gather up the saints (who have been about fulfilling His Commission of furthering the Kingdom of God on earth) to Himself before that great and dreadful day.

But it won't be a time of destruction of the world He created. It will be a time of cleansing, and restoration of the Kingdom to the people of God.

Rev 14:9 And the third angel followed them, saying with a loud voice, If any man worship the beast and his image, and receive *his* mark in his forehead, or in his hand,
10 The same shall drink of the wine of the wrath of God, which is poured out without mixture into the cup of his indignation; and he shall be tormented with fire and brimstone in the presence of the holy angels, and in the presence of the Lamb:

Rev 16:19 And the great city was divided into three parts, and the cities of the nations fell: and great Babylon came in remembrance before God, to give unto her the cup of the wine of the fierceness of his wrath.

**Jer 25:15 For thus saith the LORD God of Israel unto me; Take the wine cup of this fury at my hand, and cause all the nations, to whom I send thee, to drink it.
16 And they shall drink, and be moved, and be mad, because of the sword that I will send among them.**

Psa 75:8 For in the hand of the LORD *there is* **a cup, and the wine is red; it is full of mixture; and he poureth out of the same: but the dregs thereof, all the wicked of the earth shall wring** *them* **out,** *and* **drink** *them.*
**9 But I will declare for ever; I will sing praises to the God of Jacob.
10 All the horns of the wicked also will I cut off;** *but* **the horns of the righteous shall be exalted.**

Psalm 75 is a prophetic Psalm that ties the vision of Daniel and the vision of John in the book of Revelation together.

Psalm 75 assures us that the power of the wicked will be cut off, but the righteous shall be exalted. This is a picture of the end of the age that the disciples were asking Jesus about.

Revelation 15-18 describes the Wrath of God on the earth. After the earth has been cleansed of its wickedness, the saints of God will return to rule and reign with Christ for a thousand years. This occurs in Revelation 20.

It will be the end of this age and the beginning of something new.

Rev 21:5 And he that sat upon the throne said, Behold, I make all things new. And he said unto me, Write: for these words are true and faithful.

But when He comes back for His Church in Revelation 14, He will be coming back for those who have been actively about furthering His Kingdom on the earth. The Beast is making war with these Saints, because they are about their Father's Kingdom, and he is trying to do what he can to render them powerless and ineffective, in the Western Church, he does that primarily through false doctrine and another gospel that renders them hearers of the Word of God and not doers of the Word. *In other parts of the world, he is slaughtering them at the hands of religious extremists, or imprisoning them by laws that prohibit religion.*

Noah was all about preparing the ark before the coming of God's wrath. The True Church will be all about furthering the Kingdom of God before the coming of God's wrath.

But there will be a great number of professing Christians that have bought into the harlot system in compromise and apostasy, instead of being about the Kingdom of God.

All of the different manufactured crises' that have been formulated from the pulpit puppets of Satan, the Chicken Littles, and the political powers that be, will have contributed to the apostasy of many. They won't be a part of that first resurrection. The parables of Matthew 25 are a plain warning against that Day; the forgetful virgins, the slothful servant, and the uncaring goats.

The truth of the matter is that a lot of professing Christians will be surprised when Jesus returns, and they hear Him say "Depart from me" because they have put their trust in man's fables instead of the Word of God.

THE GENERATION JESUS WAS TALKING ABOUT IN MATTHEW 24:34
The Preterist Position concerning Matthew 24 and the Book of Revelation

One of the major questions people ask regarding Jesus' Dialogue with His disciples in Matthew 24 concerns His Statement:

Mat 24:34 Verily I say unto you, This generation shall not pass, till all these things be fulfilled.

Those of the "preterist" persuasion point to this verse and the fact the Jesus speaks in the second person (ye, or you) during His discourse, which would seem to suggest that He was telling His disciples these things would happen in their lifetime. "Preterist" means past, as in all the things Jesus spoke of in Matthew 24 regarding the three questions asked by the disciples was fulfilled in 70 AD with the destruction of Jerusalem, hence, they don't adhere to the doctrine of a future Second Coming.

Mat 24:23 Then if any man shall say unto you, Lo, here *is* Christ, or there; believe *it* not.

Mat 24:33 So likewise ye, when ye shall see all these things, know that it is near, *even* at the doors.

Mat 24:26 Wherefore if they shall say unto you, Behold, he is in the desert; go not forth: behold, *he is* in the secret chambers; believe *it* not.

Those who hold to the Preterist interpretation of Scripture interpret the Book of Revelation as being symbolic of the persecution of the Church in the 1st Century, written in code to encourage the Body of Christ who were already receiving tribulation at the hands of Caesar.

To a preterist, The "new heavens and new earth" of Revelation 21:1 is the world under the New Covenant established by Christ, just as a Christian is made a new creature in 2 Cor 5:7.

Preterists view end times prophecies as having already been fulfilled when the Kingdom of God was given into the hands of the Gentiles.

**Act 28:24 And some believed the things which were spoken, and some believed not.
25 And when they agreed not among themselves, they departed, after that Paul had spoken one word, Well spake the Holy Ghost by Esaias the prophet unto our fathers,
26 Saying, Go unto this people, and say, Hearing ye shall hear, and shall not understand; and seeing ye shall see, and not perceive:
27 For the heart of this people is waxed gross, and their ears are dull of hearing, and their eyes have they closed; lest they should see with *their* eyes, and hear with *their* ears, and understand with *their* heart, and should be converted, and I should heal them.
28 Be it known therefore unto you, that the salvation of God is sent unto the Gentiles, and *that* they will hear it.**

The futurist (those who believe that these things spoken in Matthew 24 and Revelation will happen at some point in the future) maintains that Jesus was referring to the generation that would be living when all these signs that Jesus spoke about would come to pass. They say that the second person tense is used in many passages of the Bible that speak of a future event, distant from those who are being addressed.

I believe there is a degree of validity in both positions.

From the futurist perspective, we can see that the use of the second person in scripture does not always pertain to the immediate audience that is being addressed. Take, for an example (one of many), Joseph's words to his brethren before he died:

**Gen 50:24 And Joseph said unto his brethren, I die: and God will surely visit you, and bring you out of this land unto the land which he sware to Abraham, to Isaac, and to Jacob.
25 And Joseph took an oath of the children of Israel, saying, God will surely visit you, and ye shall carry up my bones from hence.**

Though he uses the second person when he addresses his brethren concerning their departure from Egypt and his burial in the land of Promise, that was not to be fulfilled until nearly 400 years later.

If we were to take the preterist position (that the use of the 2nd person in Jesus' Dialogue with His disciples in Matthew 24 means that what He said has no relevance to us today), then we would have to apply the same rule to where ever the use of the 2nd person is found in Scripture.

Hence, if we are going to validate the preterist position, when Paul writes to the saints that are in Rome, we could argue that the instruction in the Book of Romans has nothing to do with other Christians:

Romans 1:7 To all that be in Rome, beloved of God, called [to be] saints: Grace to you and peace from God our Father, and the Lord Jesus Christ.

The same could be said of Paul's letters that were specifically addressed to the churches of Galatia, Ephesus, Philippi, Colosse, and that of the Thessalonians - since they were not addressed to Christians at large, then following the preterist reasoning, we can disregard the instruction given in any of these letters.

If that sounds foolish, then the preterist argument of dismissing Jesus' words as having any relevance for us today because of the use of the 2nd person by Jesus in Matthew 24 is (in my personal opinion) just as foolish.

Following the preterist reasoning concerning Jesus' use of the second person, then the Sermon on the Mount was intended for only His disciples when He said:

Matthew 5:44 But I say unto you, Love your enemies, bless them that curse you, do good to them that hate you, and pray for them which despitefully use you, and persecute you;

But as I said earlier, there is a degree of validity in both the preterist and the futurist positions. Solomon declared that there is no new thing under the sun, and the New Testament teaches us that the Old Testament laws and ordinances were a prophetic type and shadow of those things that were to come with the establishment of the New Covenant (Col2:17, Heb 10:1).

So what did Jesus mean by **"This generation shall not pass, till all these things be fulfilled"?**

Preterists say everything Jesus spoke of **was fulfilled** in 70 AD, and to a large degree, they are right. But I would remind the reader that the Western Wall is still standing. There are still stones of that Temple era that have remained standing. The Gospel was preached to the known world then, but not to every kingdom and nation and tribe in the world.

Futurists say the things Jesus spoke of are **yet to be fulfilled**.

I think the problem that both camps have lies in the English interpretation of the Greek word translated as "fulfilled" in Matthew 24:34.

The Greek word used here that is translated as "fulfilled" (Strong's number G1096 - *ginomai*) is different from that which is used elsewhere concerning the fulfillment of prophecy:

In passages which speak of the fulfillment of the prophetic word, the Greek word "pleroo" (Strong's number G4137) is used, which means complete, or completed. Some of those passages are here:

Mat 1:22 Now all this was done, that it might be fulfilled which was spoken of the Lord by the prophet, saying,
23 Behold, a virgin shall be with child, and shall bring forth a son, and they shall call his name Emmanuel, which being interpreted is, God with us.

Mat 2:15 And was there until the death of Herod: that it might be fulfilled which was spoken of the Lord by the prophet, saying, Out of Egypt have I called my son.

Mat 4:14 That it might be fulfilled which was spoken by Esaias the prophet, saying,
15 The land of Zabulon, and the land of Nephthalim, *by* the way of the sea, beyond Jordan, Galilee of the Gentiles;
16 The people which sat in darkness saw great light; and to them which sat in the region and shadow of death light is sprung up.

Mat 8:17 That it might be fulfilled which was spoken by Esaias the prophet, saying, Himself took our infirmities, and bare *our* sicknesses.

Mar 1:15 And saying, The time is fulfilled, and the kingdom of God is at hand: repent ye, and believe the gospel.

In the parallel passage to Matthew 24 found in Luke's account, Jesus refers to the impending destruction of Jerusalem (fulfilled in 70 AD) followed by a future period called the "times" of the Gentiles which must be fulfilled (pleroo).

Luk 21:24 And they shall fall by the edge of the sword, and shall be led away captive into all nations: and Jerusalem shall be trodden down of the Gentiles, until the times of the Gentiles be fulfilled (pleroo).

That is where we are at now, in the times of the Gentiles. Paul alludes to this time of fulfillment (the word translated as "fulness" is the same word [different tense] translated in these passages above) that would take place at some time in the future:

Rom 11:25 For I would not, brethren, that ye should be ignorant of this mystery, lest ye should be wise in your own conceits; that blindness in part is happened to Israel, until the fulness (pleroma - Strong's number 4138) **of the Gentiles be come in.**

Luke records what would happen after the times of the Gentiles were fulfilled:

Luk 21:25 And there shall be signs in the sun, and in the moon, and in the stars; and upon the earth distress of nations, with perplexity; the sea and the waves roaring;
26 Men's hearts failing them for fear, and for looking after those things which are coming on the earth: for the powers of heaven shall be shaken.
27 And then shall they see the Son of man coming in a cloud with power and great glory.
28 And when these things begin to come to pass, then look up, and lift up your heads; for your redemption draweth nigh.

From Matthew we know that this event will take place AFTER the tribulation. We have already addressed the tribulation of God's people extending since the fall of Jerusalem in 70 AD to the present time.

In Matthew 24:34, Jesus uses a different word than "pleroo", and while that word has been translated as "fulfilled", it would have been better to translate it as "done" as it was in the parallel account in Mark.

Mar 13:30 Verily I say unto you, that this generation shall not pass, till all these things be done.

I hope I didn't lose you here, but a brief summation would be that the testimony of Matthew, Mark and Luke all agree that these things would be done in the time of that generation, but the time of the fulfillment of the prophecy of the return of Christ remains known only by the Father.

Mar 13:32 But of that day and *that* hour knoweth no man, no, not the angels which are in heaven, neither the Son, but the Father.

THE WAR

In Revelation 13, the Beast is making war with the Saints. It isn't a picture of the helpless saints being mercilessly slaughtered by the Beast; there is a war going on. The Saints of God are fighting for the Kingdom of God, and the Beast is fighting for the continuance of the kingdom of this age. This is something that is taking place even now (although many of those who profess to be Christians are not engaged in the battle), but sometime in the future it will be ramped up with great intensity.

The Word of God says our warfare is not carnal. Our warfare is spiritual, and comes through pulling down strongholds and every high thing that exalts itself above the knowledge of God, walking in the supernatural. This is done primarily through Prayer and fulfilling the Great Commission on a personal level.

Daniel says that they who know their God will do exploits.

The dragon (the devil) has given the Beast the power that he has, and that power is a combination of the four ancient kingdoms that Daniel wrote about (read the section concerning the Ten Horns again). Each of those kingdoms reigned over areas that are dominated by Islam today.

As I have pointed out elsewhere, the geographical area that was in submission to ancient Babylon is the same area that we see is the most opposed to Israel's right to existence as a nation. Islam is a religion that is centered around world conquest achieved by the power of man. That hasn't been a recent development. That goal has been Islam's purpose since it's prophet founded that religion.

The culmination of the tribulation that has extended in various forms from 70 AD until the present day will be when the atrocities committed by the fundamentalist adherents of the religion of Islam and other anti Christ religions serve to usher in the full authority of the kingdom of the Beast of Revelation 13, and that kingdom with its' blasphemous *Anti Semite-Anti Christ-Anti God* agenda will dominate the world for a short time..

I have stated elsewhere that I do not believe that Islam is the Beast system, but it will be the *catalyst* that brings that system about. In the appendix[6] I discuss the harlot and the Beast that the harlot rides. I would encourage you to read that section, but let me just say right here that the Beast system will be a time when religion of all kinds will be outlawed (including Islam), and secular humanism will be the driving force of that kingdom.

Only that remnant of Christians who refuse to compromise their faith in the midst of great persecution will resist the Beast. In the midst of great persecution, Christians will be about the Father's business, and will do exploits as they contend for the Faith. Persecution against Christianity will come from all sides.

It is then that the Saints of God will be caught up with Christ, and the cleansing power of the Wrath of God will cleanse the earth of all that offends; of the anti Christ spirit that prevails on the earth, and all that is an abomination in the sight of God.

It won't take God three and a half years to do that.

The commonly held story is that there will be 144,000 Jews who evangelize the world after the Church is raptured out before the tribulation. All of this is relatively new doctrine, stemming from Darby's "revelation" in 1833.

Prior to Darby, the common consensus among Christian theologians was that of a post millennial view or a historical premillennialist view. Both views hold that *the Church is responsible here and now to further the Kingdom of God on earth, and to transform the culture of the area from a pagan or heathen dominated culture to a Christian culture.*

Mat 13:38 The field is the world (kosmos)**; the good seed are the children of the kingdom; but the tares are the children of the wicked** *one;*
39 The enemy that sowed them is the devil; the harvest is the end of the world (aion = age)**; and the reapers are the angels.**
40 As therefore the tares are gathered and burned in the fire; so shall it be in the end of this world (aion = age)**.**
41 The Son of man shall send forth his angels, and they shall gather out of his kingdom all things that offend, and them which do iniquity;
42 And shall cast them into a furnace of fire: there shall be wailing and gnashing of teeth.

The angels shall gather out of His kingdom all things that offend and them which do iniquity.

Where is His Kingdom? Here on this world (verse 38).

How is His Kingdom furthered?

Through His ambassadors on earth; Christians like you and me.

Are you neglecting your duty to further His Kingdom because of some Chicken Little teachers who have deceived you into thinking that the Kingdom is some future reality that is supposed to take place after the rapture?

The war is now.

It is a battle between righteousness and evil. Righteousness cannot be compromised. But Satan would have the Church to compromise its' Purpose, and he believes that just maybe he will win through his deception, his persecution, his professional pulpiteers that lull the saints to sleep in their pews, and all the manufactured crises' his puppets have subjected the people of God to as they anxiously await the promised rapture that will take them out of this mess.

The religion of man and the Beast is furthered by man's abilities.

Islam (as well as other religions with the exception of Christianity) cannot cast out demons. But the demonic influence that grips its adherents would behead those who oppose them.

Islam does not have the supernatural working through it. It can only resort to carnal methods to advance its kingdom. Islam beheads its enemies, as did the anti Christ religion of Catholicism in the time of the Inquisition.

Adherents of Islam (as well as other religions) are centered on works of the flesh and its adherents have to depend on works of the flesh to expand its territory.

Speaking of the devil, Jesus said : **The thief cometh not, but for to steal, and to kill, and to destroy: I am come that they might have life, and that they might have *it* more abundantly (Joh 10:10).**

All those who oppose Christianity fit that description. They are either set on stealing Christian's rights, killing them, or destroying every evidence of the True and Living God.

Christianity is centered on life in the Spirit and the Grace of God that is active in every Born Again child of God, which transforms the Christian from a life of sin to one who has victory over sin because of that Grace of God that is active in his or her life.

Muslims and others don't have that testimony. Any change that happens in their lives is attributed to their own self will, or their religious works.

Our warfare is to share our testimony with our enemies. When they become our Brethren in Christ as a result of our faithful testimony, even if it means our death *("They loved not their lives unto death")*, they are no longer our enemies, and the Kingdom of God advances one soul at a time through our witness.

Eventually there will be a proclamation heard:

Rev 11:15 And the seventh angel sounded; and there were great voices in heaven, saying, The kingdoms of this world are become *the kingdoms* of our Lord, and of his Christ; and he shall reign for ever and ever.

The early Church understood that, and they loved not their lives unto the death. The spread of Christianity in the first few hundred years was due to the living testimony of those who were willing to be martyrs for the cause of the advancement of the Kingdom.

The Epistle to Diognetus declared about 130 AD:

"The Christians, though subjected day by day to punishment, increase the more in number.... Do you not see them exposed to the wild beasts so that they may be persuaded to deny the Lord? And yet, they are not overcome! Do you not see that the more of them who are punished, the greater becomes the number of the rest? This does not seem to be the work of man. This is the power of God!

Rev 12:11 And they overcame him by the blood of the Lamb, and by the word of their testimony; and they loved not their lives unto the death.

Rev 20:4 And I saw thrones, and they sat upon them, and judgment was given unto them: and *I saw* the souls of them that were beheaded for the witness of Jesus, and for the word of God, and which had not worshipped the beast, neither his image, neither

had received *his* mark upon their foreheads, or in their hands; and they lived and reigned with Christ a thousand years.

WHAT IS THE FINAL OUTCOME?

Well, you have endured the shooting of many sacred cows, and you are still reading this book. That's a good sign.

I realize that there are a lot of things that you have read that go in direct opposition to what you have been led to believe in your Christian walk. And there are no doubt areas where you will say "But what about..." or "But he doesn't address this issue".... Please understand if you want to continue resuscitating sacred cows, that is your choice.

Throughout this book, my point is this; if you are looking to some future time when you will be taken out of this mess, and if you still persist in believing in a dispensational view point based on an erroneous interpretation of Revelation 2 and 3, and if you continue to be fascinated by the prognosticators who declare that this is going to happen at this feast or that feast, or at that blood moon or 20 years from now, go ahead and continue doing that.

I personally believe you are treading on very dangerous ground, and this book is written to be a warning. But if you still choose to continue in all that foolishness, DO NOT NEGLECT YOUR RESPONSIBILITY TO FURTHER THE KINGDOM OF GOD ON A DAILY BASIS! You WILL have to answer to God for that.

The end of the story is awesome!

Dan 7:18 But the saints of the most High shall take the kingdom, and possess the kingdom for ever, even for ever and ever.

The important thing to notice here is that the saints of the Most High shall *TAKE* the kingdom. It is in the taking of the kingdom that results in the possessing of the kingdom forever, even forever and ever.

The word "take" here in combination with the word "possess" means to receive, or to accept a thing that is given and to hold on to it. We are told that the saints of the Most High shall receive the Kingdom and will hold on to it forever and forever and ever, and the Hebrew word used here for the word "forever" is the equivalent to the Greek word translated as "age". The expression " **for ever, even for ever and ever**" means throughout the ages.

Mat 25:34 Then shall the King say unto them on his right hand, Come, ye blessed of my Father, inherit the kingdom prepared for you from the foundation of the world:

This word will be to those who are found faithful doing the work of the Kingdom when Christ returns. Those who aren't, will be told to depart from Him in to the lake of fire which is reserved for the devil and his angels. Remember that "angels" can mean messengers. What kind of messenger have you been? Have you been telling those around you that there is nothing they can do except continue being faithful to tithe, to participate in church functions and to attend "church" until the rapture?

Woe unto you in that day! It is time to repent of your wicked ways and to begin to be about the Father's Business!

Even Daniel knew that there would be a time when the kingdoms of the world would become the kingdoms of our God (Rev 11:15), and that the age in which wickedness prevails in the physical world would come to an end. ***This is what the disciples were referring to in Matthew 24 when they asked the Lord concerning the "end of the age".***

The thought of the disciples was never that the *world* would end, only the age in which Satan rules as the god of this world.

There is a theme throughout Scripture that the earth is the Lord's, not Satan's.

Psa 24:1 A Psalm of David. The earth is the LORD'S, and the fulness thereof; the world, and they that dwell therein.

Pharoah is a type of Satan who holds the people of God in Bondage. Moses stood before the Pharoah, and contended with him, declaring the earth is the Lord's.

Exo 9:29 And Moses said unto him, As soon as I am gone out of the city, I will spread abroad my hands unto the LORD; and the thunder shall cease, neither shall there be any more hail; that thou mayest know how that the earth is the LORD'S.

Satan has always sought to hold the people of God in bondage to sin, or by convincing them that he has more power than what he actually has.

Did you know that the phrase "I'm just a sinner saved by Grace" is not in the Bible? Here is what God's Grace does for us:

**Tit 2:11 For the grace of God that bringeth salvation hath appeared to all men,
12 Teaching us that, denying ungodliness and worldly lusts, we should live soberly, righteously, and godly, in this present world;
13 Looking for that blessed hope, and the glorious appearing of the great God and our Saviour Jesus Christ;
14 Who gave himself for us, that he might redeem us from all iniquity, and purify unto himself a peculiar people, zealous of good works.**

The disciples understood that their God given mission was to establish the Kingdom of God on earth as it is in heaven. That is why they inquired of the Lord if He was going to restore the kingdom to Israel at that time after His resurrection (Acts 1:6). ***They didn't ask Him if He was going to take them to heaven with him at that time and destroy the earth.*** Their focus was on the restoration of the Kingdom to the people of God.

See how Jesus prayed to the Father concerning His followers:

Joh 17:14 I have given them thy word; and the world hath hated them, because they are not of the world, even as I am not of the world.
15 I pray not that thou shouldest take them out of the world, but that thou shouldest keep them from the evil.
16 They are not of the world, even as I am not of the world.
17 Sanctify them through thy truth: thy word is truth.
18 As thou hast sent me into the world, even so have I also sent them into the world.

"I pray not that you should take them out of the world, but that you should keep them from the evil." "As You sent Me into the world, even so have I also sent them into the world." There is no escape clause here. Jesus wasn't raptured up to the Father before the cross. He laid down His life for the Kingdom of God.

Christian, I am concerned that you have given up precious ground because you bought the lie of the god of this world.

You've neglected the study of the Word of God and relied on the slick talking hireling that says he is a pastor or an evangelist or a prophet to lead you into the truth. You've been duped into thinking that ten percent of your income and membership in a congregation is a fulfillment of a Christian's "duty". You have neglected the "GO YE" of Jesus for the comfort of the pew and the tickling of your ears.

You may be thinking, "Well, Jesus just prayed that for his disciples". But look what he says next:

Joh 17:20 Neither pray I for these alone, but for them also which shall believe on me through their word;
21 That they all may be one; as thou, Father, *art* in me, and I in thee, that they also may be one in us: that the world may believe that thou hast sent me.
22 And the glory which thou gavest me I have given them; that they may be one, even as we are one:

That is the purpose of this book. I undertook a lot of study and a lot of Divine rabbit trails just to get you to see that it still isn't too late.

I am concerned that you have been so desensitized to the Purpose and Calling of God that you will fail to even allow yourself to come to a place of repentance before God. Other gospels and manufactured crises' and a clique mentality along with conformity to the world may have served to harden your heart to the Truth.

YOU have a Calling from God to impact this world in your own sphere of influence for the Glory of God. Someday it is going to get worse. But that doesn't have to be NOW, in your generation. I don't believe it is too late, like a lot of voices that you may hear are saying.

God says this (let God be true, and every man that contradicts His Word a liar):

2Ch 7:14 If my people, which are called by my name, shall humble themselves, and pray, and seek my face, and turn from their wicked ways; then will I hear from heaven, and will forgive their sin, and will heal their land.

It is important for Christians to understand that. It is important for YOU to understand that. A bunch of collective "you's" can make a difference. It has to start somewhere.

Don't look around waiting for someone else to do something. You are holding this book, and you already know too much now to just ignore it and pretend like you didn't know.

It's time to repent.

If the church you attend isn't equipping you for the work of the ministry to further the Kingdom of God, find someplace that will.

And if you can't find a place that will train you to do the work of the ministry, just do it anyway. Look for the opportunities that the Lord gives you every day to help someone, to comfort someone, to feed someone, to love someone into the Kingdom, and to warn them from their sin. The time is urgent.

Here's another sacred cow that needs to be shot

Chances are you have attended three day meetings that are labeled "revivals".

Those may have been good meetings, but they certainly are not revivals, unless they have changed your life from a pew sitting Christian to a world changing influence in the lives of those around you. All of those so called "revival" meetings are just another tool of the enemy to keep the church comfortable inside the four walls, instead of furthering the Kingdom of God in their community. The preachers that are involved in these pseudo-revivals are unwittingly furthering Satan's agenda by being a part of the program, instead of equipping the saints.

Satan doesn't really care what happens inside the building. It is what happens if that Christian begins to publically proclaim his faith that Satan is concerned with. There's nothing wrong with a good three day meeting of Hallelujahs and Amens. But if that is the extent of it, it's just a bunch of noise and heightened emotions.

In Deuteronomy 10:14, the Lord tells the people that the heaven and the earth are the Lord's.

Deu 10:14 Behold, the heaven and the heaven of heavens *is* the LORD'S thy God, the earth *also,* with all that therein *is.*

Everything is His. The thread of Deuteronomy 10 and 11 is that God is Sovereign, and it extols God's All Powerful Nature, and is a reminder to Israel of His Greatness and of the Great things He has done and that He is capable of.

Deu 10:17 For the LORD your God *is* God of gods, and Lord of lords, a great God, a mighty, and a terrible, which regardeth not persons, nor taketh reward:

He tells them throughout Chapter 11 to keep their minds stayed on Him and His Will, so that their days will be as heaven upon the earth. So many people are inclined to define their lives as hell on earth, but God promises the opposite to those who follow Him wholeheartedly:

Deu 11:21 That your days may be multiplied, and the days of your children, in the land which the LORD sware unto your fathers to give them, as the days of heaven upon the earth.

God has the ultimate say of what happens on the earth. If we submit to His Sovereignty, and obey His Commission to further the Kingdom of God, our days can be as heaven on earth.

The problem lies in getting His people to submit to His Sovereignty.

Eph 2:6 speaks of our position of authority in Christ. Although we are positioned bodily in this earth, since we are in Christ and He is in us, we are seated with Him spiritually at the Right Hand of the Father just as He is.

The same authority that He possesses is literally ours, as we submit to Him.

Eph 2:6 And hath raised *us* up together, and made *us* sit together in heavenly *places* in Christ Jesus:

His Word doesn't portray Him as ever saying "Well, Satan is greater than me so you just have to wait until it's My turn. In the end of the book, we know who wins out."

No, His Word assures us that He has (***past tense, "mission accomplished"***) triumphed over all the principalities and powers and they are subject to Him (Col 2:15), and it is His Good Pleasure to give us the Kingdom (***present tense, NOW, not some future day*** -Luke 12: 31, 32). You are supposed to be His representative to a lost and dying world.

Luk 12:31 But rather seek ye the kingdom of God; and all these things shall be added unto you.
32 Fear not, little flock; for it is your Father's good pleasure to give you the kingdom.

Col 2:13 And you, being dead in your sins and the uncircumcision of your flesh, hath he quickened together with him, having forgiven you all trespasses;
14 Blotting out the handwriting of ordinances that was against us, which was contrary to us, and took it out of the way, nailing it to his cross;
15 *And* having spoiled principalities and powers, he made a shew of them openly, triumphing over them in it.

A reader may be asking at this point, if all this is true, why do Christians not live an overcoming life?

Exactly.

The answer is that Christians have been inundated with misinformation. Christians are being worn out and living a life of compromise through all the misinformation they receive from Satan's puppets in the pulpits.

Joh 14:12 Verily, verily, I say unto you, He that believeth on me, the works that I do shall he do also; and greater *works* than these shall he do; because I go unto my Father.

The problem with the misinformation that abounds concerning the Kingdom of God is that many Christians have been caught up in unbelief.

The disciples couldn't cast out devils because of their unbelief. When is the last time *you* cast out a devil?

Christians aren't doing much today in the way of furthering the Kingdom of God, because they have been conditioned to believe the world is coming to an end soon, anyway.

Remember the "manufactured crises" I mentioned earlier in this book?

Satan's pulpit puppets have been faithful to perpetrate an end-times scenario that doesn't line up with the Word of God, so the Church will be rendered powerless in the last days. As a result of the constant cries of Chicken Little pulpeteers who have been preaching since 1830 about the rapture being right around the corner, each generation produces a generation that is less convinced about how bad the world is. While the older generation satisfy themselves with the assurance that maybe tomorrow we will fly away, and that there is nothing we can do to change the of the flood of wickedness that is covering the earth, the younger generation wonders what the relevance of the Bible is for today. As a result, each generation grows up more skeptical about the truth of the Bible, and view it as out dated.

Satan has been at it since the Garden.

2Pe 3:3 Knowing this first, that there shall come in the last days scoffers, walking after their own lusts,

4 And saying, Where is the promise of his coming? for since the fathers fell asleep, all things continue as *they were* from the beginning of the creation.

I personally believe Premillennial Dispensationalism is one of the greatest tools of deception that Satan has used to render the Church impotent.

2Ti 4:3 For the time will come when they will not endure sound doctrine; but after their own lusts shall they heap to themselves teachers, having itching ears; 4 And they shall turn away *their* ears from the truth, and shall be turned unto fables.

They've been taught to just "hold on", and that God isn't consistent in His Promises. If He wants to, He will heal you. If He wants to, He will provide for you. If He wants to, He will deliver you. That is the reasoning of a person who does not believe that God's Promises are "Yea" and "Amen", and who has been conditioned to echo "amen" when the preacher tells him to.

It is submission to Jesus that ushers us into that place of receiving the Kingdom and walking in His Authority and Power. His Word is just as true today as it was when it was recorded in Solomon's day:

2Ch 7:14 If my people, which are called by my name, shall humble themselves, and pray, and seek my face, and turn from their wicked ways; then will I hear from heaven, and will forgive their sin, and will heal their land.

It's such a simple formula, yet a seemingly insurmountable task.

The wicked reign over the people of God because the people of God choose to conform to the world of the wicked rather than the Will of God.

We engage in warfare in the physical realm, rather than the realm in which it should be fought, the Spiritual realm, even though the Word plainly states that the weapons of our warfare are NOT carnal.

We make petitions to politicians for our grievances, we pick up the sword of the flesh to battle our enemies, we walk according to sight and not according to Faith. I believe that Christians should be very vocal in the political realm, but that shouldn't be the end all. Christian standards and ethics should guide the individual's vote, but personal witness and service to God are even more essential to bring about change in our society.

For the most part, the people of God are not a people of prayer. The people cry out to God, and it seems like He no longer hears, or that He doesn't care.

**Psa 94:3 LORD, how long shall the wicked, how long shall the wicked triumph?
4 *How long* shall they utter *and* speak hard things? *and* all the workers of iniquity boast themselves?
5 They break in pieces thy people, O LORD, and afflict thine heritage.
6 They slay the widow and the stranger, and murder the fatherless.**

7 Yet they say, The LORD shall not see, neither shall the God of Jacob regard *it*.

People without understanding rise to leadership in the guise of pastors, priests, evangelists, prophets, apostles, and teachers among God's people, and they give unprecedented authority and honor to the god of this age, teaching God's people that there is no hope in this life, but sometime in the future after we all die or are raptured out of here, we will find relief.

They say "But we know what the end of the Book says", as if there is no hope this side of heaven, and their congregations passively submit to the idea of the hopelessness of the evil of the days. I apologize for this choice of words, but every time I hear something like that from the pulpit, I almost want to puke. I believe the Lord does too. It is a lukewarm message being given to a lukewarm church by a lukewarm messenger who wants to give the impression that he is on fire for God.

It's almost like there is a conspiracy in the pulpits to keep the people defeated, and from fulfilling the Lord's Commission to establish the Kingdom of God here on earth.

Eze 22:23 And the word of the LORD came unto me, saying,
24 Son of man, say unto her, Thou *art* the land that is not cleansed, nor rained upon in the day of indignation.
25 *There is* a conspiracy of her prophets in the midst thereof, like a roaring lion ravening the prey; they have devoured souls; they have taken the treasure and precious things; they have made her many widows in the midst thereof.
26 Her priests have violated my law, and have profaned mine holy things: they have put no difference between the holy and profane, neither have they shewed *difference* between the unclean and the clean, and have hid their eyes from my sabbaths, and I am profaned among them.
27 Her princes in the midst thereof *are* like wolves ravening the prey, to shed blood, *and* to destroy souls, to get dishonest gain.
28 And her prophets have daubed them with untempered *morter,* seeing vanity, and divining lies unto them, saying, Thus saith the Lord GOD, when the LORD hath not spoken.
29 The people of the land have used oppression, and exercised robbery, and have vexed the poor and needy: yea, they have oppressed the stranger wrongfully.

But God only allows the wicked to flourish as an instrument of chastisement for His people who have strayed from Him.

It is the wickedness of the People of God, specifically the leadership, that allows evil to prevail in the United States or elsewhere in the world. God promises that if His people turn from their wicked ways, He *will* heal their land.

God's Design from the beginning has been that His people would have dominion over the earth, and that they would rule in righteousness. The rule of the wicked over the people of God is only temporary. God allows it, because of the backsliding of His people. It is one of the ways He chastises His people. It only lasts until God's people get serious in their relationship with Him.

Psa 94:12 Blessed *is* the man whom thou chastenest, O LORD, and teachest him out of thy law;

13 That thou mayest give him rest from the days of adversity, until the pit be digged for the wicked.
14 For the LORD will not cast off his people, neither will he forsake his inheritance.
15 But judgment shall return unto righteousness: and all the upright in heart shall follow it.

God poses a question to His people that echoes throughout time:

Psa 94:16 **Who will rise up for me against the evildoers?** *or* **who will stand up for me against the workers of iniquity?**

God seeks a people, even a man who will make up the hedge between Good and evil.

Eze 22:30 **And I sought for a man among them, that should make up the hedge, and stand in the gap before me for the land, that I should not destroy it: but I found none**

Jer 5:1 **Run ye to and fro through the streets of Jerusalem, and see now, and know, and seek in the broad places thereof, if ye can find a man, if there be** *any* **that executeth judgment, that seeketh the truth; and I will pardon it.**

Isa 64:7 **And** *there is* **none that calleth upon thy name, that stirreth up himself to take hold of thee: for thou hast hid thy face from us, and hast consumed us, because of our iniquities.**

Isa 50:2 **Wherefore, when I came,** *was there* **no man? when I called,** *was there* **none to answer? Is my hand shortened at all, that it cannot redeem? or have I no power to deliver? behold, at my rebuke I dry up the sea, I make the rivers a wilderness: their fish stinketh, because** *there is* **no water, and dieth for thirst.**

I refuse to be a conspirator working for the devil's glory. I don't care how bad it looks out there, I know that my God is greater NOW than he that is in the world. It is my calling as a man of God who is a part of the five fold ministry of the Church to equip the saints for the work of the ministry, and to train them in fulfilling the Great Commission.

I pray this book instills a hunger in pastors and Church leaders to do that, but I also pray that each individual will see that there is a Work to do, and that this book will result in more men and women of God publically proclaiming the Name of Jesus in the Market Place and on the streets of our nation. *You* have the ability as well as the responsibility to change your sphere of influence for the Glory of God. Don't doubt it. Only believe.

That dragon (Satan) who is the god of the world system has been doing all he can to stop or at least hinder the growth of the children of the Kingdom of God from reaching maturity in Christ, and exercising their God given dominion over the earth either through apathy, persecution, the cares of the world, the pride of life and the lusts of the flesh (read the parable of the sower in Matthew 13).

But in the Book it is written that that one new man will overcome and rule and reign over the nations.

Rev 12:5 And she brought forth a man child, who was to rule all nations with a rod of iron: and her child was caught up unto God, and *to* his throne.

The Word of God tells us that though we were dead in our trespasses and sins, we have been made alive in Christ, and are seated in the heavenly places in Christ.

Eph 2:4 But God, who is rich in mercy, for his great love wherewith he loved us,
5 Even when we were dead in sins, hath quickened us together with Christ, (by grace ye are saved;)
6 And hath raised *us* up together, and made *us* sit together in heavenly *places* in Christ Jesus:
7 That in the ages to come he might shew the exceeding riches of his grace in *his* kindness toward us through Christ Jesus.

If Christ is indeed in us through the indwelling of the Holy Spirit, and if we are in Him, then we are where He is, and He is where we are. Hence we are entitled to boldly come before the Throne of Grace, and to rule and reign from His position of Authority as ambassadors of the Kingdom of God.

It is the Uniting of the Body of Christ (Jew and Gentile) together which will establish the Kingdom of God on the earth. I already included this passage earlier, but it is worth inserting it here. Jesus identifies the field as the world, but the other places where we read "world", He is using the Greek word that means "age":

Mat 13:38 The field is the world; the good seed are the children of the kingdom; but the tares are the children of the wicked *one;*
39 The enemy that sowed them is the devil; the harvest is the end of the world; and the reapers are the angels.
40 As therefore the tares are gathered and burned in the fire; so shall it be in the end of this world.
41 The Son of man shall send forth his angels, and they shall gather out of his kingdom all things that offend, and them which do iniquity;
42 And shall cast them into a furnace of fire: there shall be wailing and gnashing of teeth.
43 Then shall the righteous shine forth as the sun in the kingdom of their Father. Who hath ears to hear, let him hear.

Satan will do all he can to stop the unity of the Body of Christ because it is in the unity of the Body of Christ that the Kingdom of God will be firmly established in this world.

Most Christians today really can't grasp that fact, and surely men whose ministries are centered around their personal agendas certainly cannot drop their agendas to work with others in the Body of Christ to further the Kingdom of God. The disciples were first called

"Christians" in Antioch, not Baptists, Pentecostals, Charismatics, Church of God, Church of Christ, Assemblies of God, Presbyterians, Lutherans, Methodists, or any other denominational or non-denominational label you may want to claim.

If I offend you because I come against a pet doctrine that Western Christians hold dear to their heart, and keeps them content in their pews, so be it.

I personally know my God to be greater than sickness, disease, oppression, depression, possession, or anything else that the god of this age tries to present as insurmountable.

I do know what it says at the end of the Book, but I also know what it says throughout the Book:

Deu 10:14 Behold, the heaven and the heaven of heavens is the LORD'S thy God, the earth also, with all that therein is.

Mar 16:15 And he said unto them, Go ye into all the world, and preach the gospel to every creature.
16 He that believeth and is baptized shall be saved; but he that believeth not shall be damned.
17 And these signs shall follow them that believe; In my name shall they cast out devils; they shall speak with new tongues;
18 They shall take up serpents; and if they drink any deadly thing, it shall not hurt them; they shall lay hands on the sick, and they shall recover.
19 So then after the Lord had spoken unto them, he was received up into heaven, and sat on the right hand of God.
20 And they went forth, and preached everywhere, the Lord working with them, and confirming the word with signs following. Amen.

Mat 28:18 And Jesus came and spake unto them, saying, All power is given unto me in heaven and in earth.
19 Go ye therefore, and teach all nations, baptizing them in the name of the Father, and of the Son, and of the Holy Ghost:
20 Teaching them to observe all things whatsoever I have commanded you: and, lo, I am with you alway, even unto the end of the world. Amen. (World = age, not the physical world as we know it)

Psa 94:17 Unless the LORD *had been* my help, my soul had almost dwelt in silence.
18 When I said, My foot slippeth; thy mercy, O LORD, held me up.
19 In the multitude of my thoughts within me thy comforts delight my soul.
20 Shall the throne of iniquity have fellowship with thee, which frameth mischief by a law?
21 They gather themselves together against the soul of the righteous, and condemn the innocent blood.
22 But the LORD is my defence; and my God *is* the rock of my refuge.
23 And he shall bring upon them their own iniquity, and shall cut them off in their own wickedness; *yea,* the LORD our God shall cut them off.

The Bible plainly tells us not to be anxious for tomorrow, yet that is exactly what professional pulpiteers and those who have taken upon themselves a title of prophet have caused the Church to do.

Much of the Body of Christ is so caught up in what may happen or how bad tomorrow looks, that they believe there is no Hope.

John G. Lake: "Christianity did not come to the world to apologize for its existence or to beg a place to live. It came as heaven's champion: it has the champion soul. "It shall bruise thy head, and thou shalt bruise his heel." (Gen. 3:15). That champion consciousness is in the soul of the Christian. Being born of God, he is champion of the son of God and a demonstration His salvation. He is the champion of God. He cannot be anything else. 'As he is so are we in this world.' (1Jn. 4:17). . . . I fear sometimes that we moderns somehow have lost the spirit of original Christianity. We have lost the overcoming of it. We have lost the smash of it. We are begging the devil for a place in the world, apologizing for our faith in God, trying to conform our religion to the mind of the world."

The prophetic Word is a NOW word. It calls the people of God to repentance NOW or else these things will come upon them. The message is this, regardless if it is to the individual, a city, or a nation of people, "If you repent, none of these things will come upon you".

The remedy is to repent.

The remedy is to pray.

The remedy is to seek first the Kingdom of God and His Will in all aspects of our lives. In the midst of the prophetic vision of great and terrible things that would come, Daniel sees this:

Dan 7:13 I saw in the night visions, and, behold, *one* like the Son of man came with the clouds of heaven, and came to the Ancient of days, and they brought him near before him.
14 And there was given him dominion, and glory, and a kingdom, that all people, nations, and languages, should serve him: his dominion *is* an everlasting dominion, which shall not pass away, and his kingdom *that* which shall not be destroyed.

When was dominion given to this One who was like the Son of Man? Whether you understand it or not, this One that Daniel saw was Jesus. After His Resurrection, Jesus Himself declared when that dominion was given to Him.

Mat 28:18 And Jesus came and spake unto them, saying, All power is given unto me in heaven and in earth.

19 Go ye therefore, and teach all nations, baptizing them in the name of the Father, and of the Son, and of the Holy Ghost:
20 Teaching them to observe all things whatsoever I have commanded you: and, lo, I am with you alway, even unto the end of the world. Amen. (World = age, not the physical world as we know it)

The Kingdom of God is at HAND! Now! When the people of God awake from their apathy, and begin to seek the Face of God and His Will in their lives, the end of Satan's kingdom age will take place.

He (Satan) doesn't want you to understand that. So he gets you so caught up with the cares of this world and the lust of the flesh and pride of life that you cannot find the time or the desire to yield fully to the King of kings, and the Lord of lords. He (Satan) has used professional pulpiteers to get you caught up in religious works, such as church membership, denominational exclusivism, a tithe paying membership, exclusive attendance of one particular fellowship.

"Forget about rescuing the perishing. Just invite them to your church. Your pastor will preach a word that will get them saved, and maybe they can become paying members as well!"

"Forget about unity of the Body of Christ, or equipping the saints to preach the gospel. That is not a necessary requirement in your religious circle."

 "Sure, Jesus said 'Seek ye first', but He didn't really mean it like it sounds like he said it. Bills have the priority. You can take this Jesus thing too far, you know. When He said 'Seek ye first', He meant that you need to say a prayer and ask Him to come into your heart and forgive your sins, then after that you can live a fleshly existence, except on Sundays and Wednesdays, and don't forget to calculate your 10%!"

"As long as you are a faithful member to your fellowship, you can look forward to some wonderful future time in the Kingdom of God on that glad morning when you fly away."

Mar 16:15 And he said unto them, Go ye into all the world, and preach the gospel to every creature.
16 He that believeth and is baptized shall be saved; but he that believeth not shall be damned.
17 And these signs shall follow them that believe; In my name shall they cast out devils; they shall speak with new tongues;
18 They shall take up serpents; and if they drink any deadly thing, it shall not hurt them; they shall lay hands on the sick, and they shall recover.
19 So then after the Lord had spoken unto them, he was received up into heaven, and sat on the right hand of God.
20 And they went forth, and preached everywhere, the Lord working with them, and confirming the word with signs following. Amen

The weapons of our warfare are not carnal, but mighty through God to the pulling down of strongholds.

2Co 10:3 For though we walk in the flesh, we do not war after the flesh:
4 (For the weapons of our warfare *are* not carnal, but mighty through God to the pulling down of strong holds;)
5 Casting down imaginations, and every high thing that exalteth itself against the knowledge of God, and bringing into captivity every thought to the obedience of Christ;
6 And having in a readiness to revenge all disobedience, when your obedience is fulfilled.

Eph 6:10 Finally, my brethren, be strong in the Lord, and in the power of his might.
11 Put on the whole armour of God, that ye may be able to stand against the wiles of the devil.
12 For we wrestle not against flesh and blood, but against principalities, against powers, against the rulers of the darkness of this world, against spiritual wickedness in high *places.*

Jesus has the Dominion. Not Satan. When you cast the devil out of a person, the Kingdom of God is at hand. That authority comes from Jesus, and from intimacy with Him through seeking His Face.

Daniel's message was that the Kingdom of God was to come.

Since the days of John the Baptist, the Kingdom of God has been at hand.

Jesus sent the disciples into ALL the world to preach the Gospel, that the Power of God would be dispersed throughout the world through His Holy people. Jesus said when the gospel is preached in all the world (the Gospel of the Kingdom of God, which is demonstrated by power), then the end of the age in which Satan has rule would come about. Satan is NOT the god of this world, he is simply the god of this age (2 Cor 4:4: world = Gr Aion - AGE).

The kingdoms of the world (Gr Kosmos) *will* become the Kingdom of our God once the Church wakes up to it's Purpose.

Rev 11:15 And the seventh angel sounded; and there were great voices in heaven, saying, The kingdoms of this world are become the kingdoms of our Lord, and of his Christ; and he shall reign forever and ever.

Someone doesn't want you to know that, or to understand that God's Plan has been in effect for the last two thousand plus years.

Satan wants the Body of Christ to believe that he is the god of this kosmos. He isn't. He is merely the god of this age. And his time is running out.

Satan wants the Body of Christ to believe that God's Plan will be fulfilled in some future time. It was Finished at the death, burial and resurrection of Jesus.

The angel which dialogued with John about his vision had an interesting thing to say about the prophecy of the book of Revelation:

Rev 22:10 And he saith unto me, Seal not the sayings of the prophecy of this book: for the time is at hand.

Daniel, on the other hand, was told in his vision concerning the prophetic word he had received regarding the end of the age:

Dan 12:4 But thou, O Daniel, shut up the words, and seal the book, even to the time of the end: many shall run to and fro, and knowledge shall be increased.

In Revelation, John is told not to seal the sayings, because the time was at hand.

In Daniel the time was not yet at hand.

It is proper to read Daniel in the light of what was to happen in the future.

According to the book of Revelation those things that were spoken of were already taking place.

Daniel is about future kingdoms; the kingdoms of this world, and the Kingdom of God which was to come. In the last chapter of Daniel, the man clothed in linen gave an indication of the time span in which the fulfillment of the vision should come to pass.

Dan 12:6 And one said to the man clothed in linen, which was upon the waters of the river, How long shall it be to the end of these wonders?
7 And I heard the man clothed in linen, which was upon the waters of the river, when he held up his right hand and his left hand unto heaven, and sware by him that liveth for ever that it shall be for a time, times, and an half; and when he shall have accomplished to scatter the power of the holy people, all these things shall be finished.

Time: Heb. Moad: an appointed time.

Speaking to His disciples regarding those three questions of Matthew 24, Jesus says

Mat 24:36 But of that day and hour knoweth no *man*, no, not the angels of heaven, but my Father only.

There is a time when God has ordained an end to this age, but only He alone knows when that will be.

In Daniel 12:7, the word translated as "scatter" (when he shall have accomplished to *scatter* the power of the holy people) can also be translated as "Disperse" or "Overspread", as in the following verse:

Gen 9:19 These are the three sons of Noah: and of them was the whole earth overspread.

When the Gospel has been preached in all the world by the people of God who have taken up the Call to obey the Great Commission in demonstration of Power is when all these things shall be finished.

God is just waiting for those of us who are His children to stop buying the devil's lies, and to start doing the exploits He has called us to do.

While He was living among them, the disciples were told by Jesus to only go to the lost sheep of Israel. After His Resurrection He told them to go into all the world.

The plumbline was drawn with the establishment of the New Covenant.

Rev 22:11 He that is unjust, let him be unjust still: and he which is filthy, let him be filthy still: and he that is righteous, let him be righteous still: and he that is holy, let him be holy still.
12 And, behold, I come quickly; and my reward is with me, to give every man according as his work shall be.
13 I am Alpha and Omega, the beginning and the end, the first and the last.
14 Blessed are they that do his commandments, that they may have right to the tree of life, and may enter in through the gates into the city.
15 For without are dogs, and sorcerers, and whoremongers, and murderers, and idolaters, and whosoever loveth and maketh a lie.
16 I Jesus have sent mine angel to testify unto you these things in the churches. I am the root and the offspring of David, and the bright and morning star.

The time is at hand. The Kingdom of God is at hand. Are you working to further it, or are you looking for some future event, and hiding in the bunkers until sometime in the future? That is what the devil wants you to do. But Jesus has a different strategy:

Mar 16:15 And he said unto them, Go ye into all the world, and preach the gospel to every creature.
16 He that believeth and is baptized shall be saved; but he that believeth not shall be damned.
17 And these signs shall follow them that believe; In my name shall they cast out devils; they shall speak with new tongues;
18 They shall take up serpents; and if they drink any deadly thing, it shall not hurt them; they shall lay hands on the sick, and they shall recover.
19 So then after the Lord had spoken unto them, he was received up into heaven, and sat on the right hand of God.
20 And they went forth, and preached everywhere, the Lord working with them, and confirming the word with signs following. Amen.

Mat 28:18 And Jesus came and spake unto them, saying, All power is given unto me in heaven and in earth.
19 Go ye therefore, and teach all nations, baptizing them in the name of the Father, and of the Son, and of the Holy Ghost:
20 Teaching them to observe all things whatsoever I have commanded you: and, lo, I am with you alway, even unto the end of the world (age). Amen.

Act 1:6 When they therefore were come together, they asked of him, saying, Lord, wilt thou at this time restore again the kingdom to Israel?
7 And he said unto them, It is not for you to know the times or the seasons, which the Father hath put in his own power.
8 But ye shall receive power, after that the Holy Ghost is come upon you: and ye shall be witnesses unto me both in Jerusalem, and in all Judaea, and in Samaria, and unto the uttermost part of the earth.

He will return one day to take the Kingdom that His servants have furthered in His Name. When He comes, I want to be found being about furthering His Kingdom. How about you?

The time is at hand.

Now would be the time to consider what Jesus said after He answered the disciple's three questions.

His words are just as relevant to you and I as they were to the disciples. Notice what He says about His *servants*, not just some unbelievers:

Mat 24:42 Watch therefore: for ye know not what hour your Lord doth come.
43 But know this, that if the goodman of the house had known in what watch the thief would come, he would have watched, and would not have suffered his house to be broken up.
44 Therefore be ye also ready: for in such an hour as ye think not the Son of man cometh.
45 Who then is a faithful and wise servant, whom his lord hath made ruler over his household, to give them meat in due season?
:46 Blessed *is* that servant, whom his lord when he cometh shall find so doing.
47 Verily I say unto you, That he shall make him ruler over all his goods.
48 But and if that evil servant shall say in his heart, My lord delayeth his coming;
49 And shall begin to smite *his* fellowservants, and to eat and drink with the drunken;
50 The lord of that servant shall come in a day when he looketh not for *him*, and in an hour that he is not aware of,
51 And shall cut him asunder, and appoint *him* his portion with the hypocrites: there shall be weeping and gnashing of teeth.

I don't think you want to be categorized with the evil servant. Despite what some money grubbing hireling has told you to make you feel comfortable in your church clothes, you have a responsibility before God. You will either be a faithful and wise servant or an evil servant. Which one are you? Your church clothes really don't mean a hill of beans to God. Are you clothed in His Righteousness? Are you walking in His Righteousness? If you are not, you will find yourself standing naked before God with no excuse other than that you were a slothful servant who preferred to listen to a hireling who told you your church clothes are what's important.

Maybe you think you are insignificant, or that you are *unworthy* for God to use you. Then you are calling God a liar, because He thought you were worthy enough to give His Only Begotten Son to die for your sins, so you could become a child of God.

After this warning, Jesus told three parables. The first was the parable of the ten virgins, five of whom were wise and five who were foolish, waiting for the coming of their Lord.

The second was about the servants who had received responsibilities to perform while their Lord was departed into another country.

And the third was about the reckoning that was done at the Coming of the Lord.

In each instance, the ones who neglected their expected duty were left outside.

Are you really concerned about the course this nation or your state or your city has taken? You have more authority than you realize.

Maybe after reading this, you will choose to ignore the revealed truth that is contained herein, because you prefer the traditions that you have grown up with. If you acknowledged that even some of what I said in this book is true, the chances are that you might have to quit your clique, get out of your comfort zone, and go somewhere else where saints of God are truly being equipped to do the work of the ministry.

You just need to repent first and humble yourself before God and man, turn from your wicked ways, and seek the Face of God in prayer and supplication. God said He would heal the land when that happens. I'd rather believe Him than some hireling who philosophizes on how hopeless our situation is.

Mar 13:34 *For the Son of man is* as a man taking a far journey, who left his house, and gave authority to his servants, and to every man his work, and commanded the porter to watch.
35 Watch ye therefore: for ye know not when the master of the house cometh, at even, or at midnight, or at the cockcrowing, or in the morning: 36 Lest coming suddenly he find you sleeping.
37 And what I say unto you I say unto all, Watch.

1Co 15:34 Awake to righteousness, and sin not; for some have not the knowledge of God: I speak *this* to your shame.

As I said at the beginning of this book, it may seem like I have come out hard against pastors and churches. But there ARE pastors who are after God's own heart, pastors who will do all they know to do to further the Kingdom of God and to equip their congregation to do the same. Some pastors just don't know any better than to do what they have seen other pastors do, but their hearts are for the Lord. If you are a pastor who is about equipping your church to do the work of the ministry, I commend you, and I pray God's abundant Blessings on you.

If you find that you are one of those who love God, but have only been following what tradition teaches you, then praise the Lord, I know that you will alter your mindset and start equipping your church to get out of the pews and impact the world around you.

If you are a professional pulpiteer, then I have just one thing to say:

Repent, for the Kingdom of God is at Hand!

Get out of yourself and start being about the Father's business. Start equipping the Body of Christ you are in charge of to begin to do the work of the ministry.

And if you are a Christian who never knew any of this, it's time for YOU to do something about it! Give this book to your pastor, or those you know who are actively involved in ministry. Hopefully your pastor will have the sense to know how to equip you for the work God has called you to.

Go tell someone about Jesus. Do your part to further the Kingdom of God in this world one soul at a time.

Tell them about the Kingdom of God.

Tell them about an abundant life that could be theirs.

Let them know they don't have to be slaves to sin.

Cast out devils.

Heal the sick.

Preach the Word.

It's in you.

Let the Power of the Holy Spirit manifest itself in your life as you yield to Him.

Live your life for the Father.

The Kingdom of God is at hand.

Appendix

Setting Things In Order

Introduction To The Appendix

The initial purpose of this book was to examine the Words of Jesus as recorded in Matthew 24. There is such a large scope of prophecy concerning what is referred to as the "last days" or the "end times" that could be elaborated upon here, but that wasn't the purpose of this book. Be that as it may, I deemed it necessary to include this Appendix in the back of the book in order to address some questions that may need to be resolved concerning some of what I have written.

It is important to understand that Jesus taught His disciples this Principle:

Mat 6:34 Take therefore no thought for the morrow: for the morrow shall take thought for the things of itself. Sufficient unto the day *is* the evil thereof.

At the end of Jesus' discourse regarding His answers to the disciples' questions in Matthew 24, Jesus basically gave a warning and said if you are not about His business that He has committed to you when He comes, it won't be a good Day for you (*Matthew 24:44-25:46*).

If the Father's Will (Calling) for your life does not concern you, you might not be His child.

It doesn't matter how you want to paint that, just take a moment to read Matthew 24:42 and on through all of chapter 25.

Four times in Matthew 24 He warns His disciples to be careful that they don't be deceived concerning the "end times", and my personal opinion is that the focus on "end times" scenarios that are so prevalent in the Church are a leading cause of divisiveness and deception in the Church, *deceiving Christians into being focused on the wrong thing, when they should be focused on fulfilling the Great Commission and furthering the Kingdom of God on earth.*

An Over View Of Various Eschatological Positions

(Source: http://en.wikipedia.org/wiki/Christian_eschatological_views)

Dispensational Premillennialism: The rapture of the church occurs just prior to the seven-year tribulation, where Christ returns for his saints to meet them in the air. This is followed by the tribulation, the rise of the Antichrist_to world-rule, the return of Christ to the Mount of Olives, and Armageddon, resulting in a millennial reign of Messiah over the Jews, centered in restored Jerusalem.

☐ Prewrath/Mid-tribulation View: The rapture of the church occurs in the midst of the seven-year period. Mid-tribulation view holds that the rapture occurs halfway through; Prewrath holds that the rapture occurs sometime in the midst of the tribulation in the latter 3.5 years, but before God's wrath is poured out upon the nations.

☐ Historic Premillennialism or Post-Tribulation View: The rapture of the church (the body of true believers) happens after a period of great tribulation, with the church being caught up to meet Christ in the air and will accompany him to earth to share in his (literal or figurative) thousand year rule.

☐ Postmillennialism: Christ's Second coming_is seen as occurring after the one-thousand years, which many in this school of thought believe is ushered in by the church. This view is also divided into two sub-schools of interpretation:

• Revivalist Postmillennialism: the millennium represents an unknown period of time marked by a gradual Christian revival, followed by widespread successful evangelism. After these efforts is the return of Christ foreseen.

• Reconstructionist Postmillennialism: the Church increases its influence through successful evangelism and expansion, finally establishing a theocratic kingdom of 1,000 years duration (literal or figurative) followed by the return of Christ.

☐ Amillennialism: Non-literal *"thousand years"* or long age between Christ's first and second comings; the millennial reign of Christ as pictured in the book of Revelation is viewed now as Christ reigning at the right hand of the Father. It can be hard to draw a fine line between Amillenialism and Revivalist Postmillenialism. Amillenialism tends to believe society will, through growing rebellion, continue to deteriorate, while Postmillenialism believes the Church will influence the world producing greater righteousness.

Preterism

Preterism (from the Latin *praeteritus,* meaning "gone by") is an approach which sees prophecy as chiefly being fulfilled in the past, especially (in the case of the Book of Revelation) during the first century.   Prophecies in general, therefore, have already been fulfilled. In particular, many Preterists (whether they be Full Preterists or Partial Preterists) view The Book of Revelation as a text employing symbols in its communication of prophecy to the Early Church regarding the actors and events involved during the destruction of Jerusalem in the year 70 AD. Other Preterists

consider the Book of Revelation to be a symbolic prophetic presentation of the struggle of Christianity to survive the persecutions of the Roman Empire.

There are two major views within Preterism, that of Partial preterism (that many of the Bible's prophecies were fulfilled during the life and time of Jesus and the Early Church) and Full preterism, (that all of the Bible's prophecies were fulfilled during the life and time of Jesus and the Early Church). Preterist beliefs usually have a close association with Amillennialism, the belief that the Millennial reign of Christ began during the establishment of the Early Church. Preterists usually consider events such as the Great Tribulation as having occurred during the siege and destruction of Jerusalem from 66-70. Early Preterist theologians included Eusebius and John Chrysostom. (Source: http://en.wikipedia.org/wiki/Christian_eschatological_views)

Most (if not all) of the Church Fathers of the first few centuries held to the view that the Kingdom of God will one day prevail upon the earth through the advancement of the Church. This view is generally referred to as *post millennialism*. Origen wrote this in his treatise "Against Celsus":

"It is evident that even the Barbarians, when they yield obedience to the Word of God, will become most obedient to the Law…. Every form of worship will be destroyed except the Christian Religion, which alone will prevail. And indeed it will one day triumph as its principles take possession of the minds of men more and more every day."

Most of the central figures who were instrumental in the great moves of God in the history of the Christian Church were postmillennialists (the belief that Christ would reign through His Church over the world for a thousand years, followed by Christ's Second Coming).

The Geneva Bible, which predates the King James Bible contained a commentary on some portions of Scripture, and the authors of the commentary are decidedly postmillennial.

Dan 2:45 Where as thou sawest, that the stone was cut of the mountaine without handes, and that it brake in pieces the yron, the brasse, the claye, the siluer, and the golde: so the great God hath shewed the King, what shall come to passe hereafter, and the dreame is true, and the interpretation thereof is sure.

The commentary for this verse reads thus: "**Meaning Christ, who was sent by God, and not set up by man, whose kingdom at the beginning would be small and without beauty to man's judgment, but would at length grow and fill the whole earth, which he calls a great mountain, as in (Dan 2:35). And this kingdom, which is not only referred to the person of Christ, but also to the whole body of his Church, and to every member of it, will be eternal: for the Spirit that is in them is eternal life; (Rom 8:10). "**

The First and Second and Third Great Awakenings, revivals which impacted the moral and cultural fabric of America were led by Postmillennialists such as Jonathan Edwards and Charles Finney.

☐ **Postmillennialism:** *Christ's Second coming* **is seen as occurring after the one-thousand years, which many in this school of thought believe is ushered in by the church. This view is also divided into two sub-schools of interpretation:**

Revivalist Postmillennialism: the millennium represents an unknown period of time marked by a gradual Christian revival, followed by widespread successful evangelism. After these efforts is the return of Christ foreseen.

Reconstructionist Postmillennialism: This is also referred to as "Dominion Theology," and is embraced by many in the Word of Faith movement. It is the duty of Christians to actively further the Kingdom of God in all aspects of society in order to impact the world, and usher in the Millennium.

Although I personally dislike labels, I would have to say that my personal eschatological outlook is more closely related to the idea of Revivalist Postmillennialism, and true revival results in a radical societal change that could be viewed as Reconstructionism, just as in the early Church, Christians were accused of turning the world upside down.

However, I do believe in a specific thousand year period in which the Church will reign with a system of Theonomy (the moral law of God prevails) over the world, under the leadership of Christ. But I don't believe that will happen until God's Wrath purges the world of those who rebel against His Kingdom.

I believe before the wrath of God, but after the tribulation (which has extended from 70AD until now), Christ will take His Church out of harm's way, just as Noah was protected in the ark as God's wrath cleansed the earth in his day. I believe this happens in Revelation 14, with the simultaneous reapings of the earth in Revelation 14:14-20.

This is more in line *with* ***historic premillennialism*** as opposed to dispensational premillennialism which teaches a rapture of the Church before a seven year tribulation, which is supposedly foretold in Daniel 9:24-27 as the "seventieth week". I will deal with that seventieth week in detail on page 137.

Since Revivalist Post Millennialism does not embrace the Revelation 14:14-20 scenario of a rapture of the Church *BEFORE* the outpouring of the Wrath of God, I would like to characterize my position as a ***Partial Preterist with the leanings of a Revivalist/Reconstructionist Historic Premillennialist.***

I believe it is through the agency of the Church in Revival that the Wrath of God is delayed. 2nd Chronicles 7:14 is a continual Provision God makes for His people. If His people humble themselves, seek His face, pray and turn from their wicked ways, He promises to heal their land.

When the Church realizes the seriousness and the severity of the Judgment of God, and looks through the eyes of God at all humanity, and realizes the dreadful consequences to those who die without the Grace of God, and our failure to do anything to prevent that from happening, then revival breaks out, and the Hand of God is held back as the Kingdom of God is once again established in the earth. This has happened several times in history, the chief examples being the Reformation, the 1st and 2nd Great Awakening, Azusa Street, the Hebrides Revival, the Welsh Revival and other great moves of God that took place throughout history as Christians realized how far they had departed from their first love and brought forth fruit fit for repentance. That could happen again, if the Church would repent of neglecting it's God given duty to further the Kingdom of God on earth.

I believe that like Israel of old who experienced times of revival and the consequent Favor of God on the land, eventually perilous times will arise, and the love of the Church will wax cold as Christians become lovers of themselves more than lovers of God, having a form of godliness, but denying the Power thereof.

This is what is known as the apostasy of the Church, and it is that widespread apostasy which will usher in a time of widespread godlessness throughout the world, and increased persecution on the People of God, so that it would appear that there is no vestige of righteousness on the earth. But there will be a remnant, seen in the two witnesses who will uphold the Word of God as True.

Many will be turned to righteousness in the midst of great persecution at this time. This will be a time of the final revival of the Church. The Kingdoms of this world will become the Kingdom of God. We are told that immediately AFTER the tribulation of those days, the sign of the Son of man will appear in heaven, and He shall gather His elect in that Post tribulation Rapture. There will be a great cleansing of the earth through fire, and then the earth will be restored as it was in the time of the flood. We will live under the rule of Christ for a thousand years.

After that period of time Satan will be loosed for a season in one last effort at a revolt against the Kingdom of God.

1Co 15:24 Then *cometh* the end, when he shall have delivered up the kingdom to God, even the Father; when he shall have put down all rule and all authority and power.
25 For he must reign, till he hath put all enemies under his feet.

Most Postmillennialists don't subscribe to a "great falling away of the Church", yet the Bible is plain in that respect. It is as a result of the neglect of the Great Commission that the "Falling Away" in the last days will take place (2 Thes 2:3; 1 Tim 4:1-3; 2 Tim 3:1-9, Matt 24:12).

Jesus was about "DOING" the Will of the Father. He didn't hold seminars on the last days. He healed the sick, raised the dead, cast out devils and preached the Gospel of the Kingdom of

God, and taught His disciples to do the same thing. His model prayer included this phrase: "Thy Kingdom Come, Thy Will be done on earth, as it is in heaven.

Discussions about end times were incidental to His Ministry, but the end times was by no means His focus. His focus was raising up a people who would turn the world upside down for the Glory of God in preparation for His Return.

Mat 25:13 Watch therefore, for ye know neither the day nor the hour wherein the Son of man cometh.

14 For *the kingdom of heaven is* as a man travelling into a far country, *who* called his own servants, and delivered unto them his goods.

15 And unto one he gave five talents, to another two, and to another one; to every man according to his several ability; and straightway took his journey.

16 Then he that had received the five talents went and traded with the same, and made *them* other five talents.

17 And likewise he that *had received* two, he also gained other two.

18 But he that had received one went and digged in the earth, and hid his lord's money.

19 After a long time the lord of those servants cometh, and reckoneth with them.

20 And so he that had received five talents came and brought other five talents, saying, Lord, thou deliveredst unto me five talents: behold, I have gained beside them five talents more.

21 His lord said unto him, Well done, *thou* good and faithful servant: thou hast been faithful over a few things, I will make thee ruler over many things: enter thou into the joy of thy lord.

22 He also that had received two talents came and said, Lord, thou deliveredst unto me two talents: behold, I have gained two other talents beside them.

23 His lord said unto him, Well done, good and faithful servant; thou hast been faithful over a few things, I will make thee ruler over many things: enter thou into the joy of thy lord.

24 Then he which had received the one talent came and said, Lord, I knew thee that thou art an hard man, reaping where thou hast not sown, and gathering where thou hast not strawed:

25 And I was afraid, and went and hid thy talent in the earth: lo, *there* thou hast *that is* thine.

26 His lord answered and said unto him, *Thou* wicked and slothful servant, thou knewest that I reap where I sowed not, and gather where I have not strawed:

27 Thou oughtest therefore to have put my money to the exchangers, and *then* at my coming I should have received mine own with usury.

28 Take therefore the talent from him, and give *it* unto him which hath ten talents.

29 For unto every one that hath shall be given, and he shall have abundance: but from him that hath not shall be taken away even that which he hath.

30 And cast ye the unprofitable servant into outer darkness: there shall be weeping and gnashing of teeth.

Personally, it doesn't matter to me if you choose to believe in a pre-tribulation rapture, a mid tribulation rapture, or a post tribulation rapture, or if you don't believe in a rapture at all. It really doesn't matter to me if you are pre-millennial, post-millennial, or amillennial, or even if you are a preterist.

What concerns me is that your focus may be too centered around those things, and you are allowing them to become a dividing force between you and the rest of the Body of Christ who don't agree with your position. As a result, you may be too busy dwelling on and debating end times eschatology to fulfill the Great Commission.

Interpretation of end times events ("eschatology") are not worthy of division in the Body of Christ, but that is what the result often is. Today, if one says he or she does not believe in a pre-trib rapture, they are portrayed by others who do believe in a pre-trib rapture as not believing in the Second Coming of the Lord or of a "catching up" of the saints.

It's almost like "If you don't belong to our clique, we don't want anything to do with you". You will find that there are as many opinions on the end times as there are books about the end times. And most of the time, the profit generated from the book, the CD, the DVD or the seminar is the bottom line.

**Mar 9:38 And John answered him, saying, Master, we saw one casting out devils in thy name, and he followeth not us: and we forbad him, because he followeth not us.
39 But Jesus said, Forbid him not: for there is no man which shall do a miracle in my name, that can lightly speak evil of me.
40 For he that is not against us is on our part.**

Are you doing what you are called to do in furthering the Kingdom of God?

If not, you simply need to repent. You don't have to believe like I believe. But if you profess to be a Christian, don't be deceived: You DO need to be about your Father's business.

The root of the dispensational premillennialist's doctrine is that nothing we can do will prevent the end of the world from occurring, so why should we obey the Word of God that promises us:

**2Ch 7:13 If I shut up heaven that there be no rain, or if I command the locusts to devour the land, or if I send pestilence among my people;
14 If my people, which are called by my name, shall humble themselves, and pray, and seek my face, and turn from their wicked ways; then will I hear from heaven, and will forgive their sin, and will heal their land.**

The Western mentality is that if Western society crumbles, the end of the world is right around the corner. Americans believe that if the economy collapses and America falls, the end of the world is soon to follow.

The end of their comfort will certainly follow, but just because the United States of America may one day cease being a world power does not signal the end of the world. If that happens, I can guarantee that Christians will begin seeking God in prayer like they never have before. And that is a shame, because the truth is, it doesn't have to be that way.

We (Christians) could be the hedge that prevents the degradation of the world and the fall of the United States. But most likely the reader will put this book on the shelf, adding it to the ever growing collection of their "Last Days" inventory, and to plan to attend more "end time" seminars, all the while neglecting their responsibility to the Kingdom of God before God and men.

Don't be deceived. Charles Finney's (who was a post millennial) words are more pertinent today than they were when he spoke them two centuries ago:

"If there is a decay of conscience, the pulpit is responsible for it. If the public press lacks moral discernment, the pulpit is responsible for it. If the church is degenerate and worldly, the pulpit is responsible for it. If the world loses its interest in Christianity, the pulpit is responsible for it. If Satan rules in our halls of legislation, the pulpit is responsible for it. If our politics become so corrupt that the very foundations of our government are ready to fall away, the pulpit is responsible for it." - Rev. Charles Finney

It begins at the pulpit, but the blame lies on all of us who proclaim that we believe in Jesus Christ, and do not follow His Ways, but instead pursue after the things of this world, rather than the Will of God.

2 Chronicles 7:13 If I shut up heaven that there be no rain, or if I command the locusts to devour the land, or if I send pestilence among my people;
14 If my people, which are called by my name, shall humble themselves, and pray, and seek my face, and turn from their wicked ways; then will I hear from heaven, and will forgive their sin, and will heal their land. - The One True and Living God

What About the 70 Weeks of Daniel?

This book has addressed a lot concerning endtime prophecy, but the subject matter did not allow me to cover the 70 weeks in the body of the book. I will attempt to address Daniel's prophecy concerning the 70 weeks here.

Dan 9:24 Seventy weeks are determined upon thy people and upon thy holy city, to finish the transgression, and to make an end of sins, and to make reconciliation for iniquity, and to bring in everlasting righteousness, and to seal up the vision and prophecy, and to anoint the most Holy.
25 Know therefore and understand, *that* from the going forth of the commandment to restore and to build Jerusalem unto the Messiah the Prince *shall be* seven weeks, and threescore and two weeks: the street shall be built again, and the wall, even in troublous times.
26 And after threescore and two weeks shall Messiah be cut off, but not for himself: and the people of the prince that shall come shall destroy the city and the sanctuary; and the end thereof *shall be* with a flood, and unto the end of the war desolations are determined.
27 And he shall confirm the covenant with many for one week: and in the midst of the week he shall cause the sacrifice and the oblation to cease, and for the overspreading of abominations he shall make *it* desolate, even until the consummation, and that determined shall be poured upon the desolate.

Almost every commentator agrees that the seventy weeks is actually 70 weeks of years, which would be 490 years. This idea of one day equaling a year is used in Numbers 14:34, when the Israelites were condemned to wander for 4o years in the wilderness because of their unbelief; a year for each day that the spies were searching out the land.

The same year for a day principle was used in God's instruction to the prophet Ezekiel:

Eze 4:4 Lie thou also upon thy left side, and lay the iniquity of the house of Israel upon it: *according* to the number of the days that thou shalt lie upon it thou shalt bear their iniquity.
5 For I have laid upon thee the years of their iniquity, according to the number of the days, three hundred and ninety days: so shalt thou bear the iniquity of the house of Israel.
6 And when thou hast accomplished them, lie again on thy right side, and thou shalt bear the iniquity of the house of Judah forty days: I have appointed thee each day for a year.

The issue at debate among prophetic circles concerning end times doctrinal stances is the 70th week which is referred to in Daniel 9:27.

Dan 9:27 And he shall confirm the covenant with many for one week: and in the midst of the week he shall cause the sacrifice and the oblation to cease, and for the overspreading of abominations he shall make *it* desolate, even until the consummation, and that determined shall be poured upon the desolate

The seventy weeks spoken of in Daniel 9:24-27 are divided into three different spans of times, the first of which is seven weeks, which would represent forty nine years. Then there was sixty two weeks, and then in verse 27 we see reference to the seventieth week.

 A lot of modern commentators (primarily dispensationalists) would place a large span of time of at least 2000 years and more between the first sixty nine weeks and the seventieth week in order to make their case for their particular eschatological view point.

The problem with that is while they essentially agree with the seven weeks and the sixty two weeks as being separate yet running concurrent with one another (483 years), they then attempt to provide a huge gap between the sixty ninth and the seventieth, which is referred to by many who maintain a dispensationalist futurist position as the "*Church Age*".

 It would seem that a similar gapping of time would be just as credible between the seven weeks and the sixty two weeks of verse 25, but one finds no such method employed in the various commentaries. Prior to Darby's pre-tribulation rapture hypothesis, no such gapping from the sixty ninth to the seventieth week was embraced by theologians. It might be reasonably argued that they had no such revelation until the Grace of God visited John Darby in his "Aha" moment.

I believe that the "gapping" theory between the sixty ninth week and the seventieth leads into many errors and twisting and wrestling with scriptures to make it work.

But if we look at the seventy weeks for what they are, we can make perfect sense of the prophecy without having to wrestle or distort the scripture to fit our pet doctrine. As I said, prior to Darby's "revelation", there was some sound interpretation of the seventy weeks, and the passage in Daniel 9:24-27 is a wonderful PROOF of the viability of the prophetic word concerning the Messiah, in that it was gloriously fulfilled.

The seventieth week is separate in Daniel's prophecy as a "DON'T MISS THIS IMPORTANT EVENT THAT IS GOING TO TAKE PLACE FOUR HUNDRED AND NINETY YEARS FROM NOW!"

At this point I would like to insert Adam Clarke's observations on the passage:

From the going forth of the commandment to restore and to build Jerusalem - The foregoing events being all accomplished by Jesus Christ, they of course determine the prophecy to him. And if we reckon back four hundred and ninety years, we shall find the time of the going forth of this command.

 Most learned men agree that the death of Christ happened at the passover in the month Nisan, in the four thousand seven hundred and forty-sixth year of the Julian period. Four hundred and ninety years, reckoned back from the above year, leads us directly to the month Nisan in the four thousand two hundred and fifty-sixth year of the same period; the very month and year in which Ezra had his commission from Artaxerxes Longimanus, king of Persia, (see Ezr 7:9), to restore and rebuild Jerusalem. See the commission in Ezra 7:11-26 (note), and Prideaux's Connexions, vol. 2 p. 380.

No "gapping of time" is needed here. It all gives the prophecy in Daniel 9 a great deal of proof for the fulfillment and the accuracy and veracity of the prophetic Word by Jesus Christ. A dispensationalist view takes away from the glorious proof of the truth of the Bible.

Daniel 9:24 points us to the things that the 70 weeks would accomplish. Each of the things listed were accomplished at the cross of Christ:

Dan 9:24 Seventy weeks are determined upon thy people and upon thy holy city, to finish the transgression, and to make an end of sins, and to make reconciliation for iniquity, and to bring in everlasting righteousness, and to seal up the vision and prophecy, and to anoint the most Holy.

- **"To finish the transgression".** The law was added because of transgression. But when the seed (Jesus) came to whom the promise was made (Israel), then the covenant of Faith that was made with Abraham (that his seed would be as the sand of the sea for multitude) would be fulfilled through Faith in Christ. Jesus said on the cross, "It is finished".

Gal 3:19 Wherefore then *serveth* the law? It was added because of transgressions, till the seed should come to whom the promise was made; *and it was* ordained by angels in the hand of a mediator.

- **"To make an end of sins".**

Mat 1:20 But while he thought on these things, behold, the angel of the Lord appeared unto him in a dream, saying, Joseph, thou son of David, fear not to take unto thee Mary thy wife: for that which is conceived in her is of the Holy Ghost.
21 And she shall bring forth a son, and thou shalt call his name JESUS: for he shall save his people from their sins.

Heb 10:10 By the which will we are sanctified through the offering of the body of Jesus Christ once *for all.*
11 And every priest standeth daily ministering and offering oftentimes the same sacrifices, which can never take away sins:
12 But this man, after he had offered one sacrifice for sins for ever, sat down on the right hand of God;
13 From henceforth expecting till his enemies be made his footstool.
14 For by one offering he hath perfected for ever them that are sanctified.

- **"To make reconciliation for iniquity".**

2Co 5:18 And all things *are* of God, who hath reconciled us to himself by Jesus Christ, and hath given to us the ministry of reconciliation;
19 To wit, that God was in Christ, reconciling the world unto himself, not imputing their trespasses unto them; and hath committed unto us the word of reconciliation.

- "To bring in everlasting righteousness"

2Co 5:21 For he hath made him *to be* sin for us, who knew no sin; that we might be made the righteousness of God in him.
Php 3:9 And be found in him, not having mine own righteousness, which is of the law, but that which is through the faith of Christ, the righteousness which is of God by faith:

- "To seal up the vision and prophecy"

Luk 24:25 Then he said unto them, O fools, and slow of heart to believe all that the prophets have spoken:
26 Ought not Christ to have suffered these things, and to enter into his glory?
27 And beginning at Moses and all the prophets, he expounded unto them in all the scriptures the things concerning himself.

Luk 24:44 And he said unto them, These *are* the words which I spake unto you, while I was yet with you, that all things must be fulfilled, which were written in the law of Moses, and *in* the prophets, and *in* the psalms, concerning me.

- "And to anoint the most Holy".

Heb 9:11 But Christ being come an high priest of good things to come, by a greater and more perfect tabernacle, not made with hands, that is to say, not of this building;
12 Neither by the blood of goats and calves, but by his own blood he entered in once into the holy place, having obtained eternal redemption *for us.*

IF Christ fulfilled all of these points, then it only follows that the 70 weeks have been accomplished. Dispensationalists say that the seventieth week has not yet been fulfilled, and from that seventieth week, they manufacture the seven year tribulation and the rapture of the Church.

I will defer here once more to Adam Clarke's commentary.

Adam Clarke was a Methodist evangelist, Missionary, circuit rider, pastor, Biblical scholar and commentator who lived in service to Christ from 18 years old until his death at 72 years old (b.1760 d. 1832), who in turn, consults the writings of another man, Dean (Humphrey)

Prideaux. For the reader's convenience I will insert each of the verses that Clarke deals with in his commentary:

Dan 9:24 Seventy weeks are determined upon thy people and upon thy holy city, to finish the transgression, and to make an end of sins, and to make reconciliation for iniquity, and to bring in everlasting righteousness, and to seal up the vision and prophecy, and to anoint the most Holy.

Clarke writes:

Daniel 9:24
"Seventy weeks are determined - This is a most important prophecy, and has given rise to a variety of opinions relative to the proper mode of explanation; but the chief difficulty, if not the only one, is to find out the time from which these seventy weeks should be dated.

What is here said by the angel is not a direct answer to Daniel's prayer. He prays to know when the seventy weeks of the captivity are to end. Gabriel shows him that there are seventy weeks determined relative to a redemption from another sort of captivity, which shall commence with the going forth of the edict to restore and rebuild Jerusalem, and shall terminate with the death of Messiah the Prince, and the total abolition of the Jewish sacrifices.

In the four following verses he enters into the particulars of this most important determination, and leaves them with Daniel for his comfort, who has left them to the Church of God for the confirmation of its faith, and a testimony to the truth of Divine revelation. They contain the fullest confirmation of Christianity, and a complete refutation of the Jewish cavils and blasphemies on this subject.

Of all the writers I have consulted on this most noble prophecy, Dean Prideaux appears to me the most clear and satisfactory. I shall therefore follow his method in my explanation, and often borrow his words.

Seventy weeks are determined - The Jews had Sabbatic years, <u>Lev 25:8</u>, by which their years were divided into weeks of years, as in this important prophecy, each week containing seven years. The seventy weeks therefore here spoken of amount to four hundred and ninety years.

In <u>Dan 9:24</u> there are six events mentioned which should be the consequences of the incarnation of our Lord: -

I. To finish (לכלא lechalle, to restrain), the transgression which was effected by the preaching of the Gospel, and pouring out of the Holy Ghost among men.

II. To make an end of sins; rather ולהתם חטאות **ulehathem chataoth, "to make an end of sin-offerings," which our Lord did when he offered his spotless soul and body on the cross once for all.**

III. To make reconciliation (ולכפר **ulechapper, "to make atonement or expiation"**) **for iniquity; which he did by the once offering up of himself.**

IV. To bring in everlasting righteousness, צדק עלמים **tsedek olamim, that is, "the righteousness, or righteous One, of ages;" that person who had been the object of the faith of mankind, and the subject of the predictions of the prophets through all the ages of the world.**

V. To seal up (ולחתם **velachtom, "to finish or complete"**) **the vision and prophecy; that is, to put an end to the necessity of any farther revelations, by completing the canon of Scripture, and fulfilling the prophecies which related to his person, sacrifice, and the glory that should follow.**

VI. And to anoint the Most Holy, קדש קדשים **kodesh kodashim, "the Holy of holies."** משיח **mashach, to anoint, (from which comes** משיח **mashiach, the Messiah, the anointed one), signifies in general, to consecrate or appoint to some special office. Here it means the consecration or appointment of our blessed Lord, the Holy One of Israel, to be the Prophet, Priest, and King of mankind.**

So much for Clarke's interpretation of verse 24. As I pointed out earlier, verse 24 has already been fulfilled by Jesus Christ. If that is the case, *then there is no gap in the seventy years.* Only by twisting these scriptures into a dispensational fairy tale or fable is there a future 70th week. Now let us look at how Adam Clarke interprets verse 25:

Dan 9:25   Know therefore and understand, *that* **from the going forth of the commandment to restore and to build Jerusalem unto the Messiah the Prince** *shall be* **seven weeks, and threescore and two weeks: the street shall be built again, and the wall, even in troublous times. "**

Adam Clarke:

Daniel 9:25

"From the going forth of the commandment to restore and to build Jerusalem - The foregoing events being all accomplished by Jesus Christ, they of course determine the prophecy to him. And if we reckon back four hundred and ninety years, we shall find the time of the going forth of this command.

Most learned men agree that the death of Christ happened at the passover in the month Nisan, in the four thousand seven hundred and forty-sixth year of the Julian period. Four hundred and ninety years, reckoned back from the above year, leads us directly to

the month Nisan in the four thousand two hundred and fifty-sixth year of the same period; the very month and year in which Ezra had his commission from Artaxerxes Longimanus, king of Persia, (see <u>Ezr 7:9</u>), to restore and rebuild Jerusalem. See the commission in Ezra 7:11-26 (note), and Prideaux's Connexions, vol. 2 p. 380.

The above seventy weeks, or four hundred and ninety years, are divided, in <u>Dan 9:25</u>, into three distinct periods, to each of which particular events are assigned.

The three periods are: -

I. Seven weeks, that is, forty-nine years.

II. Sixty-two weeks, that is, four hundred and thirty-four years.

III. One week, that is, seven years.

To the first period of seven weeks the restoration and repairing of Jerusalem are referred; and so long were Ezra and Nehemiah employed in restoring the sacred constitutions and civil establishments of the Jews, for this work lasted forty-nine years after the commission was given by Artaxerxes.

From the above seven weeks the second period of sixty-two weeks, or four hundred and thirty-four years more, commences, at the end of which the prophecy says, Messiah the Prince should come, that is, seven weeks, or forty-nine years, should be allowed for the restoration of the Jewish state; from which time till the public entrance of the Messiah on the work of the ministry should be sixty-two weeks, or four hundred and thirty-four years, in all four hundred and eighty-three years.

From the coming of our Lord, the third period is to be dated, viz., "He shall confirm the covenant with many for one week," that is seven years, <u>Dan 9:27</u>.

This confirmation of the covenant must take in the ministry of John the Baptist with that of our Lord, comprehending the term of seven years, during the whole of which he might be well said to confirm or ratify the new covenant with mankind. Our Lord says, "The law was until John;" but from his first public preaching the kingdom of God, or Gospel dispensation, commenced.

These seven years, added to the four hundred and eighty-three, complete the four hundred and ninety years, or seventy prophetic weeks; so that the whole of this prophecy, from the times and corresponding events, has been fulfilled to the very letter. (italics mine)

Some imagine that the half of the last seven years is to be referred to the total destruction of the Jews by Titus, when the daily sacrifice for ever ceased to be offered;

and that the intermediate space of thirty-seven years, from our Lord's death till the destruction of the city, is passed over as being of no account in relation to the prophecy, and that it was on this account that the last seven years are divided. But Dean Prideaux thinks that the whole refers to our Lord's preaching connected with that of the Baptist. וחצי vachatsi, says he, signifies in the half part of the week; that is, in the latter three years and a half in which he exercised himself in the public ministry, he caused, by the sacrifice of himself, all other sacrifices and oblations to cease, which were instituted to signify his.

In the latter parts of <u>Dan 9:26</u> and <u>Dan 9:27</u> we find the Third Part of this great prophecy, which refers to what should be done after the completion of these seventy weeks."

So much for Clarke who concludes his summation with " *These seven years, added to the four hundred and eighty-three, complete the four hundred and ninety years, or seventy prophetic weeks; so that the whole of this prophecy, from the times and corresponding events, has been fulfilled to the very letter.*"

I don't believe he deals with the next two verses adequately, so I will attempt to add my thoughts concerning the twenty sixth and the twenty seventh verses. Verses 26 and 27 are difficult, because they speak interchangeably of Jesus, and Titus.

Dan 9:26 And after threescore and two weeks shall Messiah be cut off, but not for himself: and the people of the prince that shall come shall destroy the city and the sanctuary; and the end thereof *shall be* with a flood, and unto the end of the war desolations are determined.

What comes after the sixty two weeks? The final week which was mentioned in the entirety of the seventy weeks. That seventieth week that dispensationalists base their eschatology on. We have already looked at the seven weeks (49 years) in which Jerusalem would be rebuilt. Sixty two weeks (434 years) later was the coming of the Messiah. Which is sixty nine weeks total. After those sixty two weeks, came the final week, the seventieth, in which Messiah would be "cut off". Let's look at the definition of this word translated as "cut off":

H3772 כָּרַתkârath BDB Definition: 1) to cut, cut off, cut down, cut off a body part, cut out, eliminate, kill, cut a covenant
1a) (Qal) 1a1) to cut off 1a1a) to cut off a body part, behead 1a2) to cut down 1a3) to hew 1a4) to cut or make a covenant
1b) (Niphal) 1b1) to be cut off 1b2) to be cut down 1b3) to be chewed 1b4) to be cut off, fail
1c) (Pual) 1c1) to be cut off 1c2) to be cut down
1d) (Hiphil) 1d1) to cut off 1d2) to cut off, destroy 1d3) to cut down, destroy 1d4) to take away 1d5) to permit to perish

1e) (Hophal) cut off   Part of Speech: verb

In the seventieth week, the Messiah was cut off, or killed, and through that death, he established a New Covenant. He finished or put an end to the transgression of mankind by His Blood that He shed on the cross.

In fact in fulfillment of this important prophecy in Daniel, He declared with His last breath, "It is finished".

Through His Death on the cross, He made an end to the sacrifice and the sin offering, and reconciled us to God.

He clothed those of us who have believed in Him and imputed His Righteousness to us, completing or fulfilling the prophecies concerning Him, and entered into the Holy of Holy once and for all for us to atone for our sins (read Daniel 9:24 again).

The Septuagint, which Jesus often quoted from, actually takes away some of the obscurity of the Kings James translation,   and reads thus:

Dan 9:26 And after the sixty-two weeks, the anointed one shall be destroyed, and there is no judgment in him: and he shall destroy the city and the sanctuary with the prince that is coming: they shall be cut off with a flood, and to the end of the war which is rapidly completed he shall appoint the city to desolations.

"...and he shall destroy the city and the sanctuary with the prince that is coming: they shall be cut off with a flood, and to the end of the war which is rapidly completed he shall appoint the city to desolations."

Just as King Nebuchadnezzar was the instrument whereby God chastised the Nation of Israel, Titus was also used to fulfill this part of Daniel's prophecy in 70 AD. Jesus even mentioned the coming Judgment on Jerusalem and Israel as a nation which would come as a result of their rejection of Him.

Mat 21:33 Hear another parable: There was a certain householder, which planted a vineyard, and hedged it round about, and digged a winepress in it, and built a tower, and let it out to husbandmen, and went into a far country:
34 And when the time of the fruit drew near, he sent his servants to the husbandmen, that they might receive the fruits of it.
35 And the husbandmen took his servants, and beat one, and killed another, and stoned another.
36 Again, he sent other servants more than the first: and they did unto them likewise.
37 But last of all he sent unto them his son, saying, They will reverence my son.

38 But when the husbandmen saw the son, they said among themselves, This is the heir; come, let us kill him, and let us seize on his inheritance.

39 And they caught him, and cast *him* out of the vineyard, and slew *him*.

40 When the lord therefore of the vineyard cometh, what will he do unto those husbandmen?

41 They say unto him, He will miserably destroy those wicked men, and will let out *his* vineyard unto other husbandmen, which shall render him the fruits in their seasons.

Mat 23:33 *Ye* serpents, *ye* generation of vipers, how can ye escape the damnation of hell?

34 Wherefore, behold, I send unto you prophets, and wise men, and scribes: and *some* of them ye shall kill and crucify; and *some* of them shall ye scourge in your synagogues, and persecute *them* from city to city:

35 That upon you may come all the righteous blood shed upon the earth, from the blood of righteous Abel unto the blood of Zacharias son of Barachias, whom ye slew between the temple and the altar.

36 Verily I say unto you, All these things shall come upon this generation.

37 O Jerusalem, Jerusalem, *thou* that killest the prophets, and stonest them which are sent unto thee, how often would I have gathered thy children together, even as a hen gathereth her chickens under *her* wings, and ye would not!

38 Behold, your house is left unto you desolate.

It is important for the reader to note that Jesus' dialogue concerning the subject matter of this book in Matthew 24 continues immediately after these sayings in Matthew 23:33-38, as a part of His discourse on the three questions asked by the disciples, and that during the conversation, He refers to the prophecy in Daniel that foretold the events of Antioches Epiphanes' desolation of the temple as a foreshadow of what was to happen.

After Jesus was crucified, and the sacrificial system was officially annulled through His Sacrifice, the covenant was established in which God would write His Laws on our hearts, and give us His Spirit.

Dan 9:27 And he shall confirm the covenant with many for one week: and in the midst of the week he shall cause the sacrifice and the oblation to cease, and for the overspreading of abominations he shall make *it* desolate, even until the consummation, and that determined shall be poured upon the desolate.

Dispensationalists attribute this verse to the "antichrist", but reading from the Septuagint, we can see that the subject matter continues with the coming Messiah.

Dan 9:27 And one week shall establish the covenant with many: and in the midst of the week my sacrifice and drink-offering shall be taken away: and on the temple shall be the abomination of desolations; and at the end of time an end shall be put to the desolation.

"And he shall confirm the covenant with many for one week:"

This is Jesus.

Isa 42:6 I the LORD have called thee in righteousness, and will hold thine hand, and will keep thee, and give thee for a covenant of the people, for a light of the Gentiles;

He confirmed the covenant with His disciples and all those who would believe on Him through their witness:

Luk 22:20 Likewise also the cup after supper, saying, This cup *is* the new testament in my blood, which is shed for you.

In the midst of the week my sacrifice and drink-offering shall be taken away: The sacrifice and drink offering was done away through the Atoning Sacrifice of Jesus Christ. It was sealed by the destruction of Jerusalem and the temple in 70 AD.

"At the end of time" or the end of this season (kairos) as in the time, times and half a time we have seen elsewhere, when Israel will be brought into the New Covenant, and end shall be put to the desolation of the Jewish people, and they would be restored to their land and to their God when Israel realizes that Jesus Christ is indeed the Messiah.

Rom 11:22 Behold therefore the goodness and severity of God: on them which fell, severity; but toward thee, goodness, if thou continue in *his* goodness: otherwise thou also shalt be cut off.
23 And they also, if they abide not still in unbelief, shall be graffed in: for God is able to graff them in again.
24 For if thou wert cut out of the olive tree which is wild by nature, and wert graffed contrary to nature into a good olive tree: how much more shall these, which be the natural *branches,* be graffed into their own olive tree?
25 For I would not, brethren, that ye should be ignorant of this mystery, lest ye should be wise in your own conceits; that blindness in part is happened to Israel, until the fulness of the Gentiles be come in.
26 And so all Israel shall be saved: as it is written, There shall come out of Sion the Deliverer, and shall turn away ungodliness from Jacob:
27 For this *is* my covenant unto them, when I shall take away their sins.
28 As concerning the gospel, *they are* enemies for your sakes: but as touching the election, *they are* beloved for the fathers' sakes.
29 For the gifts and calling of God *are* without repentance.
30 For as ye in times past have not believed God, yet have now obtained mercy through their unbelief:

31 Even so have these also now not believed, that through your mercy they also may obtain mercy.

32 For God hath concluded them all in unbelief, that he might have mercy upon all.

Dan 9:27...and in the midst of the week my sacrifice and drink-offering shall be taken away: and on the temple shall be the abomination of desolations; and at the end of time an end shall be put to the desolation

"In the midst of the week" would be three and a half years. Jesus' ministry in this seventieth week was completed in three and a half years through His death on the cross.

Jamieson, Faucett and Brown write this concerning this portion:

in ... midst of ... week — The seventy weeks extend to a.d. 33. Israel was not actually destroyed till a.d. 79, but it was so virtually, a.d. 33, about three or four years after Christ's death, during which the Gospel was preached exclusively to the Jews. When the Jews persecuted the Church and stoned Stephen (Act 7:54-60), the respite of grace granted to them was at an end (Luk 13:7-9). Israel, having rejected Christ, was rejected by Christ, and henceforth is counted dead (compare Gen 2:17 with Gen 5:5; Hos 13:1, Hos 13:2), its actual destruction by Titus being the consummation of the removal of the kingdom of God from Israel to the Gentiles (Mat 21:43), which is not to be restored until Christ's second coming, when Israel shall be at the head of humanity (Mat 23:39; Act 1:6, Act 1:7; Rom 11:25-31; Rom 15:1-32). The interval forms for the covenant-people a great parenthesis.

Post millennialists maintain that those who attribute these verses in Daniel to a future Antichrist who appears after a long delayed seventieth week, destroy the wonderful prophetic Truth presented here and it's fulfillment at the cross.

What a wonderful apologetic tool this is, and dispensationalists rob God of His Glorious Omniscience in distorting the Truth that is presented here. I am inclined to agree with them.

I tried to steer clear of modern commentaries concerning Daniel 9:24-27, preferring to stick with those scholars who wrote before John Nelson Darby (Adam Clarke, Keil and Delitszch, and Jamieson, Faucett and Brown), but during my research of this subject, I came across some writings that deal with this same subject by an evangelist named Ralph Woodrow, and I also drew from his wealth of information. He also refers to Clarke, and no doubt, some of these others. I thought it necessary to include his concluding observations, because I am totally in agreement with them. He writes:

"Understanding this, we can now see real significance in certain New Testament statements which also speak of a definite established time at which Jesus would die. For example, we read: "They sought to take him: but no man laid hands on him, because his hour was not yet come" (John 7:30). In John 2:4, Jesus said, "Mine hour is not yet come." On another occasion, he said, "My time is not yet come" (John 7:6). Then just

prior to his betrayal and death, he said, "My time is at hand" (Mt. 26:18), and finally, '"the hour is come" (John 17:1; Mt. 26:45).

These and other verses clearly show that there was a definite time in the plan of God when Jesus would die. He came to fulfill the scriptures, and there is only one Old Testament scripture which predicted the time of his death—the prophecy which stated that Messiah would be cut off in the midst of the 70th week—at the close of three and a half years of ministry! How perfectly the prophecy was fulfilled in Christ!"

1

(from page 23, Section 1)
Another look at 2 Thessalonians 2

2Th 2:1 Now we beseech you, brethren, by the coming of our Lord Jesus Christ, and *by* our gathering together unto him

That there is a second Coming of the Lord there is no doubt, just as Acts 1:9-11 tells us that the same Jesus Who was caught up into heaven and received in a cloud WILL return in the same manner, and will gather His people unto Him. There is a Day which only the Father knows in which Jesus Christ will return in the Clouds. There is too much biblical evidence to say differently.

2 That ye be not soon shaken in mind, or be troubled, neither by spirit, nor by word, nor by letter as from us, as that the day of Christ is at hand

Unfortunately, the marketers in the Church who sell their goods about the terrible things that are upon us, and those who emulate them and preach their error from the pulpits across America have shaken the minds of a great many in the Church and have troubled them concerning these days that we are in now.

Their books, their CD's their DVDs have resulted in a flood of misinformation that has resigned the believer to assume an attitude of inaction: "*Nothing that we do will change anything, because this is all God's Plan for the world*". The Truth is God chooses to use men and women who are yielded to Him to bring about change.

2Ch 7:14 If my people, which are called by my name, shall humble themselves, and pray, and seek my face, and turn from their wicked ways; then will I hear from heaven, and will forgive their sin, and will heal their land.

Eze 22:30 And I sought for a man among them, that should make up the hedge, and stand in the gap before me for the land, that I should not destroy it: but I found none.
31 Therefore have I poured out mine indignation upon them; I have consumed them with the fire of my wrath: their own way have I recompensed upon their heads, saith the Lord GOD.

Note that it is **because the Lord found no one to stand in the gap on behalf of the nation that He poured out His wrath upon the land**.

The false prophets and professional pulpiteers who churn out their products to make a living for themselves have reduced a great majority of the Body of Christ to a people that are hearers but not doers of the Word. Again the attitude of too many in the Church today is "Nothing that we do will change anything, because this is all God's Plan for the world". That is the fruit of Darby's dispensationalism.

Christians no longer seek God.

They seek the next speaker who can produce lying signs and wonders and who will tickle their ears and will "bless" them with a personal word and a touch from their hand that will result in some carpet time. The Church is being deceived into powerlessness by those who deceive and who are being deceived themselves.

2 Thes 2:3 Let no man deceive you by any means: for *that day shall not come,* except there come a falling away first, and that man of sin be revealed, the son of perdition

Two things are to be noted here:

a) Before the Coming of the Lord, there must be a falling away first, an apostasy or a defection from the Truth that is in Jesus Christ. Amos tells of the Day of the Lord, that it will be a terrible and dreadful day. It will be a day of darkness, a day of terror. It will be a day of God's Wrath upon the earth.

It will happen because as we have seen in Ezekiel 22:30, there was no one to stand in the gap between God and the world. There will be no intercessors, because the Church has fallen away from God's Purpose and have sought their own agendas and purpose.

b) Before the Coming of the Lord, the son of perdition must be revealed. Most modern commentators say this son of perdition is the "Antichrist", an individual who would arise in the "last days" and who would make war with the saints.

According to most of those commentators, this one is the "Beast" who is mentioned in Revelation chapter 13, but we have seen that the Beast is actually a kingdom and we have already discussed the Anti Christ in an earlier section of this book, and have seen that 1 John 4:3 identifies the Anti Christ as a spirit that influences those who oppose Christ.

1Jn 4:3 And every spirit that confesseth not that Jesus Christ is come in the flesh is not of God: and this is that *spirit* of antichrist, whereof ye have heard that it should come; and even now already is it in the world.

Notice that 1 John says "ye have heard that it should come, and even now is already in the world."

Don't Miss This:

I think it is noteworthy that John, who wrote 1 John also wrote the Book of Revelation, and in that Book he doesn't mention the word "Antichrist" to describe the Beast or the false prophet.

This one mentioned in 1 Thessalonians 2:3 is called the "son of perdition". Jesus referred to Judas as the son of perdition. Judas betrayed Jesus for 30 pieces of silver.

Joh 17:12 While I was with them in the world, I kept them in thy name: those that thou gavest me I have kept, and none of them is lost, but the son of perdition; that the scripture might be fulfilled.

Heb 10:38 Now the just shall live by faith: but if *any man* draw back, my soul shall have no pleasure in him.
39 But we are not of them who draw back unto perdition; but of them that believe to the saving of the soul.

The Bible speaks in several places of a future apostasy or falling away of the people of God. The word "pernicious" in 2 Peter 2:2 is the same word translated as "perdition" elsewhere. The word means "destruction". The false prophets and the false teachers are the ones who emulate Judas' crime of betraying the Lord through their covetous ways.

How is that accomplished? If a teacher has the congregation focused more on claiming or pursuing material things for their life now, rather than training them to be active in their pursuit of furthering the Kingdom of God through proclaiming and demonstrating the Gospel of the Lord Jesus Christ, they are following Judas' path.

2Pe 2:1 But there were false prophets also among the people, even as there shall be false teachers among you, who privily shall bring in damnable heresies, even denying the Lord that bought them, and bring upon themselves swift destruction.
2 And many shall follow their *pernicious* ways; by reason of whom the way of truth shall be evil spoken of.
3 And through covetousness shall they with feigned words make merchandise of you: whose judgment now of a long time lingereth not, and their damnation slumbereth not.

Adam Clarke, in his commentary on 2 Thessalonians 2:3 writes this observation:

It is also remarkable that the wicked Jews are styled by Isaiah, Isa 1:4, בנים משחיתים benim mashchithim, "children of perdition;" persons who destroy themselves and destroy others.

There are actually numerous ideas as to who this "son of perdition" is.

But one thing is certain: According to 2 Thesssalonians 2:3, Jesus isn't coming back, and the Church isn't going to be gathered to Him ***until*** the son of perdition is exposed.

If by some reason I cannot comprehend, the reader still believes in a future 7 year tribulation time, he or she might as well at least abandon the pre-trib doctrine, because whereas your teachers have taught you that you would be taken out of here before the tribulation and the coming of the anti-Christ, and if this man of sin *is* the anti-Christ (which he is not) we are told plainly that isn't going to happen *until* the anti Christ is revealed.

Of this "son of perdition" we read:

2 Th 2:4 Who opposeth and exalteth himself above all that is called God, or that is worshipped; so that he as God sitteth in the temple of God, shewing himself that he is God.

I personally incline to the belief that this "man of sin" is not an individual, but rather a *personification* of a future spiritual condition of the Church. The Jewish building known as the temple of God was destroyed in 70 AD.

The temple of God today is the body of the believer in whom the Holy Spirit dwells.

1Co 3:16 Know ye not that ye are the temple of God, and *that* the Spirit of God dwelleth in you?

It could be argued, as some do that this man of sin represents not a person, but the Roman Catholic Church and the papacy. I don't adhere to that particular interpretation, but the hypothesis has some credibility (For an example of this view, I would refer the reader to Robert Hawker's "Poor Man's Commentary", John Wesley's Commentary, Jamieson, Fausset and Brown, as well as Albert Barnes [who looks at this man of sin as a system or a succession of the papacy], and Easton, to name a few).

Just as wisdom is personified in the Book of Proverbs, and described as a woman, and just as the Church (or Israel according to some interpreters) is personified in as a woman in Revelation 12, and just as the (I believe) harlot of Revelation 17 is a conglomeration of every non-Christian and non-Jewish religion, including the apostate Church, I believe the same method of personification is being used in 2 Thessalonians 2, when it describes the "son of perdition", and the man of sin. Also consider that Paul elsewhere exhorts believers to "put on the new man" and to "put off the old man".

I believe that 2 Timothy 3 speaks of the apostasy or the falling away that would come on the Church (they have a form of godliness) in the last days of this age:

2Ti 3:1 This know also, that in the last days perilous times shall come.
2 For men shall be lovers of their own selves, covetous, boasters, proud, blasphemers, disobedient to parents, unthankful, unholy,

3 Without natural affection, trucebreakers, false accusers, incontinent, fierce, despisers of those that are good,

4 Traitors, heady, highminded, lovers of pleasures more than lovers of God;

5 Having a form of godliness, but denying the power thereof: from such turn away.

6 For of this sort are they which creep into houses, and lead captive silly women laden with sins, led away with divers lusts,

7 Ever learning, and never able to come to the knowledge of the truth.

8 Now as Jannes and Jambres withstood Moses, so do these also resist the truth: men of corrupt minds, reprobate concerning the faith.

9 But they shall proceed no further: for their folly shall be manifest unto all *men,* as theirs also was.

The Doctrine of Balaam

In that description above, there is no semblance of what Christianity is, other than the fact that those who are described here have a "form" of godliness. These who once professed Christ have defiled the temple of God, by exalting themselves over the word of God. There is a teaching in some areas of Christianity that says that we are gods, since we are children of God. We are King's kids, who can have and are entitled to all the fineries this world has to offer. The teaching leads Christians into a form of covetousness, after the same error of Balaam, who esteemed the reward of unrighteousness above the Word of God (Remember that the messenger of the Church of Pergamos had those in his congregation who taught the doctrine of Balaam).

2Pe 2:14 Having eyes full of adultery, and that cannot cease from sin; beguiling unstable souls: an heart they have exercised with covetous practices; cursed children:
15 Which have forsaken the right way, and are gone astray, following the way of Balaam *the son* of Bosor, who loved the wages of unrighteousness;

At that time (and even now) there will be a widespread belief that anything goes in the Church, and the Grace of God will be (and is now) perverted to a place where those who profess Christ will say that whatever we do once we "say the prayer" is all right, because God is merciful to His children. This is in opposition to all that is called God, and is one evidence of the great falling away.

If the reader can have a moment of honest self examination in the light of the passage above, and if you see that you fit into some of these categories, the truth is you are partaking in that apostasy, and you have yielded yourself to the anti Christ spirit that is in the world, and you need to repent.

But that is not where it ends. In the end, that folly will be manifest (become wholly evident) to all men (see verse 9 above). In our passage in 2 Thessalonians, we are told that the wicked one will be revealed before the Coming of the Lord.

Throughout this book an attempt has been made to demonstrate that the Coming of the Lord was to restore the Kingdom of God on this earth, not to destroy the earth.

2Th 2:5 Remember ye not, that, when I was yet with you, I told you these things?
6 And now ye know what withholdeth that he might be revealed in his time.
7 For the mystery of iniquity doth already work: only he who now letteth *will let,* until he be taken out of the way.

"He who letteth" refers to the one who withholds ("letteth" is the same word as "withholdeth") or hinders the world wide apostasy from taking hold in the whole world.

How is that done? By abandoning the multitude of fables and compromise that has crept into the Church, and standing for the Truth while investing one's life in proclaiming and furthering the Kingdom of God.

The Word of God says that our warfare is not carnal.

My personal view is that 2 Thessalonians is speaking of the spiritual condition that the Church will be in (the apostasy) before the coming of the Lord. The spirit of Anti Christ will be so prevalent in the Church and outside the Church that if it was possible even the very elect will be deceived.

Jesus warned that there will be false Christ's and false prophets who will show great signs and wonders, and will lead many astray with their false teachings. It is very important for the reader to understand that the great signs and wonders that are performed by the "man of God" or the "woman of God" is not proof that God is working through them, or that God has given them a stamp of approval for their ministry.

Mat 24:24 For there shall arise false Christs, and false prophets, and shall shew great signs and wonders; insomuch that, if *it were* possible, they shall deceive the very elect.

Those who stand for the Truth and who stand against false doctrine are the ones who prevent this anti Christ spirit to dominate the people of God (*He who lets* 0r *withholds*). Eventually due to wide spread persecution, and prevailing false doctrine and increased conformity to the world, those who cling to the Truth of the Biblical doctrine will be "taken out of the way" (2 Thessalonians 2:7) through increased persecution that comes through the Beast system that will prevail one day prevail over the earth.

Once this happens, we are told that the "man of sin" spoken of in verse three will be revealed:

2Th 2:8 And then shall that Wicked be revealed, whom the Lord shall consume with the spirit of his mouth, and shall destroy with the brightness of his coming:

9 *Even him,* **whose coming is after the working of Satan with all power and signs and lying wonders,**

10 And with all deceivableness of unrighteousness in them that perish; because they received not the love of the truth, that they might be saved.

11 And for this cause God shall send them strong delusion, that they should believe a lie:

12 That they all might be damned who believed not the truth, but had pleasure in unrighteousness.

I believe verse ten gives support to my understanding of the meaning behind 2 Thessalonians chapter 2. The subject changes from a focus on the wicked one (verse 8) to a focus on those people IN whom he works. This wicked one who will be revealed is described as one whose coming is like the working of Satan, (who cannot be seen, but who works *in* those who are taken captive by him) whose works are accompanied with all power and signs and lying wonders, and whose works are with all deceivableness of unrighteousness *in* them that perish.

The fact that this "man of sin" works in those that perish implies that it is a spiritual entity that is being referred to rather than a physical person. He works *in* these people because they don't receive the love of the truth, hence they cannot be saved (vs 10). Because of this spirit that is at work in them like it was initially at work in Judas, they are under strong delusion, and prefer unrighteousness over Truth. I believe that this is not a description of a particular individual, but of a prevailing spirit that would permeate those who are caught up in the apostasy of the last days.

In contrast to this spirit that would permeate the world, Paul then commends the Thessalonians, who were standing in the Truth, and encourages them to stand fast and continue in the teachings that they had received. It is that Truth that hinders the world wide Apostasy from taking place.

2Th 2:13 But we are bound to give thanks alway to God for you, brethren beloved of the Lord, because God hath from the beginning chosen you to salvation through sanctification of the Spirit and belief of the truth:

14 Whereunto he called you by our gospel, to the obtaining of the glory of our Lord Jesus Christ.

15 Therefore, brethren, stand fast, and hold the traditions which ye have been taught, whether by word, or our epistle.

16 Now our Lord Jesus Christ himself, and God, even our Father, which hath loved us, and hath given *us* **everlasting consolation and good hope through grace,**

17 Comfort your hearts, and stablish you in every good word and work.

2

(From Page 27, Section 1)

The Heresy of the Nicolaitans

But this thou hast, that thou hatest the deeds of the Nicolaitans, which I also hate. Rev 2:6

In all fairness, I must point out that nobody today has a definite answer as to what the Doctrine of the Nicolaitans was. But I will endeavor to submit my opinion as to what that doctrine is. Some views as to what the Nicolaitans were are found in the writings of the early church fathers. I personally don't believe we can draw a reliable conclusion as to what the Nicolaitan doctrine is from their writings. As we will see, the reports greatly vary, as time goes by:

According to Iraneus, (A.D. 120-202) The Nicolaitans were a Gnostic sect, who preceded a heretic named Cerinthus, and who taught doctrines that were contrary to the orthodox understanding of Who God is. Iraneus wrote:

"John, the disciple of the Lord, preaches this faith, and seeks, by the proclamation of the Gospel, to remove that error which by Cerinthus had been disseminated among men, and a long time previously by those termed Nicolaitans, who are an offset of that "knowledge" falsely so called, that he might confound them, and persuade them that there is but one God, who made all things by His Word; and not, as they allege, that the Creator was one, but the Father of the Lord another; and that the Son of the Creator was, forsooth, one, but the Christ from above another, who also continued impassible, descending upon Jesus, the Son of the Creator, and flew back again into His Pleroma; and that Monogenes was the beginning, but Logos was the true son of Monogenes; and that this creation to which we belong was not made by the primary God, but by some power lying far below Him, and shut off from communion with the things invisible and ineffable." (Iraneus, Against Heresies Book 3 Chapter 11)

In the "Stromata", written by Clement, of Alexandria, (a.d. 153-217) we find that he mentions followers of Nicolaus (thought by some, but obviously not Clement, himself, to have begun the error of the Nicolaitans), comparing them to a man named Aristippus, who had embraced a doctrine of self indulgence to the extreme:

"Such also are those who say that they follow Nicolaus, quoting an adage of the man, which they pervert, "that the flesh must be abused." But the worthy man [sic Nicolaus] showed that it was necessary to check pleasures and lusts, and by such training to waste away the impulses and propensities of the flesh. But they, abandoning themselves to pleasure like goats, as if insulting the body, lead a life of self-indulgence; not knowing that the body is wasted, being by nature subject to dissolution; while their soul is buried in the mire of vice; following as they do the teaching of pleasure itself, not of the apostolic man."

It is important to note here that Clement himself defended Nicolaus, by saying that those who followed him perverted his teachings. We will see that as time goes by, Nicolaus himself is accused as becoming the perpetrator of this sect of immorality called "Nicolaitan".

Later, Tertullian (A.D. 145-220) came on the scene, and also addressed the heresy of the Nicolaitans. It should be noted here that Tertullian leaned more toward the viewpoint of Iraeneus as to what the doctrine of the Nicolaitans was:

"A brother heretic emerged in Nicolaus. He was one of the seven deacons who were appointed in the Acts of the Apostles. He affirms that Darkness was seized with a concupiscence - and, indeed, a foul and obscene one - after Light: out of this permixture it is a shame to say what fetid and unclean (combinations arose). The rest (of his tenets), too, are obscene. For he tells of certain Aeons, sons of turpitude, and of conjunctions of execrable and obscene embraces and per-mixtures, and certain yet baser outcomes of these. He teaches that there were born, moreover, daemons, and gods, and spirits seven, and other things sufficiently sacrilegious alike and foul, which we blush to recount, and at once pass them by. Enough it is for us that this heresy of the Nicolaitans has been condemned by the Apocalypse of the Lord with the weightiest authority attaching to a sentence, in saying "Because this thou holdest, thou hatest the doctrine of the Nicolaitans, which I too hate."

By the time of Hyppolytus, the heresy seems to have eventually been laid at the feet of the apostle Nicolaus, And popular opinion was that Nicolaus taught a doctrine of sexual immorality:

(Hipolytus A.d. 170-226) **"...But Nicolaus has been a cause of the wide-spread combination of these wicked men. He, as one of the seven (that were chosen) for the diaconate, was appointed by the Apostles. (But Nicolaus) departed from correct doctrine, and was in the habit of inculcating indifferency of both life and food. And when the disciples (of Nicolaus) continued to offer insult to the Holy Spirit, John reproved them in the Apocalypse as fornicators and eaters of things offered unto idols."**

By the time of Eusebius (A.D.265-239), we now have the doctrine and the extent of its heresy fully defined:

"About this time, also, for a very short time, arose the heresy of those called Nicolaites, of which also mention is made in the revelation of John. These boasted of Nicolaus as their founder, one of those deacons who with Stephen were appointed by the apostles to minister unto the poor. Clement, of Alexandria, in the third book of his Stromata, relates the following respecting him, "Having a beautiful wife, and being reproached after the ascension of our Lord, with jealousy by the apostles, he conducted her in to the midst of them, and permitted any one that wished to marry her. This they say as perfectly consistent with that expression of his, that every one ought to abuse his own flesh". And thus those that have adopted this heresy, following both this example and expression literally, rush headlong into fornication without shame."

In my search of the Stromata, from which I quoted earlier, I have found no such account written by Clement, as Eusebius charges. Rather, we have seen that Clement defended Nicolaus, and called him a "worthy man".

From this brief study of the opinions of some of the early church fathers, we can see that there is no clear HISTORICAL fact as to what the doctrine of the Nicolaitans were.

Indeed, according to the "New International Dictionary of the Christian Church," we read: **"Virtually nothing is known about these sectaries beyond John's reference to them..."**

Bullinger, in the Companion Bible, says **"History has no record of these. Tradition says much."**

Who the Nicolaitans actually were has been lost through time. But I don't believe that is an accident. We must keep in mind that the BOOK OF Revelation was written to the SEVEN CHURCHES, (BUT SPECIFICALLY TO THE SERVANTS OF GOD) CONCERNING THOSE THINGS WHICH WERE SHORTLY TO COME TO PASS...(Rev. 1:1,4).

This doctrine of the Nicolaitans is a doctrine that would prevail in that future time which we know as the "last days".

We have seen that there are several opinions as to what the Nicolaitans were, but I personally believe that the definition of this doctrine can be found in the literal meaning of the word "NICOLAITAN".

This word literally means "conquering the laity".

How does someone "conquer the Laity?"

According to Unger's Bible Handbook, **"Some take this symbolism (Nicolaitans), however, as indicating the origin of cliericalism (nikao, "conquer", and laos, "people"), making them a group that early favored a clerical system which later developed into the papal hierarchy."**

There are many in ministry who would be pleased to keep the sheep in the pew and receive their tithes and offerings and their reverence and admiration. The attitude is "I am the minister that the Lord has called".

These are men who are content to Lord it over the flock.

They want CONTROL in their church.

They CONTROL the flock through their power in the pulpit.

They may even get a few people behind them, appoint them as "elders" or "deacons", and use these men to exercise their authority over the flock of God.

There are lots of Christians who have a sincere desire to step into service for the Lord, and to fulfill the Will of God for their lives. But if there are areas in their lives that the "Overseer" doesn't agree with, they will use the "yes men" in their self-appointed "elder" or "deacon" board to "keep them in line."

"We don't think you are ready to minister on the streets, brother Joe, because, according to our records, you haven't been faithful in paying your tithes to the church." What a way to manipulate a person to "buckle under" to the whims of the controlling pastor!

A minister of God is not to "Lord it over others", but to be examples to the flock, and to instruct them so that they can reach their full potential as fellow ministers of the gospel.

In the church where the Doctrine of the Nicolaitans is upheld, people who are called to be evangelists, prophets, teachers, apostles and pastors are delegated to the pew because of the shepherds who want to control everything. They ignore Ephesians 4:11-16:

Eph 4:11 And he gave some, apostles; and some, prophets; and some, evangelists; and some, pastors and teachers;
12 For the perfecting of the saints, for the work of the ministry, for the edifying of the body of Christ:
13 Till we all come in the unity of the faith, and of the knowledge of the Son of God, unto a perfect man, unto the measure of the stature of the fulness of Christ:
14 That we *henceforth* be no more children, tossed to and fro, and carried about with every wind of doctrine, by the sleight of men, *and* cunning craftiness, whereby they lie in wait to deceive;
15 But speaking the truth in love, may grow up into him in all things, which is the head, *even* Christ:
16 From whom the whole body fitly joined together and compacted by that which every joint supplieth, according to the effectual working in the measure of every part, maketh increase of the body unto the edifying of itself in love.

But this messenger of the church in Ephesus who hates the deeds of the Nicolaitans understands that his work is to equip the saints and to make them ready for the work of the ministry.

A true servant of God is just that: a SERVANT.

He is looking to do whatever he can to help others to abound and excel in their work for the Lord.

Because those who are actively embracing the doctrine of the Nicolaitans are seeking their own good instead of the good of those who the Lord has entrusted them, they forget about their first love, because they are too busy loving themselves.

Those who do move into ministry under their instruction will fall into the same error. They will be more interested in building their own Kingdom instead of God's; because of the example they were given.

We need to be careful to walk in that first love, so the ministers our ministries beget are consumed with the same motivation:

TO LOVE THE LORD THEIR GOD WITH ALL THEIR HEART, ALL THEIR SOUL AND ALL THEIR MIGHT

Another way the laity can be conquered (or kept from finding their calling) is through encouraging them in immorality, and false doctrine, as well as compromise with the standards of the world, and conformity to those standards.

The Catholic Church is by far the most obvious church that has embraced such an erroneous practice, but I need to point out that the Catholic Church is not the only church that embraces this doctrine. Most so-called Christian churches today embrace some degree of this Nicolaitan mindset.

The Catholic Church endorses Mardis Gras, a celebration of revelry and such unbridled lust that serves to mock the atoning work of our Lord Jesus Christ. Throughout the world, similar festivals and partying are permitted on their grounds.

Adherents of the Catholic Faith are not taught to know how to possess their bodies in sanctification. This is supposedly only the duty of the Church "hierarchy". The clergy are the "holy ones"...the laity are taught and even encouraged to indulge in licentiousness to the extreme, and then to do an act of penance to be forgiven.

But as I pointed out earlier, the Catholic Church is not the only one that embraces this Nicolaitan doctrine.

Some Protestant churches also teach "once you say the prayer, it really doesn't matter what you do... the worse that could happen is that you will lose some rewards in heaven."

They call this false teaching "Unconditional Eternal Security". The endorsing of sin is a way of "conquering the laity".

The Catholic Church is laden with idolatry. Statues are everywhere, and people bow before them, praying to the dead, (which is defined as necromancy in the Bible), and putting their trust on others, instead of Jesus Christ, supposedly implying that Jesus is too busy to hear all our prayers.

Mary has become a substitute or is on a par with Jesus as an intermediator. But although the Catholic Church is so blatantly caught up in idolatry, many Protestant churches are as well.

Covetousness is idolatry, and the covetousness that abounds in many Charismatic Christian churches is running rampant. "Clergy" encourage the "laity" to "believe for big things", while "sowing" more money into their ministries .

Thieves, hypocrites, and wolves abound in the Churches today, and the laity is being conquered through their deception. The laity is being encouraged (by example) to bow before their idols and is rendered ineffective for the work of the Kingdom of God.

Promoting idolatrous practices in the hearts of the people is a way of conquering the laity.

The Catholic Church has taught it's people to compromise their faith in Christ, but so has the Protestant Church.

Compromise of the Word of God will result in conquering the laity.

The whole reason for encouraging the Nicolaitan doctrine by the messengers of today's churches is to be held in honor and prestige in the eyes of the laity.

God hates those who embrace the Nicolaitan mindset.

They seek Glory for their works.

The Priest or the Pastor thrives on the honor the laity bestows on him.

The Evangelist boasts of his "exploits".

The Prophet glories in the mystique behind his ministry.

The Apostle establishes works to be recognized by men.

The Teacher soaks up accolades from men declaring how wise and knowledgeable he is.

They all love their titles.

And they make sure their names are preceded by their titles: "Bishop so and so", "Elder such and such", "Pastor this and that", "Evangelist what and when", and "Apostle Where and How", or "Father Holy One".

Niclolaitans.

Glory seekers.

To insist on such titles, I believe is an abomination before God. There is no humility involved.

Now, If others choose to call us a teacher, or pastor, or priest, or evangelist, or apostle, or prophet (but never Father), because they recognize us as filling that office, that is quite another thing.

If your pastor, teacher, evangelist, prophet, apostle or priest is not equipping you to do the Work of the Ministry, he is just another Nicolaitan, and you need to find another church. But give him the benefit of the doubt, first. Maybe he doesn't know any better because of church tradition. Ask him to equip you. If he won't, then give him this book. Maybe he will see the Light, and realize that he NEEDS to equip you, because that is what he is called to do. If he has a heart for Jesus, he will begin to be about the Kingdom business. If he still won't, then you need to find another fellowship that is led by a pastor who is after the Lord's heart.

He that hath an ear, let him hear what the Spirit saith unto the churches; To him that overcometh will I give to eat of the tree of life, which is in the midst of the paradise of God.

3

(From Page 43, Section 2)

STATEMENTS FROM VARIOUS CHURCH SCHOLARS WHO WERE CONTEMPORIES OF JOHN DARBY CONCERNING HIS DOCTRINE.

Robert Cameron: "Now, be it remembered, that prior to that date, no hint of any approach to such belief can be found in any Christian literature from Polycarp down.... Surely, a doctrine that finds no exponent or advocate in the whole history and literature of Christendom, for eighteen hundred years after the founding of the Church - a doctrine that was never taught by a Father or Doctor of the Church in the past - that has no standard Commentator or Professor of the Greek language in any Theological School until the middle of the Nineteenth century, to give it approval, and that is without a friend, even to mention its name amongst the orthodox teachers or the heretical sects of Christendom - such a fatherless and motherless doctrine, when it rises to the front, demanding universal acceptance, ought to undergo careful scrutiny before it is admitted and tabulated as part of 'the faith once for all delivered unto the saints." (Robert Cameron, Scriptural Truth About The Lord's Return, page 72-73).

A. W. Tozer: "Here is a doctrine that was not known or taught until the beginning of this century and it is already causing splits in churches."

Philip Mauro: "The entire system of 'dispensational teaching' is modernistic in the strictest sense; for it first came into existence within the memory of persons now living; and was altogether unknown even in their younger days; It is more recent than Darwinism.""A system of doctrine that contradicts what has been held and taught by every Christian expositor and every minister of Christ from the very beginning of the Christian era—suddenly made its appearance in the later part of the nineteenth century"."

Edmund Shackleton: All who held the premillennial Coming of Christ were, till about sixty years ago, of one mind on the subject. About that time a new view was promulgated that the Coming of Christ was not one event, but that it was divided into stages, in fact, that Christ comes twice from heaven to earth, but the first time only as far as the air. This first descent, it is said, will be for the purpose of removing the Church from the world, and will occur before the Great Tribulation under Antichrist. This they call "The coming for His saints" or "Secret Rapture." The second part of the Coming is said to take place when Christ appears in glory and destroys the Antichrist. This they call "The coming with His saints." Apart from the test of the Word, which is the only final one, there are certain reasons why this doctrine should be viewed with suspicion. It appears to be little more than sixty years old; and it seems highly improbable that if scriptural it could have escaped the scrutiny of the many devoted Bible students whose writings have been preserved to us from the past. More especially in the writings of the early Christian fathers would we expect to find some notice of this doctrine, if it had been taught by the Apostles; but those who have their works declare that they betray no knowledge of a theory that the Church would escape the Tribulation under Antichrist, or that there would be any "coming" except that spoken of in Matthew 24, as occurring in manifest glory "after the Tribulation." This is all the more significant, because these writers bestowed much attention upon the subject of the Antichrist and the Great Tribulation. Augustine, referring to Daniel 7, wrote: "But he who reads this passage even half asleep cannot fail to see that the kingdom of Antichrist shall fiercely, though for a short time, assail the Church." (Edmund Shackleton, Will the Church Escape the Great Tribulation? pp. 31, 32, cited by Alexander Reese, The Approaching Advent of Christ, p. 231.)

4
(From Page 46, Section 2)
Daniel 7, 8

This is a very difficult study to follow. I did my best to try to simplify it, but it is still difficult, and I want to apologize in advance to those who wade into this. I have dealt with this elsewhere in the book, but am placing it here as well, as a "refresher" for the reader or to cover any thing I may have missed earlier.

Daniel 7 is a vision Daniel had in the first year in which Belshazzar the king of Babylon reigned, and it spoke of the future projecting all the way to the Book of Revelation. We see continued parallels between Daniel 7 and Revelation 13, in that the beast of Revelation had attributes of each of the beasts described in Daniel 7.

Rev 13:2 And the beast which I saw was like unto a leopard, and his feet were as *the feet* of a bear, and his mouth as the mouth of a lion: and the dragon gave him his power, and his seat, and great authority.

Dan 7:4 The first *was* like a lion, and had eagle's wings: I beheld till the wings thereof were plucked, and it was lifted up from the earth, and made stand upon the feet as a man, and a man's heart was given to it.
5 And behold another beast, a second, like to a bear, and it raised up itself on one side, and *it had* three ribs in the mouth of it between the teeth of it: and they said thus unto it, Arise, devour much flesh.
6 After this I beheld, and lo another, like a leopard, which had upon the back of it four wings of a fowl; the beast had also four heads; and dominion was given to it.

All commentators agree that these first three kingdoms were the Babylonian , the Medo-Persian and the Grecian kingdoms, respectively.

The interpretation

Dan 7:15 I Daniel was grieved in my spirit in the midst of *my* body, and the visions of my head troubled me.
16 I came near unto one of them that stood by, and asked him the truth of all this. So he told me, and made me know the interpretation of the things.
17 These great beasts, which are four, *are* four kings, *which* shall arise out of the earth.
19 Then I would know the truth of the fourth beast, which was diverse from all the others, exceeding dreadful, whose teeth *were of* iron, and his nails *of* brass; *which* devoured, brake in pieces, and stamped the residue with his feet;

20 And of the ten horns that *were* in his head, and *of* the other which came up, and before whom three fell; even *of* that horn that had eyes, and a mouth that spake very great things, whose look *was* more stout than his fellows.

21 I beheld, and the same horn made war with the saints, and prevailed against them;

22 Until the Ancient of days came, and judgment was given to the saints of the most High; and the time came that the saints possessed the kingdom.

23 Thus he said, The fourth beast shall be the fourth kingdom upon earth, which shall be diverse from all kingdoms, and shall devour the whole earth, and shall tread it down, and break it in pieces.

24 And the ten horns out of this kingdom *are* ten kings *that* shall arise: and another shall rise after them; and he shall be diverse from the first, and he shall subdue three kings.

25 And he shall speak *great* words against the most High, and shall wear out the saints of the most High, and think to change times and laws: and they shall be given into his hand until a time and times and the dividing of time.

26 But the judgment shall sit, and they shall take away his dominion, to consume and to destroy *it* unto the end.

27 And the kingdom and dominion, and the greatness of the kingdom under the whole heaven, shall be given to the people of the saints of the most High, whose kingdom *is* an everlasting kingdom, and all dominions shall serve and obey him.

28 Hitherto *is* the end of the matter. As for me Daniel, my cogitations much troubled me, and my countenance changed in me: but I kept the matter in my heart.

Look at verse 23 and make a mental note that the **fourth beast is NOT a man, but a kingdom.** Also refer to the section concerning the Ten Horns, and my comment on the beast there as well.

Two years after his first vision, Daniel had another. Daniel 8 is a vision that he had in the third year in which Belshazzar reigned, and it spoke of a more precise picture of the time in which the Medio Persian empire (second beast Daniel 7:5; described in Daniel 8 as a ram) would be conquered by the Grecian empire (the leopard in Daniel 7:6) under Alexander the Great (the notable horn in Daniel 8:5).

Dan 8:3 Then I lifted up mine eyes, and saw, and, behold, there stood before the river a ram which had *two* horns: and the *two* horns *were* high; but one *was* higher than the other, and the higher came up last.

4 I saw the ram pushing westward, and northward, and southward; so that no beasts might stand before him, neither *was there any* that could deliver out of his hand; but he did according to his will, and became great.

5 And as I was considering, behold, an he goat came from the west on the face of the whole earth, and touched not the ground: and the goat *had* a notable horn between his eyes.

Note that the leopard of Daniel 7:6 had four horns, and that in Daniel 8:8, the notable horn was broken and four horns came up in its place.

Dan 8:8 Therefore the he goat waxed very great: and when he was strong, the great horn was broken; and for it came up four notable ones toward the four winds of heaven.

At the death of Alexander, four kingdoms arose in his place; that of Cassander (Macedonia) toward the west, that of Seleucus (Babylonia, etc.) toward the east, that of Lysimachus (Thracia and Bithynia) toward the north, and finally that of Ptolemy (Egypt) toward the south (*Keil-Delitsch*). The one that concerns us regarding this prophecy is the Selucid (Syrian) dynasty, out of which which sprang Antiochus Epiphanes.

Dan 8:9 And out of one of them came forth a little horn, which waxed exceeding great, toward the south, and toward the east, and toward the pleasant *land*.

Keil and Delitsch:

The one of the four horns from which the little horn grew up is the Syrian monarchy, and the horn growing up out of it is the king Antiochus Epiphanes, as Josephus (*Ant.* x. 11. 7) and all interpreters acknowledge, on the ground of 1 Macc. 1:10. The south, against which he became great, is Egypt (cf. <u>Dan 11:5</u> and 1 Macc. 1:16ff.). The east is not Asia (Kranichfeld), but Babylon, and particularly Elymaïs and Armenia, 1 Macc. 1:31, 37; 3:31, 37; 6:1-4, according to which he subdued Elymaïs and overcame Artaxias, king of Armenia (App. Syr. c. 45, 46; Polyb. xxxi. 11). Besides the south and the east, Canaan, the holy land, as lying between, is named as the third land, as in <u>Isa 19:23</u>.

Concerning this "little horn" which we know to be Antiochus Epiphanes, we read this:

Dan 8:10 And it waxed great, *even* to the host of heaven; and it cast down *some* of the host and of the stars to the ground, and stamped upon them.

We need to understand that this is a vision, and as a horn represents a man, so the host and the stars represent the people of God (refer to Revelation 1:20 where the stars are interpreted as the "angels" or messengers of the churches). I am of the opinion that the host of heaven is meant to be the people of Israel in general as God's chosen people, and the stars would be the priests or those in leadership over the people of God (*see 8:24 for the interpretation where he is said to destroy the mighty and the holy people*). Antiochus did replace the priests of the temple with his own appointees.

Keil and Delitsch make a very detailed and profound argument for Daniel 8:13 and 14, to show that Daniel 8 was a prophetic word that foretold the defilement of the temple by

Antichus Epiphanes, and as such, that the 2,300 days mentioned in verse 14 has nothing to do with the vision of John (which was yet future) as recorded in the Book of Revelation.

Dan 8:13 Then I heard one saint speaking, and another saint said unto that certain *saint* which spake, How long *shall be* the vision *concerning* the daily *sacrifice,* and the transgression of desolation, to give both the sanctuary and the host to be trodden under foot?
14 And he said unto me, Unto two thousand and three hundred days; then shall the sanctuary be cleansed.

Whereas chapter 8 speaks prophetically of Antiochus Epiphanes, chapter 7 speaks of a more distant time in which a different little horn would grow up out of the fourth world-kingdom, which would bring a time of affliction upon God's people at some fixed time in the future, which time was known only to God and which is measured by a time, times and a half a time.

Just as Jesus said "whoever reads, let him understand", concerning His prophetic words about the abomination of desolation in Mathew 24, we can see that Antiochus was a type and a shadow of another future event (or events) that would take place in some future time.

There was a specific period of time in which this oppression caused by Antiochus Epiphanes would last, 2,300 days, or six years and a few months. No matter how terrible that time would be, the people of God could be assured that this would come to an end, and the same is true of any future tribulation that the people of God would endure ("except those days be shortened"...).

Keil and Delitsch wrote:

The oppression prophesied of in this chapter would visit the people of Israel at not too distant a time; and its commencement as well as its termination, announced by God beforehand, was fitted to strengthen believers in the faith of the truth and fidelity of God for the time of the great tribulation of the end, the duration of which God the Lord indeed determined accurately and firmly beforehand, but according to a measure of time whose extent men cannot calculate in advance. In this respect the designation of the time of the affliction which the horn growing up out of the third world-kingdom will bring upon God's people, becomes a type for the duration of the oppression of the last enemy of the Church of the Lord at the end of the days.

In Daniel 7 we read of a vision that Daniel received concerning events that were to happen at some time in the future. It is an over view of the things that would occur, and Daniel 8 deals more in detail those things regarding the second and third beast of Daniel 7:5 and 6. The details of the fourth beast would be expounded on in future chapters 11, 12.

The summation of what was going to happen in the future is found at the end of the chapter:

Dan 7:26 But the judgment shall sit, and they shall take away his dominion, to consume and to destroy *it* **unto the end.**

27 And the kingdom and dominion, and the greatness of the kingdom under the whole heaven, shall be given to the people of the saints of the most High, whose kingdom *is* **an everlasting kingdom, and all dominions shall serve and obey him.**

28 Hitherto *is* **the end of the matter. As for me Daniel, my cogitations much troubled me, and my countenance changed in me: but I kept the matter in my heart.**

Hallelujah! That is a beautiful summation!

As I said at the beginning of this particular study, it probably was difficult to follow. The reader might have to reread it two or three times before it makes sense. But to capsualize what we've learned: Daniel 7 foretells four kingdoms that would arise on the earth. The first was that which ruled at the time, the Babylonian kingdom. The second would be the Persian, and the third would be the Grecian kingdom. Then it goes on to tell us that there would be a fourth kingdom, and this would be the Roman kingdom.

Daniel 8 deals primarily with the Grecian kingdom era, part of which was the Selucid dynasty under Antioches Epiphanes, who eventually defiled the the temple and laid Jerusalem waste. This is the event (as a foreshadow of what was to come) that Jesus referred to concerning Daniel in Matthew 24:15:

Mat 24:15 When ye therefore shall see the abomination of desolation, spoken of by Daniel the prophet, stand in the holy place, (whoso readeth, let him understand:)

We will deal more with all of this in Appendix 6 as we discuss the harlot and the Beast.

5

(From Page 49, Section 2)

Trinitarianism or Unitarianism

BAPTISM:
IN THE NAME OF THE FATHER, THE SON AND THE HOLY GHOST, OR
IN THE NAME OF JESUS ONLY?

The Question is frequently asked by an anti-trinitarian:

"What is the name of the Father, or of the Holy Spirit, if we are to baptize in their NAME?"

The question I like to ask any son or daughter is this…what do you call your natural father? If you love him, and honor him, and respect him, though you may know him to be named Bill or Fred or John or Joseph; to you, his name will always be "father", or dad, or pa, or papa, or daddy, or some other term of intimacy.

The Son is Jesus Christ or Yeshuah, Ha Maschiah. And the Holy Spirit is Holy Spirit, or Ruach Ha Kodesh. Father, Son, and Holy Spirit are not merely *titles* for the one true God, they are Who He is... They are His Names.

See how Jesus personalized the Holy Spirit by saying "he" and "himself", instead of "it":

John 15:26   But when the Comforter is come, whom I will send unto you from the Father, even the Spirit of truth, which proceedeth from the Father, he shall testify of me: (KJV)

He proceeds from the Father just as Jesus does…They are ONE. Of the same substance, co-eternal and co-equal with one another. See another place where the word "He" is used in describing the Holy Spirit, denoting personality, instead of some impersonal active force as the Jehovah's Witnesses teach:

John 16:13 Howbeit when he, the Spirit of truth, is come, he will guide you into all truth: for he shall not speak of himself; but whatsoever he shall hear, that shall he speak: and he will shew you things to come. (KJV)

So when we baptize in the Name of the Father, the Son, and the Holy Spirit, we can see that this is the correct formula. It is important to note how Jesus commissioned the disciples and those who would come after them:

Matt 28:18 And Jesus came and spake unto them, saying, All power is given unto me in heaven and in earth.
19 Go ye therefore, and teach all nations, baptizing them in the name of the Father, and of the Son, and of the Holy Ghost:
20 Teaching them to observe all things whatsoever I have commanded you: and, lo, I am with you alway, even unto the end of the world. Amen. (KJV)

Notice that He said that they were to teach them to observe all things whatsoever He had commanded them. My question to those who baptize in the NAME OF JESUS ONLY is this: did not our Lord just command His disciples to baptize in the NAME OF THE FATHER, AND OF THE SON, AND OF THE HOLY GHOST? It seems that those who insist in baptizing in the Name of Jesus only are in direct violation of the commandment of Jesus recorded in Matthew 28:18-20.

The next question would be *"if all this is true, then why do we not see this formula used in the book of Acts, or anywhere else?"*

The classic argument for baptism in the Name of Jesus Only is based on what Peter says in Acts 2:28. Peter told the group of people he was preaching to to be baptized *in the Name of Jesus Christ for the remission of sins.* He did not say to be baptized in the Name of the Father, of the Son, and of the Holy Ghost:

Acts 2:37 Now when they heard this, they were pricked in their heart, and said unto Peter and to the rest of the apostles, Men and brethren, what shall we do?
38 Then Peter said unto them, Repent, and be baptized every one of you in the name of Jesus Christ for the remission of sins, and ye shall receive the gift of the Holy Ghost. (KJV)

There are other passages that seem to support the argument for the baptism in the Name of Jesus only, and I intend to deal with each one that I am aware of, but I will address them one at a time. There is a common thread to be seen in each of these passages.

First, we need to know who this group is that are being spoken to here. The Bible tells us that they were "devout" Jews:

Acts 2:5 And there were dwelling at Jerusalem Jews, devout men, out of every nation under heaven.
6 Now when this was noised abroad, the multitude came together, and were confounded, because that every man heard them speak in his own language.
7 And they were all amazed and marvelled, saying one to another, Behold, are not all these which speak Galilaeans?
8 And how hear we every man in our own tongue, wherein we were born?
9 Parthians, and Medes, and Elamites, and the dwellers in Mesopotamia, and in Judaea, and Cappadocia, in Pontus, and Asia,
10 Phrygia, and Pamphylia, in Egypt, and in the parts of Libya about Cyrene, and strangers of Rome, Jews and proselytes,
11 Cretes and Arabians, we do hear them speak in our tongues the wonderful works of God.
12 And they were all amazed, and were in doubt, saying one to another, What meaneth this?
13 Others mocking said, These men are full of new wine. (KJV)

According to Thayer's, "Devout" is translated thus:

2126 eulabes-
1) taking hold well a) carefully and surely b) cautiously 2) reverencing God, pious, religious

So we can see that those whom Peter was addressing were already those who had reverenced God. They knew the Father. But they did not know Jesus, and they did not know the Holy Spirit.

It is important to be mindful that the occasion for Peter's preaching was that the Holy Spirit had just been poured out on the disciples, and these devout Jews were wondering what had occurred.

See what those who had been assembled in the upper room had been told by Jesus, prior to this taking place:

Acts 1:1 The former treatise have I made, O Theophilus, of all that Jesus began both to do and teach,
2 Until the day in which he was taken up, after that he through the Holy Ghost had given commandments unto the apostles whom he had chosen:
3 To whom also he shewed himself alive after his passion by many infallible proofs, being seen of them forty days, and speaking of the things pertaining to the kingdom of God:
4 And, being assembled together with them, commanded them that they should not depart from Jerusalem, but wait for the promise of the Father, which, saith he, ye have heard of me.
5 For John truly baptized with water; but ye shall be baptized with the Holy Ghost not many days hence. (KJV)

In this passage, we see the Father (verse 4), the Son (verse 1), and the Holy Ghost (verse 2, and verse 5) all mentioned. The disciples had been baptized by John in the waters of repentance toward the Father, and they had received Jesus as the One through Whom they would receive the remission of sins. The only person of the Triune God these in the upper room had yet to receive was the Holy Ghost, and so they were instructed to wait for this to happen. This was accomplished in Acts 2:1-4.

The sermon Peter preaches to these *devout* Jews is about the Lord Jesus Christ and the Holy Spirit. They already knew the Father and they worshipped Him. That is what made them "devout". In verse 16-21, Peter addresses the issue of the Holy Spirit, showing that it was the prophecy of Joel which had come to pass. Verses 22-32 tell us of the role of the Messiah Jesus, according to the fulfillment of prophecy. Again, in verse 33, we see the Father, the Son and the Holy Ghost all mentioned at once:

Acts 2:33 Therefore being by the right hand of God exalted, and having received of the Father the promise of the Holy Ghost, he hath shed forth this, which ye now see and hear. (KJV)

Acts 2:36 Therefore let all the house of Israel know assuredly, that God hath made that same Jesus, whom ye have crucified, both Lord and Christ. (KJV)

They worshipped God. But they needed to know Who the Christ was. Here, in Peter's discourse, they learn that God made Jesus both Lord and Christ. The proof of it laid in the fact that the Holy Spirit had fallen upon these disciples, and the Jews who were present witnessed it. Having heard and received the Truth spoken by Peter, we read that they were pricked in their heart:

Acts 2:37 Now when they heard this, they were pricked in their heart, and said unto Peter and to the rest of the apostles, Men and brethren, what shall we do?
38 Then Peter said unto them, Repent, and be baptized every one of you in the name of Jesus Christ for the remission of sins, and ye shall receive the gift of the Holy Ghost.
39 For the promise is unto you, and to your children, and to all that are afar off, even as many as the Lord our God shall call. (KJV)

Though we read relatively little concerning John the Baptist, we do know that his ministry was a ministry of baptism of repentance. Through considering that which was written about him, we can tell that his ministry was one that impacted Judea and the area around it. Multitudes were baptized by him:

Mark 1:4 John did baptize in the wilderness, and preach the baptism of repentance for the remission of sins
5 And there went out unto him all the land of Judaea, and they of Jerusalem, and were all baptized of him in the river of Jordan, confessing their sins. (KJV)

Luke 7:28 For I say unto you, Among those that are born of women there is not a greater prophet than John the Baptist: but he that is least in the kingdom of God is greater than he.
29 And all the people that heard him, and the publicans, justified God, being baptized with the baptism of John.
30 But the Pharisees and lawyers rejected the counsel of God against themselves, being not baptized of him. (KJV)

It would be safe to assume that these "devout" men who were witnesses of this phenomenon in Acts chapter two had also been baptized by John's baptism of repentance toward the Father. It remained for them to be baptized into Jesus (the Son), and the Holy Spirit. I believe that as we study the various passages concerning those who had been baptized in the book of Acts, that we will find this common link: that they were *devout* people who knew the Father. It only remained for the Son and the Holy Spirit to be introduced to them.

Phillip preached Jesus in Samaria. If the reader will recall the dialogue between Jesus and the Samaritan woman at the well in John 4, we see that the Samaritans worshipped the God of Jacob, the Father (John 4:12).

So again, we see that it was Jesus Who needed to be preached in Samaria. No doubt because of the woman at the well, some seeds had already been planted regarding this man called Jesus, causing the Samaritans to be open to Philip's preaching concerning Jesus Christ. According to the Word of God, John baptized those who were in Jerusalem, all Judea, and all the region round about Jordan (Matt. 3:5) If you look at a map, you can see that this would have included Samaria.

So we see that in our account in Acts chapter 8, the people of Samaria were baptized in the Name of Jesus (the Son), but the baptism was still not complete - they needed the baptism of the Holy Spirit, which is not done with water:

Acts 8:15 Who, when they were come down, prayed for them, that they might receive the Holy Ghost:
16 (For as yet he was fallen upon none of them: only they were baptized in the name of the Lord Jesus.)
17 Then laid they their hands on them, and they received the Holy Ghost. (KJV)

Next we see the story of the Ethiopian Eunuch. Obviously, the eunuch was already a believer in the God of Israel. He was studying Isaiah's prophecy of the coming Messiah in Isa. 53:7. Philip then revealed to him Jesus, and the Eunuch understood his need for baptism.

Acts 8:36 And as they went on their way, they came unto a certain water: and the eunuch said, See, here is water; what doth hinder me to be baptized?
37 And Philip said, If thou believest with all thine heart, thou mayest. And he answered and said, I believe that Jesus Christ is the Son of God. (KJV)

DON'T LET THIS FACT SLIP BY YOU:

Notice the requirement that Phillip gave the eunuch was *that he must believe that Jesus was the Son of God.* The eunuch already knew the Father. *He needed to know the Son.* Not the Father, nor the Holy Spirit. The eunuch's profession of faith was that Jesus Christ is (present tense) the Son of God. Not *was* the Son of God, or acted like the Son of God.

There are those Christians who believe in a "modalism" of God, that the ONE God was revealed in three modes; the first being the Father of the Old Testament and as Jesus revealed Him to Israel. Jesus, Who was that same God manifested in the flesh revealed Himself as the Son of the Father while He walked on the earth, but once He died and resurrected, He is no longer the Son. Some Apostolic Pentecostals will not pray to the Father; they only address Jesus in their prayer because of this modalist or "Oneness" theology. But what took place in Acts 8:37 happened *after* the resurrection of Jesus and His ascension, and the Ethiopian eunuch's confession unto salvation was that Jesus *is* the Son of God, not was the Son of God.

Jesus had died, was buried, and rose again, and now the Son of God sits on the right hand of God the Father. A lot of people stumble at this because it seems to teach that there are three Gods, but the fact is Jesus prayed to someone in the Garden, and He called Him Father. He also acknowledged that He was with Him in the beginning, and that they were One with each other (read His prayer in John 17).. In the New Testament we see the term "Godhead" (Rom 1:20, and Col 2:9), and in 1 John 5:6-11 reveals that Triune Nature of God.

Again, in Acts chapter 10, we see another account of baptism in the Name of Jesus.

Acts 10:47 Can any man forbid water, that these should not be baptized, which have received the Holy Ghost as well as we?
48 And he commanded them to be baptized in the name of the Lord. Then prayed they him to tarry certain days. (KJV)

Who were these who were baptized? In verse two of Chapter 10, we read that Cornelius was a "devout" man, and one who feared God with all his house. Obviously, he already worshipped the Father. He already knew the baptism of John (repentance toward the Father):

Acts 10:37 That word, I say, ye know, which was published throughout all Judaea, and began from Galilee, after the baptism which John preached;(KJV)

He was a *devout* man, so we can be safe in deducing that he had been baptized with John's baptism already. The Holy Spirit fell on Cornelius and his house as Peter spoke, and then they were baptized in the Name of the Lord Jesus.

Again, in Acts 19:1, we see that they found disciples who had been baptized unto John's baptism (repentance toward the Father). They still needed to be baptized in the Name of Jesus (the Son), and in the Name of the Holy Ghost. After they had been baptized in the Name of the Lord Jesus, they then received the baptism of the Holy Ghost through Laying on of hands.

Acts 19:2 He said unto them, Have ye received the Holy Ghost since ye believed? And they said unto him, We have not so much as heard whether there be any Holy Ghost.
3 And he said unto them, Unto what then were ye baptized? And they said, Unto John's baptism.
4 Then said Paul, John verily baptized with the baptism of repentance, saying unto the people, that they should believe on him which should come after him, that is, on Christ Jesus.
5 When they heard this, they were baptized in the name of the Lord Jesus.
6 And when Paul had laid his hands upon them, the Holy Ghost came on them; and they spake with tongues, and prophesied. (KJV)

I believe that in each instance of baptism in Jesus' name, we can see that those who had been baptized were already believers in the God of Israel (the Father). The evidence points to the fact that they had already been baptized into John's baptism, which was done in the Name of the Father, and the only thing that remained was to be baptized in the Name of Jesus, and of the Holy Ghost.

Those who insist on baptism in the Name of Jesus Only are anti-trinitarians, yet I believe that Bible shows ample evidence for the Trinity.

Those who preach Jesus Only say that Jesus was the Son only while He walked the earth. But remember the profession of faith made by the Ethiopian eunuch. He said *"I believe that Jesus IS the Son of God."* (Acts 3:13,26)

After Paul's conversion, he preached that Jesus Christ IS (not was) the Son of God:

1 Cor 1:9 God is faithful, by whom ye were called unto the fellowship of his Son Jesus Christ our Lord.
10 Now I beseech you, brethren, by the name of our Lord Jesus Christ, that ye all speak the same thing, and that there be no divisions among you; but that ye be perfectly joined together in the same mind and in the same judgment. (KJV)

Gal 4:6 And because ye are sons, God hath sent forth the Spirit of his Son into your hearts, crying, Abba, Father. (KJV)

Heb 4:14 Seeing then that we have a great high priest, that is passed into the heavens, Jesus the Son of God, let us hold fast our profession. (KJV)

I Jn 1:3 That which we have seen and heard declare we unto you, that ye also may have fellowship with us: and truly our fellowship is with the Father, and with his Son Jesus Christ. (KJV)

I believe that the "Baptism in Jesus' Name Only" doctrine is a doctrine which creates division and strife among the Body of Christ. Taking it even a step farther, I would even go so far as to say that biblically, Oneness theology and Jehovah Witness type theology as well as the theology of Islam is an antichrist theology:

I Jn 2:22 Who is a liar but he that denieth that Jesus is the Christ? He is antichrist, that denieth the Father and the Son.
23 Whosoever denieth the Son, the same hath not the Father: (but) he that acknowledgeth the Son hath the Father also.
24 Let that therefore abide in you, which ye have heard from the beginning. If that which ye have heard from the beginning shall remain in you, ye also shall continue in the Son, and in the Father. (KJV)

The Word declares that God loved the world so much that He sent His Only Begotten Son.

This is the Truth of the Christ, the Messiah.

Not that the Father died for us, but that He gave His only begotten Son. It would be far easier for me to give my life in place of my son. But to give my son so someone else may live?

Jesus is at the right hand of the Father, according to the gospel which is preached in the Word of God. The only way around this for Jesus Only teachers is to allegorize it.

I Jn 2:22 Who is a liar but he that denieth that Jesus is the Christ? He is antichrist, that denieth the Father and the Son.
23 Whosoever denieth the Son, the same hath not the Father: (but) he that acknowledgeth the Son hath the Father also.
24 Let that therefore abide in you, which ye have heard from the beginning. If that which ye have heard from the beginning shall remain in you, ye also shall continue in the Son, and in the Father. (KJV)

HE IS ANTICHRIST, THAT DENIETH THE FATHER AND THE SON.

The proper teaching is that the Father sent the Son to be the Saviour of the world, not that the Father became the Son to become the saviour of the world:

I Jn 4:14 14 And we have seen and do testify that the Father sent the Son to be the Saviour of the world. (KJV)

The fact of the matter is that the fellowship a true Child of God has is with the Father, and with the Son.

I Jn 1:3 3 That which we have seen and heard declare we unto you, that ye also may have fellowship with us: and truly our fellowship is with the Father, and with his Son Jesus Christ. (KJV)

Born Again Christians don't deny the Son ship of the Lord Jesus Christ. We don't deny the Fatherhood of the Almighty God, and we don't deny the deity of the Holy Spirit.

Yet we do not profess there are three Gods.

We worship the Father as the Father.

We Worship the Son as the Son, and we Worship the Holy Spirit Who guides us into all Truth as the Holy Spirit.

And we declare them to be ONE.

I have no hang up with this, because I know that God is God, and I am not.

I understand that His Ways are far above my own ways.

If He wants to manifest Himself as three persons to me, and wants me to acknowledge Him as the Father, the Son and the Holy Spirit, I have no problem with that.

We were created in His Image as one person, but yet a threefold being consisting of Body, Soul and Spirit.

I acknowledge my Father in Heaven.

I acknowledge my Lord Jesus Christ, the only Begotten Son of the Father.

And I acknowledge the work of the Holy Spirit in my Life. According to the Word of God, I have fellowship with the Father, and with His Son, Jesus Christ.

1 Pet 1:3 Blessed be the God and Father of our Lord Jesus Christ, which according to his abundant mercy hath begotten us again unto a lively hope by the resurrection of Jesus Christ from the dead, (KJV)

2 Pet 1:16 For we have not followed cunningly devised fables, when we made known unto you the power and coming of our Lord Jesus Christ, but were eyewitnesses of his majesty. 17 For he received from God the Father honour and glory, when there came such a voice to him from the excellent glory, This is my beloved Son, in whom I am well pleased.(KJV)

Heb 1: 5 For unto which of the angels said he at any time, Thou art my Son, this day have I begotten thee? And again, I will be to him a Father, and he shall be to me a Son? (KJV)

The problem with the Jehovah witnesses and the Oneness Pentecostals and adherents to Islam is that they either are missing the Son, or the Father, and are walking in the spirit of antiChrist.

Their doctrine is based on antichrist principles, and moves them to error in other doctrines.

Oneness Pentecostals are generally immersed in legalism, like the Pharisees, and the Jehovah Witnesses deny a Hell and perpetrate a soul-sleep doctrine like the Saducees.

The words of Jesus Himself in the Book of Revelation speak loudly enough to dispel the notion that Jesus is the Father, OR that we are not to worship Jesus but the Father Only:

Rev 2: 26 And he that overcometh, and keepeth my works unto the end, to him will I give power over the nations:
27 And he shall rule them with a rod of iron; as the vessels of a potter shall they be broken to shivers: even as I received of my Father. (KJV)

Rev 3:5 He that overcometh, the same shall be clothed in white raiment; and I will not blot out his name out of the book of life, but I will confess his name before my Father, and before his angels. (KJV)

In the Book of Revelation Jesus Himself is still declaring that He is the SON of God. Nothing changed in that respect after His resurrection.

Rev 3:21 To him that overcometh will I grant to sit with me in my throne, even as I also overcame, and am set down with my Father in his throne.
22 He that hath an ear, let him hear what the Spirit saith unto the churches.
(KJV)

Those who deny the Deity of Jesus Christ need to understand that it will be Jesus who blots out the names.

That it is Jesus Who grants us Power, and that it is Jesus who permits the overcomer to sit with Him in His throne.

Those Who deny the Trinity need to see that Jesus received His Rule from His Father, and Jesus will confess the overcomers before the Father, and Jesus is seated with His Father.

I say let every man be a liar, but God's Word is True!

6

The Harlot

(From page 56, section 2)

The Harlot and the Beast

Rev 13:1 And I stood upon the sand of the sea, and saw a beast rise up out of the sea, having seven heads and ten horns, *and upon his horns ten crowns*, and upon his heads the name of blasphemy.
2 And the beast which I saw was like unto a leopard, and his feet were as *the feet* of a bear, and his mouth as the mouth of a lion: and the dragon gave him his power, and his seat, and great authority

The first thing the reader needs to be aware of is that *Revelation 17 takes place before Revelation 13.* How do I know that?

In 13:1 the ten horns which are kings have crowns.

The existence of the crowns signifies that they have received their kingdoms, whereas in Revelation 17:12 we are told that they have "*received no kingdom as yet*", and there is no mention of crowns upon the horns.

This is why we can see that chapter 17 is a summation of what happened BEFORE the events in Revelation 13. Revelation 17 and 18 is giving a historical looking back to a time before Revelation 13, and before Revelation 12. The cry "Babylon has fallen" will take place BEFORE the events described in Revelation 13.

Rev 17:12 And the ten horns which thou sawest are ten kings, *which have received no kingdom as yet;* but receive power as kings one hour with the beast.
13 These have one mind, and shall give their power and strength unto the beast.
14 These shall make war with the Lamb, and the Lamb shall overcome them: for he is Lord of lords, and King of kings: and they that are with him *are* called, and chosen, and faithful.

In the Jewish economy there are times known as the third hour, the sixth hour, the ninth hour and the 12th hour. These are also called "watches".

Each of these "hours" encompass a period of three hours in which a guard would be posted to watch for the enemy at night, or during the day. The appearance of these kings and their kingdoms will be short lived in the scheme of things.

The time of the rule of these ten kings in Revelation 13 will be a time of gross spiritual darkness, when what is good will be called evil, and what is evil will be called good. They will join the beast in his war against the saints, in an attempt to obliterate the Judeo-Christian ethic.

I hope to deal with all of this in detail as this study progresses, but for now it is important to understand that the *Beast is the spiritual power behind the world system which is prevalent during it's existence and the harlot is the Babylonian religious system which will serve to extend the global governance of the Beast.*

So now that we have determined that we need to look at chapter 17 before we can understand chapter 13, let's take a little time to study the "harlot".

The Whore of Babylon

Rev 17:1 And there came one of the seven angels which had the seven vials, and talked with me, saying unto me, Come hither; I will shew unto thee the judgment of the great whore that sitteth upon many waters:
2 With whom the kings of the earth have committed fornication, and the inhabitants of the earth have been made drunk with the wine of her fornication.
3 So he carried me away in the spirit into the wilderness: and I saw a woman sit upon a scarlet coloured beast, full of names of blasphemy, having seven heads and ten horns.

We need first to ascertain who this woman is that sits on the Beast. In verse 1, we see that she sits on many waters. Verse 15 defines those waters as being peoples, and multitudes, and nations, and tongues:

Rev 17:15 And he saith unto me, The waters which thou sawest, where the whore sitteth, are peoples, and multitudes, and nations, and tongues.

The harlot in Revelation 17 rides the beast, yet in Revelation 13, there is no mention of the woman.

If a person rides a horse, they are in control of the horse, unless that horse gets a wild streak in it. The woman has an appearance of being in control, but in Revelation 17 we are told that the ten kings who had not yet received power would hate the whore and would make her desolate and naked, and would destroy her.

Rev 17:16 And the ten horns which thou sawest upon the beast, these shall hate the whore, and shall make her desolate and naked, and shall eat her flesh, and burn her with fire.

She is tolerated for a season.

Who Is She?

Some commentators say that the harlot of Revelation 17 is Israel, or Jerusalem, and they refer to various Old Testament scriptures that refer to Israel and Jerusalem as proof texts. Others say she is the Catholic Church. Others say she is apostate Christianity. I don't believe she can be any of these.

This harlot is described as the "mother of harlots and abominations of the earth" (Rev 17:5). The fact that she is the mother shows her to be the source of all harlots and abominations of the earth.
I believe the harlot referred to in the Book of Revelation is what the passage says she is; *Babylon*, or more to the point, the Babylonian religious and economic system which existed in the days following the flood.

The cultures of most civilizations have been centered around their gods.

Babylon was a one world religion/civilization in which all spoke the same language, all were of one mind. All attempted together to build a tower which would reach unto heaven. The men who established her sought to *make themselves a name*, instead of bowing to the Name of the God Who created them for Himself.

Gen 11:4 And they said, Go to, let us build us a city and a tower, whose top *may reach* unto heaven; and let us make us a name, lest we be scattered abroad upon the face of the whole earth.

"Let us make us a name". The religion of Babylon and the economic principles of the world under the Babylonian system are centered on self.

Religion takes preeminence away from God, and instead focuses on man's manufactured concept of God, and humanity's ability to ascend to their god through works or through merit.

Idolatry is man making a god according to his imagination, instead of man acknowledging that God made man in His Image. If we are created in the Image of God, our lives should reflect God's Image. But if we make a god according to our imagination, then anything goes, and our "god" approves of it.

The Word of God says that "All things were created by God and for God" (Col 1:16). The religion of self says god is here to cater to us.

The Covenant God made with Noah and his sons was that they should bring forth abundantly in the earth and multiply therein.

Gen 9:1 And God blessed Noah and his sons, and said unto them, Be fruitful, and multiply, and replenish the earth.

Gen 9:7 And you, be ye fruitful, and multiply; bring forth abundantly in the earth, and multiply therein.

In Genesis 10:8, we read about Nimrod, the grandson of Ham. The beginning of his kingdom was Babel. Nimrod's name means "rebellion". The motivation of the building of the tower and of the city was a rebellion to God's Covenant command to replenish the earth, not just one area.

Gen 10:8 And Cush begat Nimrod: he began to be a mighty one in the earth.
9 He was a mighty hunter before the LORD: wherefore it is said, Even as Nimrod the mighty hunter before the LORD.
10 And the beginning of his kingdom was Babel, and Erech, and Accad, and Calneh, in the land of Shinar.

There has been a great deal written about Nimrod and Babylon, and it is not my intent to expound at length on the origins or the story of "Mystery Babylon".

One of the objections I hear from unbelievers when I share the Gospel of Christ with them is that all religions carry with them concepts or ideas that are similar to each other. When God confused the language of the people who were busy building the tower and they were scattered abroad, they all took their understanding of God with them.

This harlot is the religious system that rides upon the back of the world system of this current age; an occultic universalist mixture of all the world's religions that stands in opposition to Christianity and Judaism.

Rev 17:6 And I saw the woman drunken with the blood of the saints, and with the blood of the martyrs of Jesus: and when I saw her, I wondered with great admiration.

Most are aware of the Catholic Inquisition in which those Christians and Jews who did not submit to the doctrine of the Church of Rome were cruelly tortured in an effort to make them recant of their rebellion against the Pope.

In the early beginnings of the Church, Judaism had a role in persecuting Christians as well, Christianity was seen as an aberrant and blasphemous cult whose adherents threatened thousands of years of traditions.

But the truth is that in a broader sense, the religions of the world have been far more guilty of the martyrdom of Christians in a global perspective than either of these; as missionaries have been martyred throughout the world in the name of the gods of the heathen for their witness of Jesus Christ.

At the time of this writing more Christians are being martyred in the name of Allah than have been martyed by any other religion in recent history. All religions of the world with the exception of Judaism and Christianity are off-springs of the religion that began with Babylon, and have been instrumental in killing those who represent the God Who is Revealed in the Bible.

In Isaiah 47, the religion of Babylon is identified with a multitude of sorceries which she had labored with from her youth.

Isa 47:12 Stand now with thine enchantments, and with the multitude of thy sorceries, wherein thou hast laboured from thy youth; if so be thou shalt be able to profit, if so be thou mayest prevail.
13 Thou art wearied in the multitude of thy counsels. Let now the astrologers, the stargazers, the monthly prognosticators, stand up, and save thee from *these things* that shall come upon thee.
14 Behold, they shall be as stubble; the fire shall burn them; they shall not deliver themselves from the power of the flame: *there shall* not *be* a coal to warm at, *nor* fire to sit before it.
15 Thus shall they be unto thee with whom thou hast laboured, *even* thy merchants, from thy youth: they shall wander every one to his quarter; none shall save thee.

In Revelation 17, the harlot is called "Mystery". Mystery speaks of the unknown, and in this case is synonymous with the occult.

Rev 17:5 And upon her forehead *was* a name written, MYSTERY, BABYLON THE GREAT, THE MOTHER OF HARLOTS AND ABOMINATIONS OF THE EARTH.

God's people often learned the ways of the heathen who lived among them, and as a result, went after the gods of the heathen, and incorporated the worship of those gods in their worship of the One True God. As I pointed out earlier, this kind of behavior earned Israel and Jerusalem the title of a harlot. Here is one example of Jerusalem being referred to as a harlot:

Isa 1:21 How is the faithful city become an harlot! it was full of judgment; righteousness lodged in it; but now murderers.
22 Thy silver is become dross, thy wine mixed with water:
23 Thy princes *are* rebellious, and companions of thieves: every one loveth gifts, and followeth after rewards: they judge not the fatherless, neither doth the cause of the widow come unto them.

Numerous times in the Old Testament, the backslidden Israel is referred to as a harlot. But spiritual harlotry didn't stem from her, so she couldn't be referred to as the "Mother of Harlots". For that matter, neither could the Catholic Church, nor the apostate Christian Church. God warned Israel not to make a covenant with the heathen nations who He said "went whoring after other gods".

Exo 34:12 Take heed to thyself, lest thou make a covenant with the inhabitants of the land whither thou goest, lest it be for a snare in the midst of thee:
13 But ye shall destroy their altars, break their images, and cut down their groves:
14 For thou shalt worship no other god: for the LORD, whose name *is* Jealous, *is* a jealous God:
15 Lest thou make a covenant with the inhabitants of the land, and they go a whoring after their gods, and do sacrifice unto their gods, and *one* call thee, and thou eat of his sacrifice;
16 And thou take of their daughters unto thy sons, and their daughters go a whoring after their gods, and make thy sons go a whoring after their gods.
17 Thou shalt make thee no molten gods.

In Isaiah 23, God refers to a Gentile city (Tyre) as a harlot, so we can see that Jerusalem isn't the only city that is designated with that title.

Isa 23:15 And it shall come to pass in that day, that Tyre shall be forgotten seventy years, according to the days of one king: after the end of seventy years shall Tyre sing as an harlot.
16 Take an harp, go about the city, thou harlot that hast been forgotten; make sweet melody, sing many songs, that thou mayest be remembered.
17 And it shall come to pass after the end of seventy years, that the LORD will visit Tyre, and she shall turn to her hire, and shall commit fornication with all the kingdoms of the world upon the face of the earth.

The Significance Of The Harlot of Revelation 17 In Today's World

"Intolerance" is a by-word of the 21st century. The people of the world are being conditioned to be tolerant of different religions and lifestyles through the inundation of various forms of media, and by representatives of their respective governments and religions.

From September 6 to September 8 in 2000, there was a World Millennium Peace summit held in the United Nations headquarters in New York City. One of the outcomes of that summit was the World Council Of Religious Leaders.

In the Preamble of the Charter of the World Council of Religious Leaders, we read the stated goal of the Council:

As religious and spiritual leaders of the world forming the World Council of Religious Leaders, we believe that religion can serve as a positive force for achieving world peace, that conflicts among religious and spiritual groups are avoidable, and that harmony amongst them is to be consistently promoted through active discussions and dialogues. We

acknowledge that the history of humanity is replete with conflicts – even violent ones – that might have been avoided had there been a body to promote mutual understanding and equal respect among all religions. Therefore, we believe that it is our responsibility to work together to remove all causes of tension among our communities. We believe we have the will and courage to lead their followers to accept differences, to maintain self-respect, and to live in harmony with diverse communities in the world and with humankind in general.

WITH THESE ENDS IN VIEW, the World Council of Religious Leaders is formed as an independent body to be available as a resource, to work in collaboration and cooperation with, and to strengthen the United Nations and other international and national organizations that are dedicated to promoting world peace, harmony, tolerance, mutual respect among humans, and social and economic justice.

The first act of the World Council is to:

a) Affirm the charter of the United Nations

b) Reaffirm the commitment to Global Peace that was signed by the religious and spiritual leaders attending the Millennium World Peace Summit of Religious at the United Nations in August 2000.

c) Affirm that we will collectively work to promote spiritual values and practices throughout the world

It is obvious that the Christian Faith, whose founder declared "*I am the way, the truth, and the life: no man cometh unto the Father, but by me*" is an exclusive, and not an inclusive religion, so those who agree to "collectively work to promote spiritual values and practices throughout the world" may have the title "Christian", but are guilty of participating in a spiritual form of harlotry just as Israel of the Old Covenant was.

The spiritual values and practices of unadulterated Christianity are decidedly different than those of other religions.

As was stated in the Preamble above, *the World Council of Religious Leaders is formed as an independent body to be available as a resource, to work in collaboration and cooperation with, and to strengthen the United Nations and other international and national organizations that are dedicated to promoting world peace, harmony, tolerance, mutual respect among humans, and social and economic justice.*

This is not to say that the World Council of Religious leaders is the Harlot. But it is an aspect or an *attribute* of the Harlot that rides the Beast as Babylon. But we see that she is no longer in the prophetic picture in Revelation 13.

There is a move among many in the compromised church to walk in unity with the other world religions. Some influential leaders in Christianity are saying that Islam and Christianity is compatible with one another, since we worship the same God of the Old Testament. But we don't. And Islam is NOT compatible with Christianity.

These leaders and false prophets are contributors to the last days apostasy that is to come (indeed is already beginning), and this book and others like it is a call to the Church of God to come out of the religious apostasy, and to get busy about furthering the Kingdom of God on this earth:

Rev 18:4 And I heard another voice from heaven, saying, Come out of her, my people, that ye be not partakers of her sins, and that ye receive not of her plagues.

Ultimately, the world system that is in place in this "age" is different from all other world systems that existed in the past, just as the beast in Daniel 7:7 was diverse from all the other beasts.

Instead of a religiously driven age, the intent of the Beast or the principality that rules the current age is *Secular Humanism*, in which men are gods, and control their own destiny.

2Th 2:4 Who opposeth and exalteth himself above all that is called God, or that is worshipped; so that he as God sitteth in the temple of God, shewing himself that he is God.

To achieve this goal, however, those world leaders who have embraced the philosophy of Humanism must themselves tolerate the harlot's indulgences, as religion plays an important role in the present world (age), although to those key leaders, religion is irrelevant in the scheme of things, and there will be a day when religion is no longer instrumental in the agenda of the Beast. Radical Islam and other extremist religious groups including those found in Christianity are being used to further the Beast's ultimate goal of a world void of any mention God. If Satan fails, he will be cast into the Lake of Fire, and he knows his time is short.

Rev 17:16 And the ten horns which thou sawest upon the beast, these shall hate the whore, and shall make her desolate and naked, and shall eat her flesh, and burn her with fire.

In Revelation 17:1, the harlot is described as sitting upon many waters which we have seen is humanity in general. Religion has always held forth lofty ideals of an elite set of people (a priest hood) who somehow have contact with the gods of the people as mediators between the people and their gods. The mystery behind this spiritual elitism serves to foster a reverence and awe with which the "common" people view these leaders.

In 13:1, the Beast emerges from the sea of humanity, and the woman is nowhere to be seen. I believe this happens when mankind no longer sees a need for religion.

Rev 17:18 And the woman which thou sawest is that great city, which reigneth over the kings of the earth.

Some commentators say that great city is Rome and the woman is Catholicism. Some say the great city is Washington DC or New York City, and the harlot is the United States. I don't believe it is an actual city in a particular geographical location. Jesus likens His followers as a city upon a hill (Matt 5:14). Cities represent places of influence.

The Bible tells us that we don't wrestle against flesh and blood, and what we are studying here is a *vision* that John sees, and as such it is spiritual in nature. The Beast isn't really an entity that will reveal itself in the last days as having ten heads, the waters upon which the whore sat were not really waters but people, and I don't believe that the city is actually a city, but a system of governance that will one day be eliminated, and the ten horns which are upon the beast will be instrumental in its' destruction.

As I said earlier, Babylon is religion in general. Cultures of the world are generally known by their religions. The economy is part of the culture, as are the arts, education, family, and government. To a great degree the religion behind that culture will influence the arts, education, family and government as well as the economy of that culture. A good Biblical example of this is Israel itself, and the laws set forth in the Old Testament of how they were to conduct themselves in every aspect of their lives.

Another example of how the economy of a culture is effected by the religion of that culture can be found in Acts 19:19, where we see a culture being transformed because of the Gospel that Paul preached.

Act 19:19 Many of them also which used curious arts brought their books together, and burned them before all *men:* and they counted the price of them, and found *it* fifty thousand *pieces* of silver.
20 So mightily grew the word of God and prevailed.

There was a certain silversmith whose business was threatened through Paul's preaching, because he made shrines for the goddess of the area, and many craftsmen were employed and benefited through Demetrius' business.

Act 19:23 And the same time there arose no small stir about that way.
24 For a certain *man* named Demetrius, a silversmith, which made silver shrines for Diana, brought no small gain unto the craftsmen;
25 Whom he called together with the workmen of like occupation, and said, Sirs, ye know that by this craft we have our wealth.
26 Moreover ye see and hear, that not alone at Ephesus, but almost throughout all Asia, this Paul hath persuaded and turned away much people, saying that they be no gods, which are made with hands:

27 So that not only this our craft is in danger to be set at nought; but also that the temple of the great goddess Diana should be despised, and her magnificence should be destroyed, whom all Asia and the world worshippeth.

28 And when they heard *these sayings,* they were full of wrath, and cried out, saying, Great *is* Diana of the Ephesians.

29 And the whole city was filled with confusion: and having caught Gaius and Aristarchus, men of Macedonia, Paul's companions in travel, they rushed with one accord into the theatre.

30 And when Paul would have entered in unto the people, the disciples suffered him not.

31 And certain of the chief of Asia, which were his friends, sent unto him, desiring *him* that he would not adventure himself into the theatre.

32 Some therefore cried one thing, and some another: for the assembly was confused; and the more part knew not wherefore they were come together.

33 And they drew Alexander out of the multitude, the Jews putting him forward. And Alexander beckoned with the hand, and would have made his defence unto the people.

34 But when they knew that he was a Jew, all with one voice about the space of two hours cried out, Great *is* Diana of the Ephesians.

35 And when the townclerk had appeased the people, he said, *Ye* men of Ephesus, what man is there that knoweth not how that the city of the Ephesians is a worshipper of the great goddess Diana, and of the *image* which fell down from Jupiter?

36 Seeing then that these things cannot be spoken against, ye ought to be quiet, and to do nothing rashly.

37 For ye have brought hither these men, which are neither robbers of churches, nor yet blasphemers of your goddess.

38 Wherefore if Demetrius, and the craftsmen which are with him, have a matter against any man, the law is open, and there are deputies: let them implead one another.

We can see how religion affects the culture of a people.

A careful study of Revelation 18 will reveal that the description of the city is religious in nature.

Rev 18:2 And he cried mightily with a strong voice, saying, Babylon the great is fallen, is fallen, and is become the habitation of devils, and the hold of every foul spirit, and a cage of every unclean and hateful bird.

Rev 18:22 And the voice of harpers, and musicians, and of pipers, and trumpeters, shall be heard no more at all in thee; and no craftsman, of whatsoever craft *he be,* shall be found any more in thee; and the sound of a millstone shall be heard no more at all in thee;

23 And the light of a candle shall shine no more at all in thee; and the voice of the bridegroom and of the bride shall be heard no more at all in thee: for thy merchants were the great men of the earth; for by thy sorceries were all nations deceived.

24 And in her was found the blood of prophets, and of saints, and of all that were slain upon the earth.

Remember, all of this takes place before the events of Revelation 13.

Because a lot of people skim as they read, and as a result, miss some important points in the content of the book, I refer the reader again to Revelation 17:12 which says the ten horns on the beast are ten kings which had not yet received their kingdoms, and then to Revelation 13:1 where we see the horns having crowns, which implies that they have received their kingdoms.

Rev 17:12 And the ten horns which thou sawest are ten kings, which have received no kingdom as yet; but receive power as kings one hour with the beast.
13 These have one mind, and shall give their power and strength unto the beast.
14 These shall make war with the Lamb, and the Lamb shall overcome them: for he is Lord of lords, and King of kings: and they that are with him _are_ called, and chosen, and faithful.

Rev 13:1 And I stood upon the sand of the sea, and saw a beast rise up out of the sea, having seven heads and ten horns, and upon his horns ten crowns, and upon his heads the name of blasphemy.

Territorial Principalities

Again, because of the tendency of people who read books like this to skip from topic to topic instead of reading it through from page one, I will insert a portion from the section entitled "Who or What Is The Beast of Revelation 13:2", which deals with the beast of Revelation 13:2. I wrote:

There are a lot of teachers who say that the Beast of Revelation 13 is an individual, and as of this writing, I can say that during my 32 years of being a Christian, I have heard many Christian teachers proclaiming the "Beast" as being practically every United States President that has sat in office during those years, every pope, communist leaders, dictators, and even some religious leaders or celebrities.

Preterists hold the position that the "Beast" was Nero or Domitian, who ruled at the time of John's writing. A lot of people who call themselves prophets churn out books of secret Bible codes that "reveal" who this mystery man is. Did I call them prophets? They would be better termed as "profits", because that is what their endless litany of "fresh revelation" results in. This beast in Revelation 13:2 is not a man, but a _kingdom_ that will rule over the world.

If you want to know more, I would suggest you turn back to that section and read or reread what I wrote there.

Dan 7:7 After this I saw in the night visions, and behold a fourth beast, dreadful and terrible, and strong exceedingly; and it had great iron teeth: it devoured and brake in pieces, and stamped the residue with the feet of it: and it *was* diverse from all the beasts that *were* before it; and it had ten horns.
8 I considered the horns, and, behold, there came up among them another little horn, before whom there were three of the first horns plucked up by the roots: and, behold, in this horn *were* eyes like the eyes of man, and a mouth speaking great things.

The fourth beast described in Daniel is the same beast in the Book of Revelation, minus the seven heads. Most commentators agree that this fourth beast is the Roman empire, the other three being the Babylonian, the Persian and the Grecian empires. These beasts are described as a lion, a bear and a leopard, respectively, in Daniel 7:4-6:

Dan 7:4 The first *was* like a lion, and had eagle's wings: I beheld till the wings thereof were plucked, and it was lifted up from the earth, and made stand upon the feet as a man, and a man's heart was given to it.
5 And behold another beast, a second, like to a bear, and it raised up itself on one side, and *it had* three ribs in the mouth of it between the teeth of it: and they said thus unto it, Arise, devour much flesh.
6 After this I beheld, and lo another, like a leopard, which had upon the back of it four wings of a fowl; the beast had also four heads; and dominion was given to it.

Daniel 7:12 says this concerning these "beasts": "**As concerning the rest of the beasts, they had their dominion taken away: yet their lives were prolonged for a season and time.**"
We see these three beasts combining as attributes of the beast in the Book of Revelation. The Beast of Revelation has the body of a leopard, the feet of a bear and the mouth of a lion.

Rev 13:2 And the beast which I saw was like unto a leopard, and his feet were as *the feet* of a bear, and his mouth as the mouth of a lion: and the dragon gave him his power, and his seat, and great authority

What or Who is the Beast?

The "Beast" is the supernatural force that governs a world system which has been set in place by an empire that reigns over the world, or at least a great part of it. It is a ruling principality set in place by Satan who is known as the "god of this age" (2 Cor 4:4). A world system encompasses an economic, religious and social-political realm which influences the kingdoms that are a part of that system. Each particular world system is set in place by Satan to destroy the Plan of God as set forth in the Beginning of His Creation.

As I have pointed out in several areas of this book, a study of Daniel 7 will show that the Beast is a kingdom, and not a person.

Daniel 7 is a vision Daniel had in the first year in which Belshazzar the king of Babylon reigned, and it spoke of the future projecting all the way to the Book of Revelation. We see continued parallels between Daniel 7 and Revelation 13, in that the beast of Revelation had attributes of each of the beasts described in Daniel 7.

Rev 13:2 And the beast which I saw was like unto a leopard, and his feet were as *the feet* of a bear, and his mouth as the mouth of a lion: and the dragon gave him his power, and his seat, and great authority.

Dan 7:4 The first *was* like a lion, and had eagle's wings: I beheld till the wings thereof were plucked, and it was lifted up from the earth, and made stand upon the feet as a man, and a man's heart was given to it.
5 And behold another beast, a second, like to a bear, and it raised up itself on one side, and *it had* three ribs in the mouth of it between the teeth of it: and they said thus unto it, Arise, devour much flesh.
6 After this I beheld, and lo another, like a leopard, which had upon the back of it four wings of a fowl; the beast had also four heads; and dominion was given to it.

Take note of the similarity between the beast of Revelation and the beasts of Daniel. The Beast of Revelation has attributes of the three beasts of Daniel.

All commentators agree that the first three kingdoms mentioned in Daniel were the Babylonian, the Medo-Persian and the Grecian kingdoms, respectively.

The interpretation

Dan 7:15 I Daniel was grieved in my spirit in the midst of *my* body, and the visions of my head troubled me.
16 I came near unto one of them that stood by, and asked him the truth of all this. So he told me, and made me know the interpretation of the things.
17 These great beasts, which are four, *are* four kings, *which* shall arise out of the earth.
19 Then I would know the truth of the fourth beast, which was diverse from all the others, exceeding dreadful, whose teeth *were of* iron, and his nails *of* brass; *which* devoured, brake in pieces, and stamped the residue with his feet;
20 And of the ten horns that *were* in his head, and *of* the other which came up, and before whom three fell; even *of* that horn that had eyes, and a mouth that spake very great things, whose look *was* more stout than his fellows.
21 I beheld, and the same horn made war with the saints, and prevailed against them;

22 Until the Ancient of days came, and judgment was given to the saints of the most High; and the time came that the saints possessed the kingdom.

23 Thus he said, The fourth beast shall be the fourth kingdom upon earth, which shall be diverse from all kingdoms, and shall devour the whole earth, and shall tread it down, and break it in pieces.

24 And the ten horns out of this kingdom *are* ten kings *that* shall arise: and another shall rise after them; and he shall be diverse from the first, and he shall subdue three kings.

25 And he shall speak *great* words against the most High, and shall wear out the saints of the most High, and think to change times and laws: and they shall be given into his hand until a time and times and the dividing of time.

26 But the judgment shall sit, and they shall take away his dominion, to consume and to destroy *it* unto the end.

27 And the kingdom and dominion, and the greatness of the kingdom under the whole heaven, shall be given to the people of the saints of the most High, whose kingdom *is* an everlasting kingdom, and all dominions shall serve and obey him.

28 Hitherto *is* the end of the matter. As for me Daniel, my cogitations much troubled me, and my countenance changed in me: but I kept the matter in my heart.

Look at verse 23 and make a mental note that the **fourth beast is NOT a man, but a kingdom.**

We read in Revelation that the dragon, the serpent the devil and Satan are one and the same. In Genesis 3:1, we are told that the serpent was more subtil than any beast in the garden. This beast (the serpent) was an attempt by Satan to take dominion over God's Kingdom and to establish his own world system from the beginning.

Rev 12:9 And the great dragon was cast out, that old serpent, called the Devil, and Satan, which deceiveth the whole world: he was cast out into the earth, and his angels were cast out with him.

As I said earlier, whatever world system is in place at any given age is consistently against the people of the One True God (anti-Semite and Anti-Christian), with the sole design to either destroy the Kingdom of God or at least to hinder it from going forth.

A world system is more than just a kingdom. It is the principality that drives the kingdoms that are under its influence. The first three "beasts" described in Daniel were depicted as animals. The kingdoms that sprung forth under the influence of these world systems were established by sheer brute force and strength of numbers. But each empire or kingdom that sprung forth was the result of the prevailing principality that empowered it.

Our history books tell us about men's accomplishments. We learn about men like Nebuchadnezzar, Cyrus, Raamses, Alexander the Great, Napoleon, and Hitler, but the history books don't tell us about the principalities that gave them their power. The only historical book that does that is the Bible, which tells us that it really isn't flesh and blood that we are fighting against, but against principalities, against powers, against the rulers of darkness of this age, against spiritual wickedness in high places.

Eph 6:12 For we wrestle not against flesh and blood, but against principalities, against powers, against the rulers of the darkness of this world, against spiritual wickedness in high *places*.

When tempting Jesus, the devil offered Him the kingdoms of the world, if He would worship him. In Ezekiel 28, the Lord tells Ezekiel to "take up a lamentation upon the king of Tyrus", and then proceeds to describe someone who was in the Garden of Eden, one who was the anointed cherub (vs 28). I believe this describes the devil himself, who once dwelled in the Presence of God.

Eze 28:12 Son of man, take up a lamentation upon the king of Tyrus, and say unto him, Thus saith the Lord GOD; Thou sealest up the sum, full of wisdom, and perfect in beauty.
13 Thou hast been in Eden the garden of God; every precious stone *was* thy covering, the sardius, topaz, and the diamond, the beryl, the onyx, and the jasper, the sapphire, the emerald, and the carbuncle, and gold: the workmanship of thy tabrets and of thy pipes was prepared in thee in the day that thou wast created.
14 Thou *art* the anointed cherub that covereth; and I have set thee *so:* thou wast upon the holy mountain of God; thou hast walked up and down in the midst of the stones of fire.
15 Thou *wast* perfect in thy ways from the day that thou wast created, till iniquity was found in thee.
16 By the multitude of thy merchandise they have filled the midst of thee with violence, and thou hast sinned: therefore I will cast thee as profane out of the mountain of God: and I will destroy thee, O covering cherub, from the midst of the stones of fire.
17 Thine heart was lifted up because of thy beauty, thou hast corrupted thy wisdom by reason of thy brightness: I will cast thee to the ground, I will lay thee before kings, that they may behold thee.
18 Thou hast defiled thy sanctuaries by the multitude of thine iniquities, by the iniquity of thy traffick; therefore will I bring forth a fire from the midst of thee, it shall devour thee, and I will bring thee to ashes upon the earth in the sight of all them that behold thee.
19 All they that know thee among the people shall be astonished at thee: thou shalt be a terror, and never *shalt* thou *be* any more.

Satan himself is called the "*prince of the power of the air*" (Eph 2:2). He is also called the "god of this age".

To reiterate: I believe the Beasts are not the empires themselves, *but the entities or the territorial principalities (read "demons") which give the kingdoms or world empires their power.* Each of these world empires were distinguished by the god or gods they served. These gods (demons) were the personification of the spiritual principalities that gave the kingdoms their power.

Ephesians 6:12 is clear:

Eph 6:12 For we wrestle not against flesh and blood, but against principalities, against powers, against the rulers of the darkness of this world, against spiritual wickedness in high *places.*

The original Plan of God was for man to be fruitful and multiply and to have dominion over God's Creation. His Plan has not changed.

Just as God intended for man to have dominion over all of His Creation, and to have fellowship with Him, we see the same plan in effect today.

Because of the Atoning Sacrifice of Jesus, we have fellowship with God through the Holy Spirit of God living within us. "As many as received Him, to them He gave the right to become the sons of God". Because of the indwelling of the Holy Spirit, we see Power and Dominion restored to those sons of God. Through the Holy Spirit God uses His people to further the Kingdom of God one soul at a time.

Just as God uses His people to fulfill His Plan, Satan uses men who are yielded to him to fulfill his plan. Satan tried to have the Messiah destroyed in His infancy by Herod.

Mat 2:16 Then Herod, when he saw that he was mocked of the wise men, was exceeding wroth, and sent forth, and slew all the children that were in Bethlehem, and in all the coasts thereof, from two years old and under, according to the time which he had diligently enquired of the wise men.
17 Then was fulfilled that which was spoken by Jeremy the prophet, saying,
18 In Rama was there a voice heard, lamentation, and weeping, and great mourning, Rachel weeping *for* **her children, and would not be comforted, because they are not.**

In Daniel 10:13, Daniel was told that the "prince of the kingdom of Persia" hindered the angel from coming to Daniel to help him understand the vision he had received. I believe this "Prince of Persia" was the territorial spiritual principality (or ruling demon) that gave the Persian empire its power. That spiritual principality exalted itself as a god to the Persians, and their religion or worship devoted to that god impacted the society or the culture of the Persian people.

During the reign of Cyrus, Zoroastrianism was the principle religion of Persia. It was a monotheistic religion, as was Judaism. Some historians say that Judaism borrowed from Zoroastrianism, but I believe it is the other way around. We see in the Biblical texts how Daniel, and Ezra and Nehemiah were key influences in the life of king Cyrus. We find also that Esther was a Jewess who influenced the king Ahaseurus. The ancient historian Herodotus refers to this king as Xerxes, the son of Darius. Although these Hebrew men and women of God may have influenced the Persian religion, they certainly did not convert Persia to Judaism. And that ruling principality referred to as the prince of Persia is alive and well today in the Beast that the harlot rides.

Remember what Daniel 7:12 says this concerning the three "beasts" that preceded the fourth: **"As concerning the rest of the beasts, they had their dominion taken away: yet their lives were prolonged for a season and time."** "Their lives were prolonged", the essence of their antichrist nature was prolonged, and would be incorporated in the fourth beast.

Belief Systems Represented By The Three Beasts Of Daniel 7 That Comprise The Fourth Beast of Revelation

Universalism:

Zoroastrianism embraces all religions. There is no need to convert to Zoroastrianism, as they teach that the righteous of every religion go to heaven, and all religions are equal. It is the same trend that our one world society is leaning toward today. Zoroastrianism teaches that each faith leads ultimately to God, in contradiction to Jesus' Claim that He is the Way, the Truth and the Life, and no one can come to the Father except through Him. Religious Universalism is also subtly creeping into Christianity through many popular teachers today who avoid issues such as eternal punishment for those who reject Christ, or the idea that homosexuality, divorce and remarriage, and the ordination of women as pastors are all spoken against in the Bible.

Zorastrianism teaches that their god's judgment will take place in a final battle between good and evil, ultimately resulting in the destruction of evil. There will be a resurrection of the dead, and the world will be purged by molten metal, through which the righteous will wade as if it were through warm milk, and those who are evil will be burned as a punishment for their deeds, then they will be forgiven, and humanity will be made immortal and free from hunger, thirst, poverty, old age, disease and death. The world will be made perfect once again. This is called the Renovation (http://tenets.parsizoroastrianism.com/). Universalism is the nature of the 2nd beast that was to be preserved for the last days. The Beast of Revelation had the feet of the Persian empire. The feet represent the worldwide spread of the doctrine of Universalism. All would be saved.

Secular Humanism

After the Persian empire would come the Grecian empire, and there would be a spiritual principality known as the "Prince of Grecia" who would govern then (Daniel 10:20).

The religion of Ancient Greece was polytheistic. As is the case with practically every society, religion played an important role in the culture of Greek society. The gods of the Greeks had almost human qualities. They lusted for one another, they fought one another, they deceived one another and fought for their human subjects.

Secular humanism by its very nature dispenses with the idea of a need for God, and instead exalts the human intellect and elevates humanity to the level of an equality with gods. Science is ever seeking to discover the fountain of youth, and self replication and perfecting of the species through cloning and genetic manipulation. Crops are pesticide resistant, and one day if continued uninterrupted, the goal would be that humanity would be free from disease. The Bible teaches that death and disease came into the world through sin. The science of secular humanism would seek to do away with death and disease while being able to continue in our sin.

In 2 Thessalonians 2:3, we read about a "falling away" of the Church before the Coming of the Lord, and that there would be a revealing (apokalupto = the same word used as the title of the book of Revelation) of that wicked one who sits in the temple declaring himself to be god. The temple is not a temple made with hands; we are told that we who are born again children of the Most High God are temples of the Living God, and there would come a day (even now is) when the anti Christ spirit would be so prevalent on the earth that even those who profess to be Christian (but who have embraced another gospel) would embrace the humanist idea that they are gods as a result of false teachers who creep in the Church with another gospel. It is the same lie that started this mess in the first place in the Garden when the serpent told Eve that they would become as gods if they partook to the forbidden fruit.

Humanism is the nature of the 3rd beast that was to be preserved for the last days, and which would be the Body or the essence of the prevailing principality that would rule the world.

Tolerance

The Babylonian culture at the time of Nebuchadnezzar was marked by worship of Bel, Merodach, and Nebo (from whence comes the name NEBUchadnezzar) as well as a host of other gods who represented aspects of the creation (harvest, sun, moon, fertility, weather, rivers, etc). Bel was the supreme deity, the Lord of all. Merodach (or Marduk) was the god of the Creation of the universe, and Nebo was the god of the scribes.

Babylon is the oldest of man centered religions, full of idolatry and pantheism, a worshipping of the creation more than the Creator. It can be truly said that Babylon is the Mother of all apostasies and abominations of the world. The characterization of Babylon in the Book of Revelation as a harlot that sits on the Beast is the religious systems of the world as a whole (including apostate Christianity) which influence the world system (which the beast upon which she rides represents).

The beast has the mouth of a lion, which we know to represent the territorial principality of Babylon. From the mouth comes instruction and communication. Tolerance of all religions will be the norm in the end times, until the ideology of secular humanism prevails and humanity realizes that religion isn't needed. I say tolerance of all religions, with the exception of that of Judaism and Christianity, the representatives of the One True God of all Creation. Read again the Preamble of the Charter of the World Council of Religious Leaders.

That which sits on the back of a beast controls the beast on which it sits. The harlot, the mother of all apostate religions is what steers the Beast in the beginning, but in Revelation 13 the beast no longer has a rider. Karl Marx, Joseph Stalin, Mao Tse Tung and others who rose to prominence denounced religion of all kinds as being a superstition that has no relevance for humanity, and actually hindered humanity from achieving its highest state.

Darwin was used by the Satan, the enemy of God, to teach a theory that denied the existence or the necessity of God in human affairs. In Revelation 17:16, we learn that the ten horns which are on the beast will hate the whore and work to make her desolate and naked and shall destroy her.

That is why we no longer see her on the back of the beast in Revelation 13.

Once humanity has become convinced of their own ability to be gods through technological and scientific advancements, people will understand that religion is unneeded to make the world go round.

I believe the catalyst for this realization will be the appearance of a religion which is fiercer than any other, and will reinforce humanist's position that religion is a detriment to progress.

There is a mantra which is becoming increasingly common among the people of the world: "Religion has been responsible for more wars and more inhumanities than any other cause known to man".

It's not a true statement, but it is one that is being parroted by more and more people each year as humanism advances.

Rev 17:16 And the ten horns which thou sawest upon the beast, these shall hate the whore, and shall make her desolate and naked, and shall eat her flesh, and burn her with fire.

17   For God hath put in their hearts to fulfil his will, and to agree, and give their kingdom unto the beast, until the words of God shall be fulfilled.

The sum of the prophecies of Daniel and Revelation is this: There has been a war that has been waged in the heavenly realm since Adam and Eve surrendered their birth right to Satan who came in the form of the serpent, the most subtil beast in the garden. Satan's plan has been to exterminate any chance of the Messiah that was prophesied in the Garden (Gen 3:15) from occurring. The sons of God (angels - see Job 1:6, 2:1, and 38:7) saw the daughters of men, that they were fair, and they intermingled with them (Gen 6:2). As a result of this, wickedness prevailed on the earth (Gen 6:5, 6), so that there was only one righteous man to be found, and that was Noah (Gen 6:8). God saved a remnant, Noah and his house and destroyed the rest of humanity.

After the flood, God told Noah and his sons to replenish the earth and multiply. Satan was still intent on thwarting God's plan. We have already discussed the tower of Babel, so I won't re-hash that. Eventually, God made a covenant with Abraham, who was a Chaldean, but who became a friend of God because he believed God and obeyed, and as a result, God considered his obedience to be righteousness.

Jas 2:22   Seest thou how faith wrought with his works, and by works was faith made perfect?
23   And the scripture was fulfilled which saith, Abraham believed God, and it was imputed unto him for righteousness: and he was called the Friend of God.

God declared to Abraham that it was through his seed that the Blessing (the Messiah) would come. Satan got in the middle of that plan and put it in the woman's (Sarah's) heart to have her handmaiden conceive, rather than to believe it was she herself who was to bear the child who would be instrumental in bringing the promise to pass.

Ishmael was the result of that union between Abraham and Sarah's hand maiden. The descendants of Ishmael are the people of the Qu'ran, who are intent on eliminating Abraham's true seed of the promise, the descendants of Isaac.

Throughout History Satan has tried to thwart God's Plan. He tried to destroy Israel through the Pharaoh. But when the time was right, God raised up a deliverer, Moses, and He promised that sometime in the future there would be another deliverer Who would come, Who would redeem Humanity from their sin, and nothing Satan could ever do could stop it.

He tried to prevent Moses' birth through having all the first born destroyed. But he failed. He tried to prevent the Messiah's coming through putting it in Herod's heart to destroy all the firstborn in the land. But he failed.

And then redemption and reconciliation was declared not only to the Jews, but to the heathen as well, and Satan's kingdom and dominion was threatened.

Since Jesus' resurrection, those who believe in Him, Jew and Gentile alike have been invested with Authority over all the power of the enemy. Satan's last chance at success has been to prevent the Body of Christ from realizing that, to prevent that manifestation of the sons of God that is foretold in Romans 8:19; sons and daughters of God who will go forth in the Authority and Power of God to further His Kingdom here on earth as it is in heaven.

Persecution and tribulation has been his first line of defense, but that only served to scatter God's people throughout the world, and for the Name of Jesus to be proclaimed throughout the world. If you have never read Foxes' Book of Martyrs, I would suggest you do, as it will give you a good idea of the tribulation Christians have suffered since the beginning of the Church, and how God proved Himself through miracles and signs in those early days of the infancy of the Christian Church.

Tribulation has not silenced the Church, so maybe religion would. So Satan incorporated his religious twist to Christianity through the institution of the Roman Catholic Church with it's hierarchical system of elevating men to a position of god-hood.

Jesus had warned to call no man "Father", yet the Pope and priests became "Papa" and "Fathers'. The Nicolaitan heresy that Jesus hates had revived. Through sanction of the state under the rule of Constantine, clergy were put in place who would cloud the truth of the priesthood of all believers, and who would render the institution of the Catholic Church all powerful, and would keep the laity silent, to be tithe, offering and indulgences paying recipients of the Grace of God as decreed by those wicked pulpit puppets of Satan.

Every once in a while throughout history, individuals would realize that this was a distorted picture of Christianity, and would raise their voices to effect change through cries for reformation. And tribulation and persecution of the true Church would continue in order to keep the Truth of the believer's identity in Christ and their position with Him hidden.

But there has always been a remnant. Those who would understand the Commission to further the Kingdom of God and who would unselfishly commit their lives to that purpose.

And someday, the Body of Christ, that remnant who will shake themselves free from the religious trappings and restraints of the religion of man, will manifest itself as the sons of God, walking in supernatural power and authority, even in the midst of increased tribulation and persecution.

Someday religion will be outlawed, and evil will be called good and good will be called evil as Biblical morality is redefined as bigoted intolerance; and the only ones who will resist will be those who are truly the people of God. That world system that will govern will make war with the remnant of God in an effort to silence them once and for all. All the while, the people of God will do exploits in the Name of Jesus, and in the midst of the persecution, many will be turned to righteousness because of their witness.

One day the GOSPEL OF THE KINGDOM OF GOD will be preached throughout the world, and when it has, then the end of this current age in which Satan reigns will come.

Satan's message to man has always been this: "You've got this. You can be like God. You can make your destiny through your own devices." God's message has always been this: "I am God Almighty Who makes the impossible possible. I created the heavens and the earth with just my Word, I formed man from the dust of the ground, and my Plan and Purpose will come to pass, and I will use the weak things of the world to confound the strong, and the foolish tings of the world to confound those who think they are wise."

I personally believe it is His Great Mercy that tolerates Satan who was once His Chief Angel. While that may be difficult for a person to understand, it is also difficult for us to comprehend the breadth, and length and depth and height of God's Love. That is why Paul prayed that wonderful prayer in Ephesians 3:14-19:

Eph 3:14 For this cause I bow my knees unto the Father of our Lord Jesus Christ,
15 Of whom the whole family in heaven and earth is named,
16 That he would grant you, according to the riches of his glory, to be strengthened with might by his Spirit in the inner man;
17 That Christ may dwell in your hearts by faith; that ye, being rooted and grounded in love,
18 May be able to comprehend with all saints what *is* the breadth, and length, and depth, and height;
19 And to know the love of Christ, which passeth knowledge, that ye might be filled with all the fulness of God.

Throughout this book I have mentioned Satan's methods of "manufactured crises'" that he uses to blind our eyes to the True Purpose of God for our lives. Jesus plainly stated not to worry about tomorrow.

Mat 6:34 Take therefore no thought for the morrow: for the morrow shall take thought for the things of itself. Sufficient unto the day *is* the evil thereof.

Satan does all he can to get Christian's eyes fixated on the future instead of the spiritual warfare that is taking place now.

Or he tries to convince Christians to engage in spiritual warfare on a personal level (regarding themselves) rather than a territorial level. Spiritual warfare is engaging principalities such as the Prince of Persia who tried to hinder Daniel's prayers. The Kingdom of Persia must bow to the Kingdom of God. It is engaging authorities of darkness with the Truth of the Word of God. The authority of demons over an area or a person has no authority over the Authority that accompanies the Name of Jesus. It is engaging the spiritual rulers of this world and furthering the Kingdom of God in this world. It is engaging the spiritual moral depravity that is encroaching in the world, and lifting up a standard of righteousness.

There will be a proclamation made one day because of the remnant that has not bought the lie of vain religion, or who have not compromised to the world system. They will do exploits and turn many to Christ in the midst of Great tribulation. And one day will be heard these wonderful words:

Rev 11:15 And the seventh angel sounded; and there were great voices in heaven, saying, The kingdoms of this world are become *the kingdoms* of our Lord, and of his Christ; and he shall reign for ever and ever.

In the meantime, there are those who will look with fascination on the things which the modern day profits say are coming upon the world, and neglect their calling today.

Which category do you fit in?

If you are a part of that harlot religion system, the Word of God is telling you to come out of her, and be not partakers of her sin. Awake to righteousness, because many don't have the knowledge of God, and if you profess Christ, your primary purpose is to further the Kingdom of God in your realm of influence. Jesus said take heed that you be not deceived...and he finishes His discourse in Matthew 24 and 25 with the command to be found obeying His Commission when He comes.

7

(From Page 65, Section 2)

A Brief Word Study To Dispel Some Objections Concerning the Time, Times and Half a Time

There is a difference in the Word structure of this phrase in these passages and that in Daniel 7. In Daniel 7, we have seen that the word translated as "time" is a set period of time like a year, or a century or a millennium. God knows the precise Chronological time down to the year, the day, and the hour of when His Plans will be fulfilled. In fact Jesus in His answer to the disciple's questions we are addressing in Matthew 24 said this:

Mat 24:35 Heaven and earth shall pass away, but my words shall not pass away.
36 But of that day and hour knoweth no *man*, no, not the angels of heaven, but my Father only.

Another example of that Chronology of particular events occurring in God's Plan is found in the following passage:

Rev 9:15 And the four angels were loosed, which were prepared for an hour, and a day, and a month, and a year, for to slay the third part of men.

The words used here in Daniel 12 and Revelation 12 and translated as "time" is defined as a season or a designated time, like a festival or an appointed time, or times that are to be fulfilled. We see that Jesus came at an *appointed time*.

Gal 4:4 But when the fulness of the time was come, God sent forth his Son, made of a woman, made under the law,

Mar 1:14 Now after that John was put in prison, Jesus came into Galilee, preaching the gospel of the kingdom of God,
15 And saying, The time is fulfilled, and the kingdom of God is at hand: repent ye, and believe the gospel.

We see that there is a time known as the "times of the Gentiles" that are to be fulfilled.

Luk 21:24 And they shall fall by the edge of the sword, and shall be led away captive into all nations: and Jerusalem shall be trodden down of the Gentiles, until the times of the Gentiles be fulfilled.

Rom 11:25 For I would not, brethren, that ye should be ignorant of this mystery, lest ye should be wise in your own conceits; that blindness in part is happened to Israel, until the fulness of the Gentiles be come in.

And there is a time of restitution of all things; the restoration of God's Kingdom on the earth, when Jesus Christ will return.

Act 3:20 And he shall send Jesus Christ, which before was preached unto you:
21 Whom the heaven must receive until the times of restitution of all things, which God hath spoken by the mouth of all his holy prophets since the world began.

The disciples asked Jesus of this time before He was received in the clouds:

Act 1:6 When they therefore were come together, they asked of him, saying, Lord, wilt thou at this time restore again the kingdom to Israel?
7 And he said unto them, It is not for you to know the times or the seasons, which the Father hath put in his own power.
8 But ye shall receive power, after that the Holy Ghost is come upon you: and ye shall be witnesses unto me both in Jerusalem, and in all Judaea, and in Samaria, and unto the uttermost part of the earth.

The significance of the difference between the words used for "time" in Daniel 7 and Daniel 12 is Daniel 7 speaks of a specific period of time, such as 3 1/2 years or 3 1/2 centuries, or 3 1/2 millennia. It speaks of the little horn which shall speak great words of the Most High and shall wear out the saints of the Most High, and think to change times (seasons) and laws, and there will be a specific time period in which he will be allowed to do these things.

On the other hand, the "time" mentioned in Daniel 12 speaks of an appointed time that will be fulfilled.

In essence, they are the same in meaning, but carry a different sense with them.

Your appointment (time) is at 5:00 (time).

8

(from page 68)

WHAT HAPPENS WHEN THE PEOPLE OF GOD DIE?

Since Christ's Resurrection, those who are have died in Christ (have their names written in the Book of Life) are in the Presence of the Lamb.

Revelation 7:9 talks of those who have come out of great tribulation and where they are:

Rev 7:9 After this I beheld, and, lo, a great multitude, which no man could number, of all nations, and kindreds, and people, and tongues, stood before the throne, and before the Lamb, clothed with white robes, and palms in their hands;
10 And cried with a loud voice, saying, Salvation to our God which sitteth upon the throne, and unto the Lamb.
11 And all the angels stood round about the throne, and *about* the elders and the four beasts, and fell before the throne on their faces, and worshipped God,
12 Saying, Amen: Blessing, and glory, and wisdom, and thanksgiving, and honour, and power, and might, *be* unto our God for ever and ever. Amen.
13 And one of the elders answered, saying unto me, What are these which are arrayed in white robes? and whence came they?
14 And I said unto him, Sir, thou knowest. And he said to me, These are they which came out of great tribulation, and have washed their robes, and made them white in the blood of the Lamb.
15 Therefore are they before the throne of God, and serve him day and night in his temple: and he that sitteth on the throne shall dwell among them.
16 They shall hunger no more, neither thirst any more; neither shall the sun light on them, nor any heat.
17 For the Lamb which is in the midst of the throne shall feed them, and shall lead them unto living fountains of waters: and God shall wipe away all tears from their eyes.

Paul himself went through great persecution, or tribulation as he served the Lord, and he understood that Jesus was the Resurrection and the life.

Whereas prior to the death, burial and resurrection of Christ, those who were God's people were preserved in a place called Abraham's Bosom (read Luke 16:19-31), now after Christ's Resurrection, those who die in Christ are immediately in His Presence. Hence, Paul could confidently write this statement:

Php 1:21 For to me to live *is* Christ, and to die *is* gain.
22 But if I live in the flesh, this *is* the fruit of my labour: yet what I shall choose I wot not.

23 For I am in a strait betwixt two, having a desire to depart, and to be with Christ; which is far better:
24 Nevertheless to abide in the flesh *is* more needful for you.

In Daniel 12:2 we read what happens when the people of God are "delivered" at that time mentioned as a time of trouble (tribulation):

Dan 12:2 And many of them that sleep in the dust of the earth shall awake, some to everlasting life, and some to shame *and* everlasting contempt.

Rev 7:13 And one of the elders answered, saying unto me, What are these which are arrayed in white robes? and whence came they?
14 And I said unto him, Sir, thou knowest. And he said to me, These are they which came out of great tribulation, and have washed their robes, and made them white in the blood of the Lamb.

Those who have given their lives for the furtherance of the Kingdom of God are in the Presence of God (Rev 7:9-17) right now.

Cults like Seventh Day Adventists and Jehovah's Witnesses insist that the dead are asleep (doctrine of soul sleep) due to some scriptures found in the Old Testament, like this one in Ecclesiastes:

Ecc 9:5 For the living know that they shall die: but the dead know not any thing, neither have they any more a reward; for the memory of them is forgotten.

But Jesus is (present tense) the Resurrection and the Life.

Joh 11:25 Jesus said unto her, I am the resurrection, and the life: he that believeth in me, though he were dead, yet shall he live:
26 And whosoever liveth and believeth in me shall never die. Believest thou this?

Jesus obtained the keys to death and hell, and as such they have no hold on the believer under the New Covenant. If we are in Christ, we pass from death to life, and Jesus Himself declared that whereas the dead once knew nothing, now from the time of His Coming to dwell with mankind on earth and to walk among them as a man, the dead would hear His Voice.

There is no more death for the believer. The outward man may perish, but that inward man which is continually being renewed and refreshed passes from death to life.

Joh 5:24 Verily, verily, I say unto you, He that heareth my word, and believeth on him that sent me, hath everlasting life, and shall not come into condemnation; but is passed from death unto life.

25 Verily, verily, I say unto you, The hour is coming, and now is, when the dead shall hear the voice of the Son of God: and they that hear shall live.

Through his Resurrection, Jesus abolished the power of death over those who come to Him.

2Ti 1:10 But is now made manifest by the appearing of our Saviour Jesus Christ, who hath abolished death, and hath brought life and immortality to light through the gospel:

9

(from section 2, Page 69)
Who are the Two Witnesses

It is not my intention to expound at length on this, but whereas MOST commentators believe that the two witnesses mentioned in Revelation 11 are Elijah and Moses, or Enoch and Elijah (There are also many individuals who believe that they themselves will be one of the two witnesses). I reject that notion by allowing the Scripture to interpret itself.

I believe that the two witnesses are the two Churches mentioned in Revelation 2 and 3 whose leadership (angels= messengers) the Lord does not call to repentance, Smyrna and Philadelphia.

To break it down a little further, I believe these Churches represent the Gentile and the Messianic Church, the Church in Smyrna is the Messianic Body of Christ who walk circumspectly before the Lord, and the Church in Philadelphia is the Gentile Body of Christ who also walk circumspectly before the Lord. Or vice-versa, but I am inclined to believe it is how I stated it is.

Rev 2:8 And unto the angel of the church in Smyrna write; These things saith the first and the last, which was dead, and is alive;
9 I know thy works, and tribulation, and poverty, (but thou art rich) and *I know* the blasphemy of them which say they are Jews, and are not, but *are* the synagogue of Satan.
10 Fear none of those things which thou shalt suffer: behold, the devil shall cast *some* of you into prison, that ye may be tried; and ye shall have tribulation ten days: be thou faithful unto death, and I will give thee a crown of life.
11 He that hath an ear, let him hear what the Spirit saith unto the churches; He that overcometh shall not be hurt of the second death.

Rev 3:7 And to the angel of the church in Philadelphia write; These things saith he that is holy, he that is true, he that hath the key of David, he that openeth, and no man shutteth; and shutteth, and no man openeth;
8 I know thy works: behold, I have set before thee an open door, and no man can shut it: for thou hast a little strength, and hast kept my word, and hast not denied my name.
9 Behold, I will make them of the synagogue of Satan, which say they are Jews, and are not, but do lie; behold, I will make them to come and worship before thy feet, and to know that I have loved thee.
10 Because thou hast kept the word of my patience, I also will keep thee from the hour of temptation, which shall come upon all the world, to try them that dwell upon the earth.

11 Behold, I come quickly: hold that fast which thou hast, that no man take thy crown.
12 Him that overcometh will I make a pillar in the temple of my God, and he shall go no more out: and I will write upon him the name of my God, and the name of the city of my God, *which is* new Jerusalem, which cometh down out of heaven from my God: and *I will write upon him* my new name.
13 He that hath an ear, let him hear what the Spirit saith unto the churches.

In Revelation 11, the two witnesses are identified as the two candlesticks that stand before the Lord God Almighty.

Rev 11:3 And I will give *power* unto my two witnesses, and they shall prophesy a thousand two hundred *and* threescore days, clothed in sackcloth.
4 These are the two olive trees, and the two candlesticks standing before the God of the earth.

Revelation 1:20 identifies who or what the candlesticks are in John's vision.

Rev 1:20 The mystery of the seven stars which thou sawest in my right hand, and the seven golden candlesticks. The seven stars are the angels of the seven churches: and the seven candlesticks which thou sawest are the seven churches.

We can see that the candlesticks in John's vision are the churches.

While there is an expected falling away in the last days (described in detail in 2 Tim 3:1-8, 1 Tim 4:1-3, and 2 Thessalonians 2:3, as well as the words of rebuke given to the other 5 messengers to the churches in Revelation chapters 2 and 3), there is a remnant in the Body of Christ who will not waver from the Truth that is in Jesus Christ, as we see in the letters to the Smyrnan and the Philadelphian leadership.

It is important to make a distinction here. The majority of Christians in the pulpit or out of the pulpit refer to the letters of Revelation 2 and 3 as the letters to the churches. But that is not the proper exegesis of these chapters. "The Letters to the Churches" position stems from Darby's Dispensationalist eschatology.

Those who subscribe to Dispensationalism see each of the letters as a particular "dispensation" of the Church. According to them, we are in the final dispensation of the "Church Age", which would be the Laodocean age. Dispensationalism is necessary to support the idea of a pre-trib rapture, and other errant end time doctrines that Darby came up with, and that many messengers unthinkingly repeat in their messages to the Body of Christ.

In my introduction to the Appendix, I deal in depth with the verses of Daniel 9:24-27, and the fact that these 70 weeks of Daniel have in truth been absolutely fulfilled. But dispensationalists maintain that the 70th week of Daniel 9 is somehow tied in with their prefabricated antichrist beast, and the pretrib rapture.

But this book is not an in-depth exposition of the whole of end times eschatology.

My intent is just to show the Church that we have been duped into focusing on the wrong thing instead of the important thing; taking personal responsibility for the furtherance of the Kingdom of God on this earth in this age NOW. The Kingdom of God is within you! What are you doing looking for some future kingdom while allowing the kingdoms of this world to distract you from your real God Given purpose?

The fact is that the introduction to each of the letters is to the Angel (which doesn't only refer to a heavenly being, but also to a messenger) of the Church. Five of these messengers (not the churches) are told to repent of their bad doctrine. Only two are *not* told to repent.

The two witnesses are identified as the two candlesticks, which we see in Revelation 1:20 are two churches. There will be (or is now) a great falling away from the Truth.

The Truth is Before Jesus went to be with the Father, He gave assignment to the disciples and to those who would believe on Christ through their witness (that is all Christians). That assignment was to Preach the Gospel of the Kingdom of God and Make disciples. The five messengers of the churches who were told to repent lost focus of their calling.

Only two types of messengers will lead their fellowship in the Truth. The Messianic Church of Smyrna, who will further the Kingdom of God even in the midst of great persecution, and the Gentile Church of Philadelphia who operates in the Love of Christ.

The Beast will make war with these witnesses. Revelation 11 is a description of what takes place in Revelation 13.

Of course, questions concerning the periods of time that are mentioned in Revelation 11:2, 3 and 11 as well as chapter 12, and the Book of Daniel arise as a result of investigating who these two witnesses are. Revelation 11:3 says that the two witnesses will prophesy 1,260 days. Interestingly, in Revelation 12:6, we read that the woman flees into the wilderness and is sustained for 1,260 days.

Rev 11:3 And I will give *power* unto my two witnesses, and they shall prophesy a thousand two hundred *and* threescore days, clothed in sackcloth.

Rev 12:6 And the woman fled into the wilderness, where she hath a place prepared of God, that they should feed her there a thousand two hundred *and* threescore days.

There are various interpretations concerning the periods of time that are mentioned in the Book of Revelation and the Book of Daniel. I would submit one more interpretation for the reader's consideration. Whether this is on point or not, the reader can be the judge.

I have no "Thus saith the Lord" concerning this, but during my studies of the subject at hand, this is what I found.

It is significant that these two witnesses (or two churches) prophesy (witness of the Kingdom of God) for 1,260 days, after which time the Beast makes war with them and kills them.

If we date the time that the Islamic Abomination of Desolation was set up in the Holy Place (an abomination because the substitution of any other temple designed to worship another god other than the god of Israel would be an abomination) we can come up with a pretty interesting statistic:

The dome of the Rock was constructed from 687-691) and add 1260 years to it (a year for a day), we can get the years 1947, 1948 and 1949, all of which were significant concerning the founding of the modern day nation of Israel. In 1947, the first Jewish immigrants to Israel disembarked at the Port of Eilat, and the UN decreed the partitioning of Palestine for the birth of the Nation of Israel. From 1947 - 1949, Israel was engaged in the War of Independence with the surrounding Islamic countries in its quest to become a nation.

Ever since Israel's foundation as a Nation, Islam has been at war with Israel and with the Christians who support her.

10

(From Page 77, Section 2)

More on Revelation 12 And The War In Heaven

Rev 12:6 And the woman fled into the wilderness, where she hath a place prepared of God, that they should feed her there a thousand two hundred *and* threescore days.

7 And there was war in heaven: Michael and his angels fought against the dragon; and the dragon fought and his angels,

8 And prevailed not; neither was their place found any more in heaven.

9 And the great dragon was cast out, that old serpent, called the Devil, and Satan, which deceiveth the whole world: he was cast out into the earth, and his angels were cast out with him.

10 And I heard a loud voice saying in heaven, Now is come salvation, and strength, and the kingdom of our God, and the power of his Christ: for the accuser of our brethren is cast down, which accused them before our God day and night.

11 And they overcame him by the blood of the Lamb, and by the word of their testimony; and they loved not their lives unto the death.

12 Therefore rejoice, *ye* heavens, and ye that dwell in them. Woe to the inhabiters of the earth and of the sea! for the devil is come down unto you, having great wrath, because he knoweth that he hath but a short time.

13 And when the dragon saw that he was cast unto the earth, he persecuted the woman which brought forth the man *child.*

14 And to the woman were given two wings of a great eagle, that she might fly into the wilderness, into her place, where she is nourished for a time, and times, and half a time, from the face of the serpent.

Mat 16:13 When Jesus came into the coasts of Caesarea Philippi, he asked his disciples, saying, Whom do men say that I the Son of man am?

14 And they said, Some *say that thou art* John the Baptist: some, Elias; and others, Jeremias, or one of the prophets.

15 He saith unto them, But whom say ye that I am?

16 And Simon Peter answered and said, Thou art the Christ, the Son of the living God.

17 And Jesus answered and said unto him, Blessed art thou, Simon Barjona: for flesh and blood hath not revealed *it* unto thee, but my Father which is in heaven.

18 And I say also unto thee, That thou art Peter, and upon this rock I will build my church; and the gates of hell shall not prevail against it.

19 And I will give unto thee the keys of the kingdom of heaven: and whatsoever thou shalt bind on earth shall be bound in heaven: and whatsoever thou shalt loose on earth shall be loosed in heaven.

The war in heaven mentioned in Revelation 12:7 took place at the Crucifixion of Christ. Prior to that, Satan had access to the Throne of God and to stand before God to bring accusations against the people of God (Read Job 1:6-12 to see the Accuser of the Brethren in action):

Job 1:6 Now there was a day when the sons of God came to present themselves before the LORD, and Satan came also among them.

7 And the LORD said unto Satan, Whence comest thou? Then Satan answered the LORD, and said, From going to and fro in the earth, and from walking up and down in it.

8 And the LORD said unto Satan, Hast thou considered my servant Job, that *there is* none like him in the earth, a perfect and an upright man, one that feareth God, and escheweth evil?

9 Then Satan answered the LORD, and said, Doth Job fear God for nought?

10 Hast not thou made an hedge about him, and about his house, and about all that he hath on every side? thou hast blessed the work of his hands, and his substance is increased in the land.

11 But put forth thine hand now, and touch all that he hath, and he will curse thee to thy face.

12 And the LORD said unto Satan, Behold, all that he hath *is* in thy power; only upon himself put not forth thine hand. So Satan went forth from the presence of the LORD.

The next chapter presents another example of Satan's access to the presence of God in Heaven:

Job 2:1 Again there was a day when the sons of God came to present themselves before the LORD, and Satan came also among them to present himself before the LORD.

2 And the LORD said unto Satan, From whence comest thou? And Satan answered the LORD, and said, From going to and fro in the earth, and from walking up and down in it.

3 And the LORD said unto Satan, Hast thou considered my servant Job, that *there is* none like him in the earth, a perfect and an upright man, one that feareth God, and escheweth evil? and still he holdeth fast his integrity, although thou movedst me against him, to destroy him without cause.

4 And Satan answered the LORD, and said, Skin for skin, yea, all that a man hath will he give for his life.

5 But put forth thine hand now, and touch his bone and his flesh, and he will curse thee to thy face.

6 And the LORD said unto Satan, Behold, he *is* in thine hand; but save his life.

7 So went Satan forth from the presence of the LORD, and smote Job with sore boils from the sole of his foot unto his crown.

Prior to Jesus' death burial and resurrection, Satan had the right to access the Presence of the Lord in a kind of legal wrangling with God Himself as the Accuser of the Brethren. Through

Adam and Eve's fall in the garden, he rightfully gained the dominion and authority over the people groups and kingdoms of the world, and ruled as their god in many different guises. To some people groups he was known as Chemosh, to others he was known as Dagon, and to others he was known as Ashtoreth, and Baal and Milcom and Molech.

Today he is known as a myriad of other names to a myriad of other people groups, but since the crucifixion, Jesus Christ has been given a Name above every name, and has been about reconciling His Creation to Himself.

Rom 5:10 For if, when we were enemies, we were reconciled to God by the death of his Son, much more, being reconciled, we shall be saved by his life.
11 And not only *so,* but we also joy in God through our Lord Jesus Christ, by whom we have now received the atonement.

In His obedience to God as a man, Jesus became the second Adam, and reestablished the Kingdom of God on the earth, restoring humanity's position of dominion over the earth.

Php 2:8 And being found in fashion as a man, he humbled himself, and became obedient unto death, even the death of the cross.
9 Wherefore God also hath highly exalted him, and given him a name which is above every name:
10 That at the name of Jesus every knee should bow, of *things* in heaven, and *things* in earth, and *things* under the earth;
11 And *that* every tongue should confess that Jesus Christ *is* Lord, to the glory of God the Father.

Jesus' Gospel was about the Kingdom of God and how it functions, and how citizens of the Kingdom of God are to live.

After the war in heaven that took place at the time of the Crucifixion, where Michael and his angels fought against the dragon and his angels, the dragon was cast out of heaven into the earth.

Rev 12:10 And I heard a loud voice saying in heaven, Now is come salvation, and strength, and the kingdom of our God, and the power of his Christ: for the accuser of our brethren is cast down, which accused them before our God day and night.

Satan no longer has the right to stand before God and act as the Accuser of the Brethren, so he was cast down to the earth for a season (an age) until the Gospel of the Kingdom of God would be preached in all the world. Since then, Satan has used every device he could to prevent that from happening. The first course of action he uses are distractions that cause people to forget the message of the Gospel of the Kingdom of God.

Mat 13:19 When any one heareth the word of the kingdom, and understandeth *it* **not, then cometh the wicked** *one,* **and catcheth away that which was sown in his heart. This is he which received seed by the way side.**

The second course of action that Satan uses to hinder the Truth of Gospel of the Kingdom of God from going forth is persecution. Remember that in context when Jesus mentions hearing the word, He is referring to the word of the Kingdom (see verse 19 above).

Mat 13:20 But he that received the seed into stony places, the same is he that heareth the word, and anon with joy receiveth it;
21 Yet hath he not root in himself, but dureth for a while: for when tribulation or persecution ariseth because of the word, by and by he is offended.

Rev 12:13 And when the dragon saw that he was cast unto the earth, he persecuted the woman which brought forth the man *child.*

And the most successful of his devices are the distractions that this present age under Satan's dominion bring to humanity as a whole, and Christians in particular:

Mat 13:22 He also that received seed among the thorns is he that heareth the word; and the care of this world, and the deceitfulness of riches, choke the word, and he becometh unfruitful.

Through his various schemes, Satan has succeeded in preventing the Truth contained in the Gospel of the Kingdom of God **(the authority of the believer, and the restoration of humanity's dominion over the earth and over sin, sickness and disease, and his position of Righteousness and the right to walk in that righteousness through Jesus Christ)** from being revealed to humanity as a whole. Hence Paul's letter to the Ephesians about the Christian's inheritance in Christ and his prayer for them:

Eph 1:15 Wherefore I also, after I heard of your faith in the Lord Jesus, and love unto all the saints,
16 Cease not to give thanks for you, making mention of you in my prayers;
17 That the God of our Lord Jesus Christ, the Father of glory, may give unto you the spirit of wisdom and revelation in the knowledge of him:
18 The eyes of your understanding being enlightened; that ye may know what is the hope of his calling, and what the riches of the glory of his inheritance in the saints,
19 And what *is* **the exceeding greatness of his power to us-ward who believe, according to the working of his mighty power,**
20 Which he wrought in Christ, when he raised him from the dead, and set *him* **at his own right hand in the heavenly** *places,*
21 Far above all principality, and power, and might, and dominion, and every name that is named, not only in this world, but also in that which is to come:

22 And hath put all *things* under his feet, and gave him *to be* the head over all *things* to the church,
23 Which is his body, the fulness of him that filleth all in all.

Jesus said seek FIRST the Kingdom of God and His Righteousness. Those who have their eyes of understanding enlightened are engaged in a spiritual battle for the establishment of the Kingdom of God in this world.

Satan has succeeded in distracting the majority of Christians from this goal by using professional clergy to further another gospel which is not the Gospel of the Kingdom of God. He no longer can stand before God and accuse them, but he can blind their minds of understanding and cause them to look at some future time when the Kingdom of God would come, and get them caught up in various debates of "end time" events, and false doctrines and deception being preached from the pulpit:

Rev 12:15 And the serpent cast out of his mouth water as a flood after the woman, that he might cause her to be carried away of the flood.

2Ti 4:3 For the time will come when they will not endure sound doctrine; but after their own lusts shall they heap to themselves teachers, having itching ears;
4 And they shall turn away *their* ears from the truth, and shall be turned unto fables.

Rev 12:16 And the earth helped the woman, and the earth opened her mouth, and swallowed up the flood which the dragon cast out of his mouth.

I love what Clarke has to say about this passage:

The earth helped the woman - "Nothing, and indeed," as Bishop Newton excellently observes, "was more likely to produce the ruin and utter subversion of the Christian Church than the irruptions of so many barbarous nations into the Roman empire. But the event proved contrary to human appearance and expectation: the earth swallowed up the flood; the barbarians were rather swallowed up by the Romans, than the Romans by the barbarians; the heathen conquerors, instead of imposing their own, submitted to the religion of the conquered Christians; and they not only embraced the religion, but affected even the laws, the manners, the customs, the language, and the very name, of Romans, so that the victors were in a manner absorbed and lost among the vanquished."

We see that which is described above in the history of Roman Catholicism. Though many pagan customs were incorporated into Christian holy days such as Easter (Easter eggs and rabbits) and Christmas (both festivals occur on the Spring Solstice and the Winter Solstice, respectively), the basic meaning concerning the death burial and resurrection of Christ, and the Birth of Christ have not been lost. Though the Roman Catholic Church itself became lost in idolatry and necromancy (prayers to dead saints) and other pagan customs and rituals, the message of Christ has not been lost, although the Gospel has been woefully distorted. But since the inception of the Church there has always been a remnant who have not lost sight of Christ's Purpose of establishing the Kingdom of God throughout the world. It is those who Satan seeks to silence.

Rev 12:17 And the dragon was wroth with the woman, and went to make war with the remnant of her seed, which keep the commandments of God, and have the testimony of Jesus Christ.

But the message has been the same since Christ began to establish His Church:

The Kingdom of God is at hand.

2Co 4:3 But if our gospel be hid, it is hid to them that are lost:
4 In whom the god of this world hath blinded the minds of them which believe not, lest the light of the glorious gospel of Christ, who is the image of God, should shine unto them.

11

(Page 88 Section 2)
The Qu'ran And It's Relation To 666

Sura 1+Sura 2=3+Sura 3=6 + Sura 4 =10 +Sura 5 =15 + Sura 6 =21 + Sura 7 = 28 + Sura 8 = 36 + Sura 9 = 45 + Sura 10 = 55 +Sura 11 = 66 + Sura 12 =78 + Sura 13 =91 + Sura 14 = 105 +Sura 15 = 120 + Sura 16 = 136 + Sura 17 = 153 + Sura 18 = 171 + Sura 19 = 190 + Sura 20 =210 + Sura 21 = 231 + Sura 22 = 253 + Sura 23 = 276 + Sura 24 = 300 + Sura 25 = 325 + Sura 26 = 351 + Sura 27 = 378 + Sura 28 = 406 + Sura 29 = 435 + Sura 30 = 465 + Sura 31 = 496 + Sura 32 = 528 + Sura 33 =561 + Sura 34 = 595 + sura 35 = 630 + Sura 36 = 666

From our understanding of Daniel and Revelation concerning the four Beasts, we know that the beasts represent kingdoms. We have seen that the Beast of Revelation is a combination of the Median-Persion, Babylonian and the Grecian empires as described in Daniel chapter 7. These are the Beasts who had their dominion taken away, but their lives were prolonged.

Dan 7:12 As concerning the rest of the beasts, they had their dominion taken away: yet their lives were prolonged for a season and time.

We have seen that the territories of these kingdoms are the same territories that are under Islamic influence in this present age. Mohammad is the prophet that founded the kingdom of Islam, and the Qu'ran that he recited and the Sura that gives him endorsement from "Allah" just happens to carry within it the number 666.

According to Islam, all those who have been conquered must declare that there is no god but Allah and Mohammed is his prophet. The anti Christ spirit behind Islam demands that Christians deny the Son-ship of Jesus Christ and the Fatherhood of God.

Christianity is not a religion of death and destruction, but the principle of jihad brings death and destruction to all who oppose Islam.

The dragon and those who follow him and his religion can only war through physical means. Slaughter those who cannot or will not defend themselves, or either put a tax (*Jizya*) upon those who will not submit to Islam or behead them in the name of their god. The prophet of Islam recited these words (the People of the Book are Jews and Christians):

Surah 9.29 Fight those who believe not in Allah nor the Last Day, nor hold that forbidden which hath been forbidden by Allah and His Messenger, nor acknowledge the religion of Truth, (even if they are) of the People of the Book, until they pay the Jizya with willing submission, and feel themselves subdued. 30 The Jews call 'Uzair a son of Allah, and the Christians call Christ the son of Allah. That is a saying from their mouth; (in this) they but imitate what the unbelievers of old used to say. Allah's curse be on them: how they are deluded away from the Truth!

Six hundred years before the prophet of Islam came into being, Jesus said this:

Joh 10:10 The thief cometh not, but for to steal, and to kill, and to destroy: I am come that they might have life, and that they might have *it* more abundantly.
11 I am the good shepherd: the good shepherd giveth his life for the sheep.

The prophet of Islam and his god is about extortion, death, destruction and forceful submission. Jesus and His Father are about Life.

Rev 12:17 And the dragon was wroth with the woman, and went to make war with the remnant of her seed, which keep the commandments of God, and have the testimony of Jesus Christ.

Elsewhere in this book, I inserted a quote from Adam Clarke concerning Catholicism and the papacy, which he thought was the Beast and the false prophet of Revelation 13:

But I neither lay stress upon nor draw conclusions from these dates. If the Church of Rome will reform itself, it will then be the true Christian Church, and will never be destroyed. Let it throw aside all that is ritually Jewish, all that is heathen; all that which pretends to be of God, and which is only of man, all doctrines that are not in the Bible; and all rites and ceremonies which are not of the appointment of Christ and his apostles; and then, all hail the once Roman, but now, after such a change, the Holy, Catholic Church! Every true Protestant would wish rather the reform than the extinction of this Church.

I could sincerely echo Adam Clarke's sentiments in relation to those who follow Islam.

If Islam would reform itself, it could then be a part of the Kingdom of God.

Let it throw aside its Anti Christ doctrine, all that is of the evil one, all that pretends to be of the God of Abraham, Isaac and Jacob, and which is only of man; all doctrines that are not in the Bible, and all rites and ceremonies which are not of the appointment of Christ and His apostles. Let them embrace the only One that God has highly exalted above every Name, whether in Heaven or on earth, and let them bow their knee to Him in sincerity, the One Who shed His Blood for their redemption, the ONLY begotten Son of God, Jesus Christ, then those who were once deceived and destined for a flaming Hell because of their murderous ways will become a living part of the Christian Church. Every true Christian would wish the salvation rather than the eternal condemnation of these deceived people for whom Christ died.

2Pe 3:8 But, beloved, be not ignorant of this one thing, that one day *is* with the Lord as a thousand years, and a thousand years as one day.

9 The Lord is not slack concerning his promise, as some men count slackness; but is longsuffering to us-ward, not willing that any should perish, but that all should come to repentance.

It is the Blood of the Lamb and the Testimony of Jesus that causes men to repent and come to a saving knowledge of Christ. While their weapons are carnal, the Christian's weapons are spiritual. There are nominal or cultural Muslims everywhere, just as there are nominal Christians, the kind who go to Church because it is part of their culture, but who do not embrace the Bible as the True Word of God.

These Muslims who are Muslims because of their heritage, or because of their desire to "fit in" also have not embraced the Qu'ran as a true revelation from God. There are many who profess Islam, but who have not really read the Qu'ran. These Muslims who witness the murderous ways of those who are engaged in Jihad against the world, want no part of the wickedness they see them commit in the name of Allah. When they discover that they cannot divorce the writings of the Qu'ran from their religion, cultural Muslims are turning to Christ, because they see the difference between a god of hatred and the God of Love and Mercy.

2Co 10:3 For though we walk in the flesh, we do not war after the flesh:
4 (For the weapons of our warfare *are* not carnal, but mighty through God to the pulling down of strong holds;)
5 Casting down imaginations, and every high thing that exalteth itself against the knowledge of God, and bringing into captivity every thought to the obedience of Christ;

Rev 20:4 And I saw thrones, and they sat upon them, and judgment was given unto them: and *I saw* the souls of them that were beheaded for the witness of Jesus, and for the word of God, and which had not worshipped the beast, neither his image, neither had received *his* mark upon their foreheads, or in their hands; and they lived and reigned with Christ a thousand years.
5 But the rest of the dead lived not again until the thousand years were finished. This *is* the first resurrection.
6 Blessed and holy *is* he that hath part in the first resurrection: on such the second death hath no power, but they shall be priests of God and of Christ, and shall reign with him a thousand years.

Those who follow the preterist line of reasoning do not believe that the book of Revelation has anything to do with the future, so this that I am about to write will not ring true to them.

Although the chapter of the Qu'ran that endorses Mohammad and speaks of the "last days" and confirms that Jesus is not God's Son add up to the number 666, I do not believe the Mark of the Beast (which is a kingdom, not a man) is the Qu'ran. I believe it is a foreshadow of what is to come.

Just as those who are brought into submission by Islamic jihadists whose goal is to usher in the twelfth Mahdi, and the eventual submission of the world to Islam must declare "there is no god but Allah and Mohammed is his prophet", or die, there will be a time when people of all religions (including Islam) will have to denounce their belief in their god, or be imprisoned or die.

My Opinion?

MY OPINION IS NOT THE SAME AS THUS SAITH THE LORD.

The number is the number of a man. It was in the Creation that God created man on the 6th day, a threefold being created in the image of a triune God. The serpent's temptation was that man could be as God. In the time before the flood, the sons of God (angels - see Job 1:6, 2:1, 38:7) intermingled with the daughters of men.

Gen 6:5 And GOD saw that the wickedness of man *was* great in the earth, and *that* every imagination of the thoughts of his heart *was* only evil continually.

The problem with man trying to ascend to godhood is that man isn't naturally endowed with the Wisdom that is necessary to be God. As we become Born of the Spirit, or Born Again, we begin to become conformed to the Image of God and we grow in wisdom, but the unregenerate man can only pretend to attain to Spiritual enlightenment as he acquires knowledge concerning the supernatural.

Although Islam is an Anti Christ Religion, I do not believe that Islam is The Anti Christ. 1st John defines what the Anti Christ and the spirit of Anti Christ is.

I believe the radical adherents of Islam will serve to further the agenda of the beast, which is a world void of religion, and where secular humanism prevails. I believe this time is foretold in Revelation 13.

When the people of the world get fed up with the extremism of various religions, leaders will rise up who will outlaw religion. Rev 17:12-16.

Sound farfetched? Remember Stalin and Lenin, Marx and Mao, and others who succeeded in doing just that. Look at North Korea, where religion is forbidden. To those who embrace the humanist mindset, Christianity is really the one threat to their goal of a universal governance devoid of religion.

The Bible says the thief comes to kill steal or destroy. People can become convinced to kill or to oppress in the name of their gods. But they can also do that in the name of an ideology that may be absent from any god.

Christians are painted by the anti-Christ leaning left as intolerant, and a threat to individual happiness.

Muslims are creating atrocities in the name of their god. Hindus are slaughtering Christians. Muslims are slaughtering Christians and Hindus.

Rev 13:3 And I saw one of his heads as it were wounded to death; and his deadly wound was healed: and all the world wondered after the beast.

Communism lost its grip on Russia, but I believe Communist Russia will return to power soon, and the communist socialist republic of Russia will be back on the scene with greater influence and power.

I believe that could be the head that was wounded to death, or another possibility is that it was wounded in the war with the saints.

How would that happen? Through an awakening of the Body of Christ to its Purpose and Calling. You can call it a revival or a reformation, when the Church repents of its apathy and starts to walk in its authority and actively furthered the Kingdom of God one soul at a time. When the Church wakes up and says "NO!" And the Gospel of the Kingdom begins to be preached throughout the world, the Lord working with them, with signs following.

But there will be a time when the Church just stops caring and stops being the Church. In Daniel, we are told that Satan will wear out the saints. When that happens, then that is the great falling away that will bring the times of the Gentiles to a fulfillment. Just as the time of Israel came to an end, so too will the times of the Gentiles. It's the way of humanity.

Is that time now? That's left up to those who call themselves Christians. Has Satan's deception been so great that he finally managed to render the Church powerless? Or will there be one more time when the Church rises up like it did with the Anabaptists, in the 1st and 2nd great Awakening, in Azusa Street, among the Moravians, the Hebrides, and on other occasions? Some will automatically and emphatically say "No". And that is what concerns me. That attitude will usher in the beast of Revelation 13:11.

But there will always be a remnant, a few who will be faithful unto the end. Those who love not their lives unto the death.

The second beast is a kingdom which exercises all the power of the first beast kingdom. He has two horns like a lamb, in that he appears to promise peace, but he speaks like a dragon. We know the dragon is the devil. We have seen that horns represent kings. This probably represents two kings, or two leaders representing the Western and the Eastern world who are all about the "good" of mankind; tolerance and personal happiness will be the chief aim; and all of this can be accomplished through technology and world unity. The issue of Climate Change could be the common cause that brings the East and the West together. For that to happen, religion will have to be eliminated. The creed of Satanism is "do as thou wilt is the whole of the law". So it will be in the last of the last days of the end of this age.

Rev 13:11 And I beheld another beast coming up out of the earth; and he had two horns like a lamb, and he spake as a dragon.
12 And he exerciseth all the power of the first beast before him, and causeth the earth and them which dwell therein to worship the first beast, whose deadly wound was healed.
13 And he doeth great wonders, so that he maketh fire come down from heaven on the earth in the sight of men,

In Isaiah we read how Lucifer had exalted himself in his heart, and this humanist centered kingdom will do the same thing. "We can be like God", is the belief of those who reject God.

Isa 14:12 How art thou fallen from heaven, O Lucifer, son of the morning! *how* **art thou cut down to the ground, which didst weaken the nations!**
13 For thou hast said in thine heart, I will ascend into heaven, I will exalt my throne above the stars of God: I will sit also upon the mount of the congregation, in the sides of the north:
14 I will ascend above the heights of the clouds; I will be like the most High.

Whatever it is called, whether Communism, Atheism, Secular humanism, the beast(s) of Revelation 13 will someday be a government without religion, a godless society that arises and does what it can to eliminate any mention of God.

Rev 13:6 And he opened his mouth in blasphemy against God, to blaspheme his name, and his tabernacle, and them that dwell in heaven.
7 And it was given unto him to make war with the saints, and to overcome them: and power was given him over all kindreds, and tongues, and nations.

I believe we who profess Christ are not far from a time of great persecution in America unless we act now.

There is a lot being said at the time of this writing about Blood moons and the shemita of 2014-2015. By the time this book is published the Blood moons and the Shimetah will have already occurred. Many prophetic voices have been speaking out about judgment which will be visited upon America because of America's departure from the Morality of the Bible.

I don't disagree that there *may* be something of epic proportions that takes place at this time. Something of epic proportions can happen any time...

The world's economy has been looking very dismal the past few years. America may truly undergo a great financial crises.

There is an Islamic group known as Isis who are right now wreaking havoc in the name of Allah as they jihad for the 12th Imam.

Christians are being slaughtered around the world. Another attack within America on the scale of 911 may take place soon. Time will only tell.

But where I disagree with these prophetic voices proclaiming God's judgment upon America, is while all these things may indeed take place in America, if they do, it will be God's Judgment upon the Church which has done *nothing* to be the light to the lost and to further the Kingdom of God in this nation. It is only because of the negligence of the Church that these things can happen.

The preachers preach imminent destruction, and an escape clause for those who are "in Christ". But there is no escape clause. Ask our brothers and sisters who are being slaughtered throughout the world if there has been an escape clause. Wake up! It is because of that godless doctrine that the Church has stopped caring and has ceased being a hedge between good and evil. It is because the Body of Christ has been assured that these things will happen anyway, so don't worry, because God will rapture you out that the Church is impotent today.

What would it be like if Pastors continuously preached the importance of being a hedge between good and evil? What would it be like if the Church was not reduced to a spectator clique, but if every member of the Body was trained and equipped to do the work of ministry, instead of being conditioned to believe that only some are called to "go ye"?

The world will unify with one another. But the pastors keep the Body of Christ divided.

Even now it isn't too late. Even now the Church can rise up and be the Force that holds back the advance of the enemy. God has left it up to us. He has given us the authority to further His Kingdom.

2Ch 7:14 If my people, which are called by my name, shall humble themselves, and pray, and seek my face, and turn from their wicked ways; then will I hear from heaven, and will forgive their sin, and will heal their land.

We are not so different from what Israel was in the days of Ezekiel:

Eze 22:3 Then say thou, Thus saith the Lord GOD, The city sheddeth blood in the midst of it, that her time may come, and maketh idols against herself to defile herself.
4 Thou art become guilty in thy blood that thou hast shed; and hast defiled thyself in thine idols which thou hast made; and thou hast caused thy days to draw near, and art come *even* unto thy years: therefore have I made thee a reproach unto the heathen, and a mocking to all countries.
5 *Those that be* near, and *those that be* far from thee, shall mock thee, *which art* infamous *and* much vexed.

6 Behold, the princes of Israel, every one were in thee to their power to shed blood.

7 In thee have they set light by father and mother: in the midst of thee have they dealt by oppression with the stranger: in thee have they vexed the fatherless and the widow.

8 Thou hast despised mine holy things, and hast profaned my sabbaths.

9 In thee are men that carry tales to shed blood: and in thee they eat upon the mountains: in the midst of thee they commit lewdness.

10 In thee have they discovered their fathers' nakedness: in thee have they humbled her that was set apart for pollution.

11 And one hath committed abomination with his neighbour's wife; and another hath lewdly defiled his daughter in law; and another in thee hath humbled his sister, his father's daughter.

12 In thee have they taken gifts to shed blood; thou hast taken usury and increase, and thou hast greedily gained of thy neighbours by extortion, and hast forgotten me, saith the Lord GOD.

13 Behold, therefore I have smitten mine hand at thy dishonest gain which thou hast made, and at thy blood which hath been in the midst of thee.

14 Can thine heart endure, or can thine hands be strong, in the days that I shall deal with thee? I the LORD have spoken *it*, and will do *it*.

15 And I will scatter thee among the heathen, and disperse thee in the countries, and will consume thy filthiness out of thee.

16 And thou shalt take thine inheritance in thyself in the sight of the heathen, and thou shalt know that I *am* the LORD.

17 And the word of the LORD came unto me, saying,

18 Son of man, the house of Israel is to me become dross: all they *are* brass, and tin, and iron, and lead, in the midst of the furnace; they are *even* the dross of silver.

19 Therefore thus saith the Lord GOD; Because ye are all become dross, behold, therefore I will gather you into the midst of Jerusalem.

20 *As* they gather silver, and brass, and iron, and lead, and tin, into the midst of the furnace, to blow the fire upon it, to melt *it;* so will I gather *you* in mine anger and in my fury, and I will leave *you there,* and melt you.

21 Yea, I will gather you, and blow upon you in the fire of my wrath, and ye shall be melted in the midst thereof.

22 As silver is melted in the midst of the furnace, so shall ye be melted in the midst thereof; and ye shall know that I the LORD have poured out my fury upon you.

23 And the word of the LORD came unto me, saying,

24 Son of man, say unto her, Thou *art* the land that is not cleansed, nor rained upon in the day of indignation.

25 *There is* a conspiracy of her prophets in the midst thereof, like a roaring lion ravening the prey; they have devoured souls; they have taken the treasure and precious things; they have made her many widows in the midst thereof.

26 Her priests have violated my law, and have profaned mine holy things: they have put no difference between the holy and profane, neither have they shewed *difference* between the unclean and the clean, and have hid their eyes from my sabbaths, and I am profaned among them.

27 Her princes in the midst thereof *are* like wolves ravening the prey, to shed blood, *and* to destroy souls, to get dishonest gain.

28 And her prophets have daubed them with untempered *morter,* seeing vanity, and divining lies unto them, saying, Thus saith the Lord GOD, when the LORD hath not spoken.

29 The people of the land have used oppression, and exercised robbery, and have vexed the poor and needy: yea, they have oppressed the stranger wrongfully.
30 And I sought for a man among them, that should make up the hedge, and stand in the gap before me for the land, that I should not destroy it: but I found none.
31 Therefore have I poured out mine indignation upon them; I have consumed them with the fire of my wrath: their own way have I recompensed upon their heads, saith the Lord GOD.

His Word is true, but the dispensationalists are in the camp that says there is no hope this side of heaven. It was because the priest hood and the prophets and the people of God were all gone out of the Way, and God could find no one to make up the hedge, that His Wrath fell upon Israel.

As Israel was so will the Gentile Church be one day...Is that time now? THAT is up to YOU.

I know I have been rough on the pastors and the prophets and the evangelists during the course of this book. But there really is no time to write another feel good book. It is time for the Church and those who are in ministry to repent and drop their agenda and get busy equipping the saints to do the work of the ministry before it is too late.

Martin Niemöhler, a pastor who lived during Hitler's time wrote:

First they came for the communists, and I didn't speak out because I wasn't a communist.

Then they came for the socialists and I didn't speak out because I wasn't a socialist.

Then they came for the Jews, and I didn't speak out because I wasn't a Jew.

Then they came for me, and there was no one left to speak for me.

This is the voice of a pastor who had the Authority of Jesus Christ to change the world in which he lived, and did nothing, because he felt those things happening around him had no bearing on him or his sphere of influence. The leadership of the Church needs to get it's head out of the sand, and begin to make a stand for the Kingdom of God.

You deny Christ through your actions or your lack thereof. The Kingdom of God isn't about your territorial church kingdom if you just keep everything primarily within your four walls. That' your ego at work.

To experience the Saving Grace of Jesus Christ for one's life, a person has to come to the point where they acknowledge that they have sinned. They have to come to the place where they take responsibility for their rebellion against God, stop blaming others for their sin, and surrender to His Will for their lives.

It's time for the Body of Christ to take responsibility for its' negligence.

Even now, at the time of this writing when there are so many voices saying "all hope is lost" there is still hope.

Christian, it is NOT the Government.

It is NOT the Liberals.

It is NOT Isis.

It is NOT homosexuals.

It is NOT Corporate America, or the Republicans or the Democrats that is the problem.

It is because we have been distracted by the cares and the lusts of this world, and have relegated the Kingdom of God to a place of least importance in our lives that we are in the place where we are today.

There is not one man who is the Beast or the Anti-Christ.

As I tried to point out throughout this book, the beasts spoken about in Daniel and Revelation are kingdoms, or more to the point, the spiritual principalities that hold influence over those kingdoms. And Satan is the ultimate one who gives power to the last days kingdom which is defined as the beast (Rom 13:4).

The rule of the kingdom described in Revelation 13:1-10 will be relatively short.

True Christians won't submit, neither to the harlot, or the beast on which she rides, or to the seven heads that are part of the beast. They will love not their lives unto the death.

But there will be in the midst of the persecution, a reawakening to the Truth of God. Even now there is a grassroots movement in the Body of Christ where "everyday Christians" are going out into the streets and manifesting the Power of God in healing and deliverance of people they encounter. More and more men and women of God are rising up to equip the believer to do the work of the ministry in furthering the Kingdom of God. Their motive for doing this is one of compassion for the lost.

I believe the "This is that" that Peter spoke about in the Book of Acts is still the Power of God unto salvation to all who believe, even unto the end of the age.

To the last breath, the true witness of God will declare his or her faith in Jesus. And as a result of that witness, many who once opposed Christ will come to His Saving Grace. The Word of God to the People of God is "to him who overcomes". God has called us to be over comers in this world.

Another kingdom will arise, and it will be a kingdom which purports to be founded in the name of peace. Once the divisive nature of religion is done away with, then the world can have peace. Science and technology is the god of this world. Medical miracles are performed in the name of scientific advances.

I personally believe the image of the beast can be seen in televised media.

Rev 13:11 And I beheld another beast coming up out of the earth; and he had two horns like a lamb, and he spake as a dragon.
12 And he exerciseth all the power of the first beast before him, and causeth the earth and them which dwell therein to worship the first beast, whose deadly wound was healed.
13 And he doeth great wonders, so that he maketh fire come down from heaven on the earth in the sight of men,
14 And deceiveth them that dwell on the earth by *the means of* those miracles which he had power to do in the sight of the beast; saying to them that dwell on the earth, that they should make an image to the beast, which had the wound by a sword, and did live.
15 And he had power to give life unto the image of the beast, that the image of the beast should both speak, and cause that as many as would not worship the image of the beast should be killed.
16 And he causeth all, both small and great, rich and poor, free and bond, to receive a mark in their right hand, or in their foreheads:
17 And that no man might buy or sell, save he that had the mark, or the name of the beast, or the number of his name.
18 Here is wisdom. Let him that hath understanding count the number of the beast: for it is the number of a man; and his number *is* Six hundred threescore *and* six.

The mark is what we think and what we do. It determines how we conduct ourselves in this world, and who we worship. Israel was told to have "frontlets between their eyes, and phylacteries upon their wrists".

Deu 6:4 Hear, O Israel: The LORD our God *is* one LORD:
5 And thou shalt love the LORD thy God with all thine heart, and with all thy soul, and with all thy might.
6 And these words, which I command thee this day, shall be in thine heart:
7 And thou shalt teach them diligently unto thy children, and shalt talk of them when thou sittest in thine house, and when thou walkest by the way, and when thou liest down, and when thou risest up.

8 And thou shalt bind them for a sign upon thine hand, and they shall be as frontlets between thine eyes.

9 And thou shalt write them upon the posts of thy house, and on thy gates.

Jesus said that we can't serve two masters. Either we are serving God, or we are serving mammon; the pursuit of these temporal worldly treasures instead of God.

Conformity to the world system is the mark of the Beast. Conformity to the Kingdom of God is the Mark of God.

Rom 12:1 I beseech you therefore, brethren, by the mercies of God, that ye present your bodies a living sacrifice, holy, acceptable unto God, *which is* your reasonable service.

2 And be not conformed to this world: but be ye transformed by the renewing of your mind, that ye may prove what *is* that good, and acceptable, and perfect, will of God.

What all of this looks like in actual fulfillment of the prophetic Word of Revelation and Daniel, I cannot say. But I do know that at this point in history, the American Church has failed in her responsibility. I don't believe it is too late to repent and to be about our Father's Kingdom Business.

The Church can still effect great change in this world.

Dispensationalists say it's too late for that.

I say dispensationalist premillennialism is a tool used by the enemy to render the Church powerless and irrelevant in this day and age.

Rather than fear those things that may be coming on the earth because of the wickedness of man, and his hatred toward the things of God, Christians should fear standing before God as slothful unproductive servants who knew their Master's Will, but didn't do it.

Heb 10:28 He that despised Moses' law died without mercy under two or three witnesses:

29 Of how much sorer punishment, suppose ye, shall he be thought worthy, who hath trodden under foot the Son of God, and hath counted the blood of the covenant, wherewith he was sanctified, an unholy thing, and hath done despite unto the Spirit of grace?

30 For we know him that hath said, Vengeance *belongeth* unto me, I will recompense, saith the Lord. And again, The Lord shall judge his people.

31 *It is* a fearful thing to fall into the hands of the living God.

Get away from the ear ticklers who aren't equipping you in the work of the ministry. Get into the fields, and begin to reap. If you don't know how, find someone who will teach you. The battle is real. The war is now. Souls are at stake. YOU are called.

**Rev 14:6 And I saw another angel fly in the midst of heaven, having the everlasting gospel to preach unto them that dwell on the earth, and to every nation, and kindred, and tongue, and people,
7 Saying with a loud voice, Fear God, and give glory to him; for the hour of his judgment is come: and worship him that made heaven, and earth, and the sea, and the fountains of waters.**

Conclusion

This book was begun as an answer to a friend who asked me a question concerning the end times, specifically the Rapture and the Second Coming. As I started to answer, I realized it would take some in depth study of the Word to give an adequate answer. The result of that study is this book which you have just read. You may not agree with all of what you have read. I realize that a lot of it goes against what has been traditionally taught by some denominations. But your particular denominational position is NOT necessarily compatible with the apostle's doctrine. As I said earlier, I am not writing a THUS SAITH THE LORD. But by the same token, I wouldn't be writing it if I didn't believe in the truth of what I am writing. And the Truth is that the Church needs a wake up call!

Where Is YOUR Heart?

Are you looking with an eager anticipation for Judgment to fall on this Nation?

Too many are.

They swear it is too late for the United States of America.

They raise their pathetic (*I mean "prophetic"*) voices and speak of the evil of the Nation while failing to look at their own evil heart.

Pharisees who delight in the fact that they are not like those sinners...they fast, witness on the street, pray and gobble up as many conspiracy theories as they can, prophesying "Thus saith the Lord" when the Lord hasn't spoken, as they echo their You Tube gleaned theology.

Just as Jesus rebuked James and John, the same rebuke applies to them:

"You know not what spirit you are of".

Forget the possibility that the Church could come to repentance and God could heal our land as a result of the people of God coming to repentance for neglecting the Commission of Christ.

They prefer to be Jonah's who would be mad if God spared this wicked nation.

They sit in the Judgment seat and pronounce a curse upon our nation instead of standing in the gap and interceding on behalf of the nation and its' leaders.

Our nation is running toward judgment and collapse because the Pharisees would rather point fingers and do nothing to see it turn around while they build their cieled houses and call their elaborate buildings the church!

Woe to these white washed tombs who jump on the bandwagon to take delight in the approaching calamity.

Do YOU think YOU will escape? No, I tell you it will be a day of darkness and despair as you realize too late that you should have been the Church instead of compromising the Word of God.

Your sons and daughters will perish at the hands of the godless ones, because you were too busy pointing fingers at those outside and inside the Church instead of working for and being a part of reform in the Church.

Wake up!

Many don't know God, and wickedness is increasing, and it is because of your unwillingness to show them the Way.

Hard words? Not near enough, if they don't result in repentant hearts.